Investigating Science
Through Bears

Investigating Science Through Bears

Karlene Ray Smith
Anne Hudson Bush

Illustrated by
Sherri Keys

1994
TEACHER IDEAS PRESS
A Division of
Libraries Unlimited, Inc.
Englewood, Colorado

This book is dedicated to the authors' parents—
Mr. and Mrs. Walter H. Ray and Mr. and Mrs. Clyde B. Hudson—
and to the many students who have enjoyed learning about
bears as much as we have enjoyed teaching about them.

TEACHER IDEAS PRESS
A Division of
Libraries Unlimited, Inc.
P.O. Box 6633
Englewood, CO 80155-6633
1-800-237-6124

Library of Congress Cataloging-in-Publication Data

Smith, Karlene Ray.
    Investigating science through bears / Karlene Ray Smith, Anne
Hudson Bush ; illustrated by Sherri Keys.
        xvi, 211 p. 22x28 cm.
        Includes bibliographical references and index.
        ISBN 1-56308-072-9
        1. Science—Study and teaching (Elementary) 2. Zoology—Study and
teaching—Activity programs. 3. Bears. I. Bush, Anne Hudson.
II. Title.
LB1585.S58 1993
372.3—dc20   93-4956
                                                                        CIP

Contents

Acknowledgments

The authors wish to thank Sherri Keys for her illustrations. A special acknowledgment to C. R. Smith for his assistance in typing and proofreading the manuscript during its preparation. In addition, the authors are grateful for the patience and understanding of their families and loved ones, who endured the frustrations and long hours that writing a book requires. And finally, the authors wish to thank those individuals who helped with research and information and who work in the various city, state, and national zoos; the National Park Service; the Pennsylvania Game Commission; and the many municipalities and universities.

Introduction

Welcome to the wonderful world of bears! *Investigating Science Through Bears* presents unique and exciting experiences in science that the elementary student will remember and treasure for a lifetime. Life science at the elementary level becomes an adventure with every new concept taught. The goal of this book is to provide elementary teachers and their students with exciting learning experiences related to the real bear. The activities are unusual, provide unique presentations, and, in general, employ recycled or throwaway materials and items for the various projects.

The sciences represent the future for our nation's success as a world leader. The elementary-classroom science teacher holds the key to creating a base for the science-literate students of the future. Studying bears of the real world will establish a background of knowledge about mammals in the animal kingdom. Through the study of bears and one political event of the past, students will establish the connection between the world of the real bears and the well-known teddy bear.

The authors of *Investigating Science Through Bears* are elementary science teachers with a total of 40 years of teaching experience at the elementary level. This experience has helped identify and develop the need for exciting and innovative methods for classroom instruction. These methods are important in presenting the many different science concepts first provided the students at the elementary level. Science in the classroom is fun with hands-on experiences, and the activities in this book employ this concept. Although activities are targeted for students from second grade to fifth grade, many activities can be adapted to both lower and higher grade levels. Consideration is given to the classroom teacher who must wrestle with supply shortages, limited budgets, and insufficient time in the day. In suggesting supplies for the activities, consideration has been given to those available in the classroom, recycled and throwaway items found in the classroom or at home, and items from nature such as rocks, sand, twigs, and so on.

While investigating bears, the integration of whole language concepts are encouraged for use by the students in their learning experiences. Whole language implies that the student should learn to read for information, ideas, insight, and entertainment. The activities presented in this book meet the criteria for the whole language approach. The reading activities and writing activities that characterize the whole language concept are presented. The arts, including literature, are also explored as they relate to bears and teddy bears. The teacher is provided the flexibility to develop the reading and other activities to fit the particular classroom situation. Cooperative learning experiences were also considered in the design of the activities that are developed in this book. In addition, the activities are designed to provide learning tools for the individual student, for small groups within the classroom, or for the class as a whole.

The opening chapters of this book address the bears found in North America. Later, bears found in other parts of the world are included to present a comprehensive look at the bear family. These chapters provide reproducible facts packs for the students, giving them important information about the bears discussed. Activities are provided at the end of each chapter that complement the interesting facts about the bears.

The transition from real bears to teddy bears is made with the story of President Theodore Roosevelt's involvement with a bear cub. *Investigating Science Through Bears* moves into the world of fantasy with Gala Affairs. Four Gala Affairs are developed, each with science concepts based on a specific theme. Each of the four affairs includes a special section about a real bear that relates fact and fantasy to the theme.

Science is exciting. New facts and information are discovered every day in the scientific world, and new ways of presenting the science concepts in the classroom are always in demand to keep the students' inquisitive minds asking questions. *Investigating Science Through Bears* provides the elementary teacher with aids in creating hands-on activities, developing whole language concepts, and exploring life science in many unique ways. Science is fun, exciting, and always present in the world in which we live!

1

The Polar Bear

Overview of Learning Experiences for the Polar Bear

The Polar Bear chapter presents methods and learning experiences designed to stimulate the young, inquiring mind in the areas of life science, social studies, and language arts. These methods and experiences, designed for use in the classroom, maximize creative, divergent thinking by the students and are structured to apply to individual students and students working as a team. The following is an overview of the specific experiences addressed in this chapter.

Life Science

- identifying the size, shape, and other physical characteristics of the polar bear

- explaining the importance of the polar bear's multilayered fur coat

- describing the structure of the polar bear's eyes and feet and determining how they help polar bears adapt to their environment

- investigating the relationships among the polar bear, other Arctic animals, and man

- comparing the different seasons of the Arctic region and determining how the seasons affect the food sources of the polar bear

Social Studies

- identifying the areas of the world where the polar bear lives

- reviewing the relationship between the polar bear and the Inuit people who live in the Arctic regions

- constructing typical habitats for the Inuit people and the polar bear and identifying the differences and similarities between the two

Language Arts

- reading the Polar Bear Facts Pack included in the chapter, plus magazines, library books, and travel brochures to acquire information related to the polar bear

- utilizing literary works about the polar bear with the goal of differentiating between fact and fantasy

- collecting supplemental information about the polar bear through the use of films, filmstrips, and videos

- reading and writing poetry about the polar bear

Polar Bear Facts Pack

Far to the north of mainland United States is the Arctic Circle. This area includes the North Pole and northern parts of Europe, Asia, and North America, and it covers more than 5 million square miles (or nearly 13 million square kilometers). Most of this area is ocean. This is the habitat of one of the world's largest land carnivores, the polar bear. For many years scientists have traveled to the Arctic Circle to study the polar bear in its natural habitat. Most people know the polar bear from visits to the zoo. Some people learn about the polar bear from reading books and watching movies. No matter how one learns about the polar bear, it is one of the most fascinating animals in the world.

On the following pages you will learn many interesting facts about polar bears. Because they live in a very cold environment, some parts of the polar bears' lives are quite different from the lives of other North American bears. You will learn how polar bears grow and become adults. How have the polar bears' bodies adapted to their habitat? Animals encompass most of the food in the Arctic. How does this affect the eating habits of polar bears? Like other bears, do polar bears fear man? After reading the Polar Bear Facts Pack you will be able to answer these and many more questions about this bear.

The Life of a Polar Bear

What's in a Name? Scientists give special names to the animals they study. These names are written in Latin. The polar bear is known as *Ursus maritimus*. This means "bear of the sea." Arctic folk call the polar bear *Nahnock*, and the Cree Indians named it *Wahb'esco*.

The Polar Bear Family. Polar bears do not live together as a family. The male and female are together only during mating season. Since male bears will eat young cubs, mother bears will not allow them around. Polar bear cubs stay with their mother until they are old enough to live on their own. Once the cubs are grown, the female will live alone until she gives birth again.

Polar Bear Cubs

Polar bear cubs are born in late December or early January. Usually the mother polar bear gives birth to two cubs. At the time of birth, the cubs weigh about $1\frac{1}{2}$ pounds (681 grams) each. They measure 12 inches (30.5 centimeters) long. This is the length of a rat. Their tiny, pink bodies are covered with soft, fuzzy hair. The cubs are born deaf and blind.

By the end of March the cubs are ready to leave their den. They then weigh about 25 pounds (11.4 kilograms). Since they were a month old, the cubs have had their sight and hearing. Their fur has become coarse and very long.

When the cubs leave the den for the first time, mother bear begins teaching them. Learning to hunt for food and protecting themselves are two big jobs. This takes weeks of practice before they are able to travel safely with their mother.

As spring turns into summer, the cubs become quite large. Full of energy, they spend hours playing with each other. All of a sudden, young polar bears become quite curious. This is a real problem for the males. Once the young cubs become yearlings they do not need to fear that they will be eaten by adult polar bears. The yearlings are too large and too smart to become a food source. They will try to eat food that belongs to older male bears. This makes the older bears angry. Many times the older bears will swipe the young bears with their paws or chase after them. Once the young bears discover that they are in trouble, they will cry for mother.

Cubs are known as yearlings on their first birthday. As they grow older, the cubs become better hunters. Hours of practice make the cubs more patient. They must learn not to chase their prey away. Mother is no longer needed for supplying food or protection. The cubs can live on their own.

By the end of most polar bears' second summer they are ready to go out on their own. Weighing between 150 and 200 pounds (68.2-90.9 kilograms), yearlings leave their mother. Summer is a good time for the young bears to find a new home. There is plenty of food for them. Hunting should not be difficult.

The Male Polar Bear

When a male yearling leaves its mother, it often looks for other male polar bears. Usually male polar bears live alone. But it is not a problem if another male polar bear is living nearby.

No longer is the young male polar bear interested in playing. It may be starving, since its hunting skills are not very good. Hours are spent looking for food. A young adult male will often attack other males' food supply. Fighting begins. At this age many young males are killed.

Slowly, the male polar bear begins to grow up. Its hunting skills have greatly improved. The polar bear has learned how to protect itself. Hours may be spent playing on the ice with other polar bears its age. They will push, roll, hit, and grab. The polar bears are careful not to hurt one another. Playing at this age helps the males to prepare for battle when they are older.

By the time the male is eight or nine years old it is very strong. The male, known as the boar, can weigh as much as 1,300 pounds (589.6 kilograms). It is not unusual for the polar bear to stand between 11 and 12 feet (3.35-3.66 meters) high. Playing days for this heavily muscled animal are over. The male is ready to be strong and powerful.

Adult male polar bears seldom fight with one another. When a fight occurs, it is usually during mating season. Males will fight until death for a female polar bear. Luckily for males, mating season lasts just a few weeks.

Hunting grounds can also cause problems between males. Each polar bear has its own territory. It hunts within that area. Although the polar bear may share its hunting ground with other small mammals, it does not want to share it with another polar bear. A polar bear returns to the same hunting ground year after year. If it loses its territory to another polar bear, a new hunting ground must be found.

A boar, the male polar bear, will remain strong for many years. As it grows older the polar bear may get arthritis. This disease makes it difficult for the polar bear to move quickly. The younger bears begin to take over. Most polar bears living in the Arctic habitat have a life span of 30 years.

The Female Polar Bear

A female polar bear will leave its mother at the same time as its brother. It must also learn to hunt and live by itself.

The female polar bear is known as the sow. It will have its first set of cubs when it is four or five years old. Cubs are born every two or three years. The sow will be able to have cubs until she is 25 years old. Most of the female's adult life is spent raising cubs. When the cubs are near their second birthday, the mother polar bear will chase them away from its territory.

Female polar bears are not as aggressive as males. They do not spend hours fighting other females. But if their cubs are in danger of being attacked, the mother polar bears will protect them. Mothers are sometimes killed while defending their cubs. Most of the time male polar bears will back away from a mother bear.

The sow is smaller than the male. By the time it is four years old, the sow weighs between 500 and 700 pounds (227.3-318.2 kilograms). It is between 7 and 9 feet (2.1-2.7 meters) tall.

Hibernation

Once the weather begins to turn cold, polar bears return to the territory where they learned to hunt as cubs. Boars may build a shelter for some of winter's coldest days, but they do not sleep all winter long. Sows, awaiting the birth of cubs, will build a den for a long winter's sleep. Yearlings share a den with their mother also.

Sows do not hibernate like many small animals. Animals that hibernate cannot be easily awakened. Their body temperature falls far below normal. Breathing slows down. Sometimes these animals will awaken to eat. Sows go into a deep winter's sleep. Their body temperature falls several degrees. Breathing is almost normal. Since the sows have eaten plenty of food during the summer and fall, they will not need to awaken during their winter's nap to eat. Their body functions such as urination and defecation stop. Sometimes loud noises will awaken them.

Sows build dens while they are awaiting the birth of their cubs. They usually build them at the edge of woods. Sometimes other female polar bears have their dens nearby. These dens form a colony.

A den is always built facing the south. This is the main direction of the sun. A tunnel, between 5 and 7 feet (1.52 and 2.13 meters) long, connects the den to the outside world. The den is very large, usually with just one room. The female uses its paws to build the strong walls of the den. Claw marks on the side of a den show where it has patted the snow to make bricklike walls. An air hole is found in the roof of the den. This allows fresh air to come and stale air to leave. Mounds of snow are put at the entrance of the tunnel by the sow to keep out the cold. When it is finished, the den gives the sow and her cubs a warm and safe place to live. Scientists have found that temperatures inside the den are about 40°F (4.4°C) warmer than the temperatures on the outside.

Physical Characteristics

All bears have similar body characteristics. Since polar bears live in an environment unlike the home of other bears, some of their body parts are different. These parts allow polar bears to adapt easily to their Arctic environment.

Body Shape. Polar bears have bodies that are thick and muscular. Their necks are longer than those of other bears. The heads of polar bears are the smallest of all North American bears. They have stubby tails.

Feet. Polar bears have feet that work well in ice and snow. Their feet are covered with large, rough, leatherlike pads. Fur is between the toes. The pads help the polar bears from slipping on the ice. Most polar bears have front feet that measure 12 inches (30.5 centimeters) wide and 18 inches (45.7 centimeters) long. Front feet, with sharp claws, act as weapons. Being hit with a front foot is like being hit with a 30-pound (13.6-kilogram) rock. Since polar bears are left-handed, they will use that foot when attacking prey.

Unlike many other animals, polar bears are flat-footed. This is known as plantigrade. Because they are flat-footed polar bears can stand and walk on their hind feet. They usually do not do this unless they are fighting.

Polar bears' feet also work well in the water. They are webbed, just like ducks' feet. The front feet are used as paddles when swimming. The back feet are used for steering.

Skin and Fur. Polar bears are covered with thick layers of yellowish white fur. The top layer is made of long, hollow hairs. It acts as a heat trap to keep the polar bears warm. These hairs also help the polar bears to float in water. Underneath the top layer is another coat of fur that is much thicker, fluffier, and softer. This layer of fur never gets wet and helps keep the polar bears dry.

Polar bears also stay warm because of their skin. Underneath the fur, black skin covers a thick layer of fat known as blubber. Blubber, sometimes as thick as 4 inches (10.16 centimeters), acts as an extra layer of warmth.

Polar bears are well protected against the wind and snow. Their heavy coats make them uncomfortable in warm weather. Zoos must have water in the polar bears' habitat so that the bears can keep cool during the warm weather.

Sense of Smell. Polar bears have an excellent sense of smell. Their long noses allow them to smell a dead whale 15 miles (24 kilometers) away. A seal hiding under 6 inches (15.2 centimeters) of ice cannot escape a polar bear's nose. Polar bears also use their noses to sense danger. People, the polar bears' worst enemy, can be smelled long before they can be seen.

Sense of Hearing. Polar bears have very small ears. Since they live in a cold climate, large ears would stick out from their heads and easily freeze. Small ears, close to the head, solve this problem. Polar bears do not hear well because of the size of their ears. But this is not a problem, because they rely on their sense of smell to hunt for food and protect themselves.

From *Investigating Science Through Bears,* ©1994. Teacher Ideas Press, P.O. Box 6633, Englewood, CO 80155-6633.

Eyesight. Scientists haven't been able to decide how well polar bears see. They think polar bears can see as well as people. Their excellent sense of smell makes up for potentially limited eyesight.

Living in a world that is always white and sunny can be very hard on animals' eyes. Polar bears' eyes are protected from snow blindness and glare by a third eyelid known as "Arctic sunglasses." This eyelid covers their eyes and makes it easier for the polar bears to see in their white environment.

Strength. Polar bears are one of the strongest animals in the world. Because of their strength they are excellent swimmers and hunters. They swim about 3 miles (4.8 kilometers) per hour. Scientists have seen them swimming 50 miles (80 kilometers) from shore in the icy Arctic Ocean. When hunting, polar bears are able to attack large prey since they have a well-muscled, big-boned body. Strong teeth and jaws allow polar bears to drag a dead seal or walrus for many miles.

Habitat Requirements

Like most animals, polar bears have needs that must be met in their habitat in order to survive. It is not always easy for them to live in their natural environment because other animals share it. Food and water supplies are as important to polar bears as shelter, space, and a safe place to live. If all of these needs are met, polar bears should continue to live in the Arctic Circle.

Home Range. The polar bears' habitat is found within their home range. This is the area that the polar bears travel to find food and a place to live and mate. The polar bears' home range can stretch for hundreds of miles. Females usually stay in the home range where they were raised. Males look for a new home range.

During the year, polar bears travel great distances within their home range. When the ice floes begin to melt, the polar bears travel from the sea to land. Depending on where they live, polar bears travel inland or along a coastline. Here they find a new source of food. Once the weather turns cold, the polar bears return to their winter homes. Polar bears travel to the same areas year after year. This journey is known as migration.

Territories. Within the polar bears' home range, each polar bear has its own territory. That is the area that the polar bear calls its own. No other polar bear can live there. The area is marked by the polar bear's scent. A fight may occur if another polar bear comes into the territory. Animals other than polar bears can share a polar bear's territory.

Shelters. During the winter the females and their cubs are asleep in their dens. Males, who usually do not take a winter's sleep, rest on the ice or in a snowdrift. Once a mother polar bear and her cubs are out of their winter's den, the female digs a pit in the ice or snow. There the female feeds and rests with the cubs. Summer dens have been found in some parts of the Arctic region. These dens are built deep into the tundra, allowing the polar bears to stay cool in the summer's heat. Many summer dens are used year after year.

Food Supply. Polar bear cubs depend on their mother for food during the first months of their life. By drinking their mother's rich milk, cubs grow quickly. Once outside of the den, the female finds plants and moss for the cubs to eat. After the female has fed herself and the cubs, they are ready to make the trip to the sea. There they find their favorite meal—the ringed seal. Seals are plentiful during spring and early summer.

In July and August food can be difficult to find, so polar bears must change their diets. Because the ice floes melt at this time, many polar bears move to land in search of food. Once living on land, polar bears begin to act like other bears looking for food. They can be found eating wild berries, seaweed, and grass. Polar bears will also dine on snow geese, lemmings, and birds' eggs. Dead whales and walrus also serve as much needed food.

Not all polar bears look for food in the summer. Males often spend the summer sleeping in sandy pits near the seashore. Because they ate so much food during the spring and early summer months, they choose to live off their stored body fat.

By fall most male polar bears are hungry—so hungry that they attempt to hunt animals, such as walrus or whales, that could kill them. Walrus and whales are often stronger than the polar bears. But if these animals are injured or stranded on the ice, then they become easy prey for the polar bear.

The Great White Hunter

Polar bears are excellent hunters. But hunting for ringed seals is a long and boring job. Wherever ringed seals can be found, polar bears are close by. Adult ringed seals weigh 130-155 pounds (58.8-70.1 kilograms) and are 5 feet (1.52 meters) long. Most ringed seals have bright, oval rings around their grayish black coats. Adults live most of their lives under thick layers of ice. They are found in the Arctic, North Atlantic, and North Pacific Oceans.

By using their great sense of smell, patience, and different hunting methods, polar bears can successfully attack a seal about every five days. Catching them is not an easy job—especially in the summer or fall. Ringed seals are scarce at that time of the year.

The polar bears' favorite seal-hunting method is to sit patiently outside the seal's air hole in the ice. They know that the seal must come up for air. When the seal appears, the polar bear takes its paw and quickly hits the seal. The seal dies instantly.

Polar bears also use several other methods for hunting seals. Sometimes a polar bear will crawl quietly across the ice to sneak up behind a seal. They are so quiet that the seal never knows the polar bear is behind it. Another method used by the polar bear is surprising the seal by coming up through the ice. Seals often sun themselves by lying on the ice floes. The polar bear will swim under the ice floe until it is near the seal. Suddenly, the polar bear will come through the ice and kill the seal.

When adult seals are scarce, baby seals make a delicious meal. By using its great sense of smell, a polar bear can often find a lair of baby seals. The polar bear uses its strong paw to break the thick ice on top of the lair. The ice that covers the lair is usually between 3 and 4 inches (7.62 and 10.16 centimeters) thick. After breaking the ice, the polar bear enters the lair and eats the young seals.

Predators and Prey

Animals of all sizes live in the polar bears' territories. Because polar bears are mainly carnivorous, they feed off these animals. Larger animals, such as seals and walrus, are the polar bears' usual prey. These animals are large enough to fill up the hungry bears' stomach. When food is scarce, polar bears search out smaller animals.

The arctic foxes will follow polar bears as they hunt for food. Since polar bears eat only parts of their prey, there is plenty of food left for the foxes. Always patient, the arctic foxes wait until the polar bears are finished, then they eat the leftovers. The foxes must be careful around the polar bears. If the polar bears are still hungry, they will try to eat the foxes.

Man is the polar bears' only real predator. Years ago, before guns were used, polar bears did not fear man. Hunters at that time fought the polar bears with great skill, using knives and spears. When hunters began to use guns, hunting polar bears became much safer for the hunter. No longer did the hunter have to get close to the polar bears to kill them. Although guns permitted hunters to kill more polar bears than before, polar bears still had a chance to run from the hunter.

That ability to escape has been lost in the past 25 years. Using airplanes and snowmobiles has become a popular way of hunting polar bears. The speed of these machines has made it impossible for the polar bear to escape man's guns. Man has become a dangerous enemy.

Polar Bears and Man— A Unique Relationship

Polar bears live out their lives in the Arctic world of blue sky and ice. For years the Inuit, the native people of Alaska, have depended on the polar bears for food, shelter, and clothing. But because of their size and beauty, the polar bear became prized trophies for sportsmen around the world. After years of being overhunted, the polar bears' population grew smaller and smaller. Scientists placed polar bears on the endangered-species list, and in the 1970s laws were written to protect the polar bears. Today the polar bear population is growing, and man has learned to live within the laws governing the hunting of this great bear.

The Polar Bear and the Inuit People

Polar bears have been important in the lives of the Inuit. For hundreds of years the Inuit have watched and learned from the polar bear. Scientists are certain that the early Inuit used the polar bear's den as a model when building an igloo. This small snow hut looks very much like the den that a female polar bear builds before the birth of her cubs.

Inuit Art. Artists who live in the Arctic often use the polar bear as their subject. The polar bear is so admired by the Inuit that it is used more often than any other Arctic animal in the people's artwork. Photographers love to use the polar bear in pictures because people enjoy looking at them.

Inuit Folktales, Legends, and Beliefs. Inuit folktales, legends, and beliefs often include the polar bear. In these stories the polar bear sometimes has supernatural powers. Many times the polar bear appears bigger than life. The spirit of the polar bear is everywhere.

Polar Bear Products

The body of the polar bear has given many products to the Inuit. Polar bear meat is very tasty. Blubber, which can be plentiful in a large male polar bear, is used for food and making oil for eating and heating.

The polar bears' fur makes the warmest clothing. Man has been unable to make any material as warm as polar bear fur. The polar bears' fur is very oily and dries quickly. Clothing and household goods made from the fur include boots, shoes, mittens, pants, and coats. For an Inuit to have any of these goods from polar bear fur means that a member of the family used great courage and hunting skills to kill a polar bear.

Most Inuit hunters consider killing a polar bear their greatest prize. Polar bear hunting can be very dangerous, especially if the polar bear is hungry. Hunting this giant of the north is a true test of bravery. Inuit boys dream of the day when they will kill their first polar bear. After a successful polar bear hunt, boys are considered men in the Inuit community.

Conservation—
The Polar Bear's Future

Today, governments in the United States, the former Soviet Union, Canada, Denmark, and Norway work together to protect the polar bears. During the past 300 years, thousands of polar bears were killed for sport as well as food and clothing. By the 1970s, scientists feared that the polar bear would soon become extinct. Strict laws were written to protect them.

Hunting polar bears from airplanes is no longer permitted. Most countries only allow their own citizens to kill polar bears, and there is a limit on the number of polar bears killed each year. These laws have greatly increased the polar bear population.

Research

How many polar bears are left in the Arctic? No one knows for sure. Experts think there are between 25,000 and 30,000 polar bears living in the wild. By using ear tags and radio-transmitting collars, scientists have been able to learn much about the polar bear population. Size of families, migration routes, life span, location of home range, and eating habits are some of the important information found through research. More money has been spent on polar bear research than on research about any other bear species. Because scientists have learned so much about the polar bear and its condition has improved, it has an excellent chance of being removed from the endangered-species list.

The Polar Bear in
the Twenty-First Century

Even though scientists have learned much about the polar bear, they are concerned about its future. People are moving into areas and businesses are being built where only wildlife once lived. Slowly the polar bears' habitat is being invaded by humans. Air pollution can easily become a problem. Business and the environmentalists must work and plan together so that the beauty of the Arctic and its animals is not harmed by progress. Saving the resources of this part of the world will not be an easy job. Cooperation is a first step.

Polar Bear Activities

Activity No. 1
The Cold Winter Arctic Winds—
Survival of Man and Animal

The multilayered fur coat worn by the polar bear includes two layers of fur over black skin. This skin covers a layer of blubber. The polar bear always builds its den facing the south and with a connecting tunnel to the outside world. The polar bear has an important influence on the lives of the Inuit. Students will identify facts and investigate this relationship between the polar bear and the Inuit. Using familiar materials, the activity will give the students the opportunity to construct a polar bear coat and to test its unique qualities. Modeling a polar bear's winter home and comparing it to an igloo built by the Inuit demonstrates man's relationship to animals

Background Information

The unique qualities of the polar bear's coat are not found in the coats of other bears. The individual, hollow hairs of the top layer of fur act as a kind of ultraviolet radiation trap that conducts the heat from the sun to the polar bear's black skin. The hollow hairs also increase the bear's buoyancy when swimming. The fur consists of an outer layer of glossy guard hair over a thick and woolly layer of underhair.

The survival of people and animals living in the Arctic is difficult because of the extreme cold temperatures. Nature has helped animals adapt to their environment by providing them with unique body structures and coverings. People's need for survival in the Arctic leads them to employ many of the animals' survival techniques.

The polar bear became a source of survival materials for the Inuit. The unique fur coat of the polar bear gave the Inuit a source of fur skins for warm winter clothing. And because the polar bear fur skin is highly prized by the Inuit, their hunters and their families wear the polar bear fur proudly.

The polar bear's first home is a den built in a snowbank. Bear cubs spend the first winter of their lives sleeping, eating, and playing in this shelter built by the mother. Scientists believe that the early Inuit people used the polar bear's den as a model when building the first winter igloos.

The Multilayered Coat

In learning about how polar bears survive in the cold Arctic climate, students will:

- discuss the importance of the multilayered fur coat of the polar bear in its survival in the Arctic regions;

- construct a model of the polar bear's multilayered fur coat, and then test its unique qualities;

- analyze the importance of the polar bear's fur and skin in the life of the Inuit people.

Materials
- oaktag paper
- polar bear patterns
- 8-x-10-inch (20.3-x-25.4-centimeter) pieces of black plastic garbage bags
- 4-x-6-inch (10.2-x-15.2-centimeter) pieces of poly-fiber sheets
- 4-x-6-inch (10.2-x-15.2-centimeter) pieces of disposable diapers
- spray bottle (empty window-cleaner bottle)
- stapler, scissors, and crayons
- white glue or paste
- learning sheet:
    No. 1. The Multicolored Coat

Preparation
1. Prepare the materials—including staplers, white glue, crayons, and learning sheets—for this activity.

2. Cut polar bear patterns for students to trace (see pp. 15-16), or have the polar bear pattern preprinted on oaktag paper ready for cutting.

3. Cut the plastic garbage bags, diapers, and poly-fiber sheets to specified sizes.

Procedure
1. After preparing the materials and reading sources, conduct discussions related to the harsh, cold winter of the Arctic regions.

2. Discuss the physical characteristics, body structure, and unique qualities of the polar bear.

3. Following the above discussions, construct a multilayered polar bear coat, and test its unique water-resistant characteristics.

4. Each student should prepare the shape of the polar bear on the oaktag paper. Then the students cover the oaktag bear with a piece of black plastic garbage bag and use staples to hold it down.

5. The students then attach the piece of disposable diaper over the top of the black plastic, using staples or glue to hold it down.

6. The final layer of the multilayered polar bear coat is the poly-fiber sheet. It is stapled in place over the disposable diaper layer. The students have created the protective layers that keep the polar bear warm and dry.

7. To demonstrate the characteristics of the simulated polar bear coat, take the spray bottle of water and spray the multilayered polar bear coat first very lightly and then heavily. Discuss the following questions during the construction and testing of the simulated polar bear coat:
    a. Why do you think black garbage bags were selected for the polar bear's skin?
    b. The poly-fiber sheet represents what layer of the polar bear's coat?
    c. What happened to the water as it went into the disposable diaper?
    d. Why do you think the garbage bag is dry?
    e. How is the polar bear protected when swimming in icy water, and why does the polar bear not freeze?
    f. What qualities does the polar bear's coat have that protects the polar bear temperatures many degrees below zero?

8. Continue to Winter Homes, and construct the polar bear's habitat and the igloos of the Inuit.

Winter Homes

In learning about the polar bear's winter home and the Inuit's winter home, students will:

- compare the similarities between the polar bear's home and the Inuit's temporary winter home—the igloo;

- build a polar bear's winter home as it would be in the Arctic environment, and compare it with the igloo—the winter home of the Inuit;

- research the design of the igloos built by the Inuit, and then construct an igloo from items found in the home.

Materials
- miniature marshmallows
- Styrofoam popcorn
- blue plastic wrap
- blue construction paper
- cotton balls
- sugar cubes
- scissors and stapler
- crayons

Preparation
1. Prepare materials and supplies—including staplers, crayons, sugar cubes, marshmallows, and so on—for this activity.

2. Collect pictures of polar bears, Arctic regions, and Arctic animals for display and pictorial reference.

3. Select from the library suitable books for classroom discussions on polar bears, Arctic animals, and the Inuit and for student use as references and as leisure reading.

Procedure
1. Display past and present pictures of Arctic life, including polar bear pictures, photographs of Arctic regions, and pictures of Inuit life.

2. As the discussion of the survival of man and the polar bear develops, compare the similarities between the polar bear's home and the Inuit's winter home. Students may then design and build both a polar bear home and an Inuit winter home.

3. Each student should receive the following materials for the design and construction of the homes:
   a. Two 18-x-24-inch (45.7-x-61-centimeter) pieces of pale blue construction paper.
   b. Cotton balls, miniature marshmallows, sugar cubes, and Styrofoam popcorn.
   c. Scissors, crayons, and white glue or paste.

   The following guidelines should be given for the basic design:
   a. Pale blue construction paper is used as background for the homes.
   b. Miniature marshmallows, Styrofoam popcorn, sugar cubes, and cotton balls represent the snow and ice.
   c. The blue plastic wrap represents the water.

4. Once all directions are clear to the students, the class may work at their own pace designing and constructing both a polar bear habitat and an Inuit winter home.

From *Investigating Science Through Bears,* ©1994. Teacher Ideas Press, P.O. Box 6633, Englewood, CO 80155-6633.

5. When the projects are complete, the students should write descriptive paragraphs explaining the completed models.

6. To create an Arctic region atmosphere in the classroom, display the completed polar bear habitats, the multilayer polar bear coats, and the Inuit's winter homes, using the collected photographs and pictures as a background.

Bear Extensions

1. Polar bears are often taken to zoos that are located in areas of the world that have a much warmer climate than that of the polar bears' Arctic home. What special changes would a zoo in a warm climate have to make to keep the polar bears healthy and happy?

2. To expand the students' knowledge of the polar bear and man in the Arctic regions, the following books are suggested. They give additional information about the Inuit people who share the Arctic world with the polar bear.

   - Alexander, Bryan, and Cheryl Alexander. *An Eskimo Family*. Minneapolis, Minn.: Lerner, 1985.

   - Hughs, Jill. Illustrated by Maurice Wilson. *Eskimoes*. New York: Glouchester Press, 1984.

   - Kalman, Bobby. Photography by William Belsey. *An Arctic Community*. New York: Crabtree, 1988.

   - Kimble, George H. Illustrated by Jean Zollinger. *Hunters and Collectors*. New York: McGraw-Hill, 1970.

   - Yue, Charlotte, and David Yue. *The Igloo*. Boston: Houghton Mifflin, 1985.

3. The long, cold winter days are spent indoors by the Inuit people. During this time, games are played, toys are made, and stories are told. Following are examples that may be shown to the students as they imagine they are living in the Arctic.
   a. Cat's cradle is one of the Inuit's favorite string creations. Demonstrate how this string design is made, and discuss how the Inuit use these string figures to represent animals and spirits in their world. Conduct a contest to see who can design the best string creation.
   b. Storytelling is an important pastime for the Inuit. Generations of children have heard about the hunting exploits of their forefathers through storytelling. Start a class story about hunting polar bears. Ask each student to add a sentence to the story, and write their responses on chart paper. When all the students have contributed and the story is finished, read it back to the class. Ask volunteers to illustrate it. Subjects can include any interesting part of life in the Arctic.

Vocabulary Words
- multilayered
- igloo
- Inuit

Learning Sheet No. 1
Making a Multilayered Coat

Student Copy

Name_____

Date_____

1. Cut out shape of polar bear.

2. Cut black plastic sheet to fit the bear.
    Glue it onto the polar bear shape.

First layer: black plastic garbage-bag
material

3. Cut disposable diaper sheet to fit
    the bear shape.

Second layer: disposable diaper material

From *Investigating Science Through Bears,* ©1994. Teacher Ideas Press, P.O. Box 6633, Englewood, CO 80155-6633.

4. Cut the bear shape from the poly-fiber material.

Third layer: poly-fiber material

5. Place second layer on bear shape. Place third layer on top of second layer.

6. Staple across top of bear's back.

7. Lightly spray multilayered coat with water, and then spray heavily. Check each layer, and observe the results. Discuss the special qualities of the polar bear's coat.

Activity No. 2
Arctic Sunglasses

Polar bears living in the Arctic regions have specially designed eyes that permit them to see in the intense brightness of their ice and snow environment. This unique eye feature is a third eyelid and is often referred to as the polar bear's Arctic sunglasses. To reduce the amount of light in their eyes, early Arctic explorers tried to protect their eyes by wearing covers over them that had only small horizontal and vertical slits. Modern science has found ways to protect people's eyes in the Arctic environment.

The students 1) create slit-type sunglasses to simulate what polar bears have available in their Arctic sunglasses, and 2) create simulations of the modern sunglasses that are worn by people when they visit the Arctic regions. From this activity, students may study the human eye and compare its functions to that of the polar bear. In addition, they should review the potential dangers to the human eye under bright conditions, why animals in the Arctic need special eye features, and what humans are doing to protect their eyes from natural and human-made hazards.

Background Information

Summer's sun is so bright that it is difficult to see objects without squinting or partially closing one's eyes. Many people wear sunglasses in the summer to protect their eyes from the bright summer sun. In the winter they wear these glasses to protect their eyes from the glare of the ice and snow. Although the polar bears do not have any real sunglasses, they do have a third eyelid that simulates the squinting that humans do.

The third eyelid reduces the amount of light entering polar bears' eyes and thus reduces the glare and possible damage to their eyes. The early Arctic explorers used this concept to make sunglasses with small horizontal and vertical slits. These slits significantly reduced the amount of high-intensity glare and reflection from the ice and snow.

Modern people use sophisticated sunglasses to protect their eyes in the Arctic environment. These include sunglasses with ultraviolet filters, tinted lenses, mirrorlike outer surfaces, and leather side shields. The combined results of these modern sunglasses are to 1) filter out most of the ultraviolet radiation (particularly in the Arctic regions where the ultraviolet-filtering ozone has been seriously depleted), 2) employ tinted lenses to reduce the intensity of the visible portion of the light spectrum available to the eyes, and 3) use the mirror effect on the lens to reflect incoming glare from the sun and the reflected glare from the ice and snow.

Nature has provided polar bears with an excellent safety device for protecting their eyes in the glare of the Arctic environment. Early explorers to the Arctic used this concept, but modern people use their scientific knowledge and technical expertise to develop sunglasses that effectively protect the eyes.

Eyes as Sunglasses

In learning about how polar bears are able to see in the intense brightness of their Arctic environment, students will:

- study the functions of the special features of polar bears' eyes;

- analyze the need for a special protective eye feature for the polar bear's survival in the Arctic region;

- study the ozone layer in the atmosphere around the Earth and how it controls the amount of ultraviolet radiation that penetrates to the Earth's surface and affects humans and the animal kingdom;

- discuss the basic functions of the human eyes and the dangers to the eyes that can result from overexposure to the ultraviolet rays of the sun;

- identify methods that early explorers used to protect their eyes from the glare of the sun and the reflection from the snow and ice;

- analyze the potential dangers that may face man and the polar bear in the future if the ozone layer continues to lessen in the Arctic regions;

- construct sunglasses like the early explorers wore, and discuss their advantages and disadvantages;

- design modern sunglasses that simulate those that present researchers and vacationers would wear in the Arctic regions.

Materials
- empty cereal boxes (for glasses frames)
- plastic six-pack holders (for glasses frames)
- multicolored oaktag paper (for glasses frames)
- scraps of construction paper
- scissors
- white glue or paste
- pencils and crayons or paints
- old sunglasses or goggles

Preparation
1. Display pictures related to the Arctic regions, polar bears, human eye, explorers, researchers, skiers, and so on.

2. Initiate the discussion of polar bears' eyes by having the students wear their sunglasses from home. Ask the following questions to introduce the topic:
   - Why do you wear sunglasses?
   - Are all sunglasses the same?
   - How can sunglasses protect your eyes?

3. Discuss the function of polar bears' eyes and the need for special protection of their eyes to ensure their survival in the Arctic regions.

4. Continue the discussion of polar bears' eyes, and compare their functions to that of human eyes.

5. Expand the life and earth science discussions of polar bears to include the following:

   • the dangers of the sun's ultraviolet radiation to humans and polar bears;

   • the atmosphere around the Earth and the effects of the ozone layer on the survival of both polar bears and humans;

   • the attempts of the early explorers to protect their eyes in the Arctic from the effects of sun reflected from the snow and ice, particularly at higher altitudes;

   • modern eye coverings;

   • speculation on what the future will bring if the sun's ultraviolet radiation becomes stronger on the surface of the Earth.

6. Compare the styles of early explorers' sunglasses with today's technically designed sunglasses.

7. Follow up these discussions by letting the students choose the materials for their sunglasses that they will design to simulate those of the early explorers.

8. Assign the students the activity of using the materials listed to design a set of sunglasses that will simulate the present-day, high-technology sunglasses;

9. After the construction of the sunglasses has been completed, make a bulletin board to display all the projects.

Bear Extensions

1. Students can do further research by writing to the National Aeronautics and Space Administration (NASA) and requesting the latest information on the patterns of ozone depletion around the Earth and on the outlook for the Earth's protective ozone layer. The NASA address is:

   Centralized Technical Services Group
   NASA Scientific and Technical Information Facility
   P.O. Box 8757
   Baltimore/Washington International Airport
   Baltimore, MD 21240

2. Invite a local optician to the classroom for a discussion of types of glasses, benefits of different sunglasses, and dangers to the eyes from sunlight.

Vocabulary Words
• sunglasses
• ultraviolet rays
• explorers
• hazards
• filters
• light spectrum

Activity No. 3
The Bear's Bare Feet

Polar bears must have feet that will work well in the snow and ice of the Arctic regions. The unique construction of polar bears' feet permits them to hunt for food while walking like a dog or standing like a human. The students should contrast the anatomical features of bears' feet with those of human feet. By identifying how polar bears' feet are designed to meet specific needs, the students can relate this to how the different kinds of shoes they wear are designed to meet specific needs. The students can, by listing their own types of shoes at home, develop a sorting and classification process that may then be integrated into a classwide activity.

Background Information

Polar bears have feet designed specifically for walking on ice and snow. Their feet are covered with large, rough, leatherlike pads that give the polar bears the traction needed to move quickly and safely. Although most other large animals—including dogs, horses, and elephants—walk on their toes, polar bears, like humans, put their feet down flat on the ground when they walk. This flat-footed stance of polar bears makes it easy for them to stand up as straight as humans. But, unlike humans, they rarely walk when standing up. Though there are many similarities between polar bear feet and human feet, there are also a number of differences. Polar bears' front feet are webbed like duck feet for greater efficiency when used as paddles during swimming. The rear feet are used like rudders for steering. In addition, polar bears' claws have a very different function from that of human's toenails!

A comparison of the anatomical features and uses of polar bear feet with that of human feet demonstrates the similarities and differences. Such a comparison shows that polar bears' feet are designed specifically to permit them to live and survive in the Arctic regions. Human's feet, however, are primarily a mechanism for moving from one place to another.

Polar bears are born with fur-covered feet. Humans, though born with smooth skin on their feet, immediately put on shoes of different kinds. All their lives humans wear different kinds of foot coverings to permit them to carry out different activities. In today's busy life-style, many activities cannot be successfully undertaken unless the correct foot covering or shoe is worn.

Different Kinds of Feet

In learning about how polar bears' feet meet the needs of their Arctic environment, students will:

- study the structure of polar bears feet, and determine how this design has been adapted for the ice and snow of the Arctic regions;

- investigate why polar bears' front and back feet make them such efficient and powerful swimmers;

- analyze and compare polar bear feet with the feet of other bears that live in different environments around the world;

- discuss the structure of human feet and why human feet are called plantigrades;

- compare the anatomical features of polar bear feet with human feet to identify similarities and differences;

- list activities that require different types of shoes to perform different tasks, jobs, sports, and so on;

- sort and classify different types of shoes according to their use, sole construction, and activities.

Material
- shoes
- slips of paper for labels
- chart paper
- anatomical model of the human foot
- polar bear foot pictures
- foot pictures of other types of bears
- pictures of all types of human shoes
- learning sheets:
  - No. 1. Who's Who of Feet
  - No. 2. Sole Power

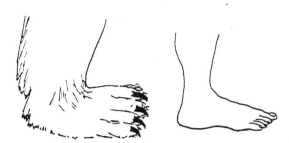

Preparation
1. Collect foot pictures of polar bears, other kinds of bears, and humans and also pictures of shoes worn by humans for different activities.

2. Borrow an anatomical model of the human foot from a local podiatrist's office for classroom study.

3. Prepare slips of 3-x-9-inch (7.6-x-22.8-centimeter) paper or oaktag paper for labels to be placed in the shoes.

4. Prepare learning sheets.

5. Assign students to bring to class shoes of different types from their closets at home.

Procedure
1. Display on the bulletin board some pictures of the polar bear's feet and human feet. Also display pictures of different types of shoes.

2. Label the shoes with the students' names when they bring them in for display.

3. Discuss the structure and characteristics of the human foot and the foot of the polar bear. Use the anatomical model of the human foot to demonstrate how the mammal foot works.

4. Assign the learning sheet Who's Who of Feet. The students are able to complete this learning sheet by looking for similarities and differences between the human foot and the polar bear foot. Follow with a discussion and question period, and record answers on chart paper.

5. Continue discussion of the foot coverings of the human foot and the polar bear foot. Then list on chart paper or on the chalkboard the different types of activities that require different types of foot coverings. These activities should include sports, dancing, bad weather, activities around the house, play, special jobs, and special occasions.

6. Have the students sort and classify the shoes a number of times. The many choices that can be made when sorting and classifying students' shoes include a focus on color, velcro closures, shoelaces, sneakers, or high tops. Use a different attribute each time.

From *Investigating Science Through Bears,* ©1994. Teacher Ideas Press, P.O. Box 6633, Englewood, CO 80155-6633.

7. Continue this study by comparing the soles of polar bear feet with those of human feet. Then investigate the different types of soles found on the different kinds of shoes.

8. Assign the learning sheet Sole Power. By following the chart titles, the students will compare shoe soles.

9. Discuss the shoe-sole drawings, and then analyze the relationship between the various types of soles and the corresponding shoe purpose.

10. Conclude the activities by analyzing the information recorded on the charts for similarities and differences between polar bear feet and human feet and for the different types of foot coverings needed by humans. The students may design a poster to summarize the foot story in a pictorial presentation.

Bear Extensions

1. Continue the sorting activities. There are many choices that can be made when sorting and classifying the students' shoes. These choices include sport shoes divided into all the different types of sports, the color and sizes of shoes, types of closure, and the color of shoelaces.

2. Expand the activity by having the students design a pair of shoes for a special purpose. Have the students write a paragraph describing their unique design. Display the designs on a bulletin board.

Vocabulary Words
- anatomical
- plantigrade
- webbed
- sole
- rudder
- paddle

Learning Sheet No. 1
Who's Who of Feet

Student Copy

Name_____

Date_____

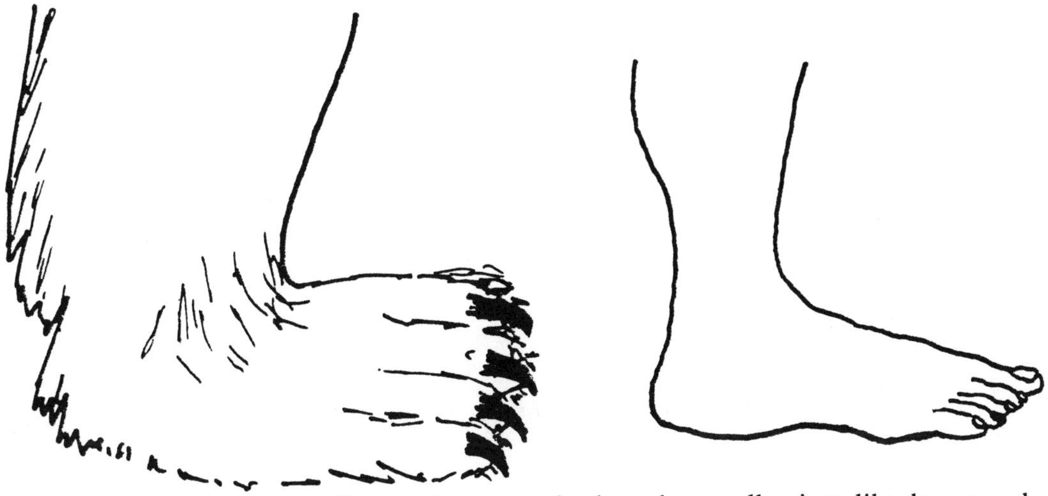

Bears put their feet down flat on the ground when they walk—just like humans do. This flat-footed walk is called a plantigrade walk. Bears use a flat-footed stance when they stand up straight—just as humans do—but they rarely walk when standing up. Compare the polar bear foot with the human foot. List at least five similarities and differences of each foot in the chart below.

Similarities	**Differences**

Analyze these similarities and differences between the feet of polar bears and humans. List possible answers to the following questions.

1. Grown male polar bears can weigh more than 1,300 pounds (589.6 kilograms). Why would four legs and feet support their body better than only two feet?

2. People's feet are small compared to the rest of their bodies. Why do our feet support us so well?

3. Polar bears have webbed feet similar to ducks; this makes them more efficient swimmers. Since human feet are not webbed, what ways or devices might be useful to help humans swim faster?

Learning Sheet No. 2
Sole Power

Student Copy

Name_____

Date_____

The polar bears have feet that work well on ice and snow. Their feet are covered with large, rough, leatherlike pads, and there is fur between their toes. This structure allows the polar bear to move easily and quickly on the ice and snow. Because humans' feet are bare, they must be covered to protect them and aid in daily activities. Let's check on the Sole Power of your shoes. Fill in the chart below.

Name of Shoe	For what activity do you wear this shoe?	Describe the soles of your shoe	Draw a picture of the sole	How does the sole of this shoe help with your activity?

1. Are the soles on all the shoes the same? Explain.

2. What would happen if you wore the wrong shoe for a special activity?

3. Describe what would happen to the polar bears if they had a different type of foot?

4. If the polar bear were going to wear one of your pairs of shoes in the ice and snow, which pair would the polar bear choose? Explain.

Vocabulary for
Polar Bear Chapter

anatomical—pertaining to the anatomy or structure of any part of an animal or a plant.

Arctic—the northern polar region; at or near the North Pole.

Arctic Ocean—the ocean of the northern polar region.

arthritis—soreness and swelling of a joint or joints of the body.

Asia—the largest continent—east of Europe and west of the Pacific Ocean. China, India, and Israel are countries in Asia.

blubber—the fat of whales and some other sea animals.

Canada—a country in North America that is north of the United States.

carcass—a body of a dead animal.

citizen—a person who by birth or choice is a member of a nation.

collar—a leather or plastic band or a metal chain for the neck of a dog or other animal.

curiosity—an eager desire to know.

Denmark—a country in northwestern Europe.

endangered—pertaining to a species whose existence is threatened.

energy—the power to work or act; force.

entrails—the internal organs; the intestines of animals.

environment—all of the surroundings that influence the growth, development, and well-being of a living thing.

Europe—the continent west of Asia and east of the Atlantic Ocean.

exhausted—to become tired.

explorer—a person who explores in traveling over little-known lands and seas for the purpose of discovery.

extinct—no longer existing.

filter—a device for passing light through a transparent material.

floe—a field or sheet of floating ice.

folktale—a story or legend originating with and handed down through the common people.

genus—a category of organisms ranking below a family and above a species.

governments—the ruling organizations of a country, state, district, or city.

grazing—to feed on growing grass.

habitat—a place where a living thing is naturally found.

harsh—rough to the touch, taste, eye, or ear; cruel; unfeeling; severe.

hazards—risks; dangers.

igloo—an Eskimo hut shaped like a dome that is often built of blocks of hard snow.

intelligent—having or showing understanding; able to learn and know; quick of learning.

Inuit—native people living in the Arctic regions of North America.

keen—able to do work quickly and exactly; quickly aware.

lair—a den or resting place of a wild animal.

legend—a story that has come down from the past and that many people have believed.

lemming—a small animal that looks like a mouse with a short tail and furry feet.

light spectrum—the band of colors formed when a beam of light is passed through a prism.

mammals—one of a group of warm-blooded animals with a backbone and usually having hair. Mammals feed their young with milk from their mothers' breasts. Human beings, cattle, bears, cats, and whales are all mammals.

migration—a moving from one place to another.

mound—a bank or heap of earth, stones, snow, or other material.

multilayered—more than one thickness of a material.

muscular—having well-developed muscles; strong.

North America—a continent northwest of South America and west of the Atlantic Ocean. It is the third largest continent; the United States, Canada, and Mexico are countries in North America.

Norway—a country in northern Europe.

paddle—to move the hands or feet about in the water.

patience—a willingness to put up with waiting.

plantigrade—a way of walking flat-footed.

pollution—the dirtying of any part of an environment; anything dirtying an environment.

population—all the living things of one kind that live in a single place.

rudder—a movable, flat surface by which a boat or ship can be steered.

scientist—a person who has expert knowledge of some branch of a science; a person specially trained in and familiar with the facts and laws of such fields of study as biology, chemistry, mathematics, physics, geology, and astronomy.

seaweed—a mass or growth of marine plants; plants growing in the sea.

situation—circumstances; case; condition.

snowmobile—a vehicle used in traveling on snow. Wooden runners in front are steered by handlebars. A snowmobile is powered by an engine.

sole—the bottom or undersurface of the foot.

Soviet Union—a former country reaching from eastern Europe across Asia to the Pacific Ocean.

species—a group of related living things that have certain basic characteristics in common.

stale—not fresh.

suitable—right for the occasion; fitting; proper.

sunglasses—eyeglasses to protect the eyes from the glare of the sun.

supernatural—something beyond the observable universe; attributed to an invisible agent, such as a ghost or spirit.

survive—to live longer than; to continue to live or exist; remain.

territory—land; region; an area such as a nesting ground in which an animal lives and from which it keeps out others of its kind.

tracking—keeping track of; to keep within one's sight or attention; to follow with electronic equipment; to observe or monitor a trail a bear follows by use of a radio-finding device.

trophy—an award, often in the form of a statue or cup; an award for a contest.

ultraviolet—the ultraviolet part of the light spectrum, just beyond the violet part of the visible spectrum.

webbed—having the toes joined by a web.

wilderness—a wild place; a region with no people living in it.

yearling—a one-year-old animal.

Teacher Educational Resources

Books

Ahistrom, Mark. *The Polar Bear*. Riverside, N.J.: Crestwood House, 1986.

Bailey, Bernadine. *Wonders of the World of Bears*. New York: Dodd, Mead, 1975.

"Bears." *Compton's Encyclopedia*. 1986 ed., Vol. 3, 116-118.

"Bears." *The World Book Encyclopedia*. 1987 ed., Vol. 2, 137-141.

Bright, Michael. *Polar Bear (Project Wildlife)*. New York: Franklin Watts, 1989.

Bruemmer, Fred. *World of the Polar Bear*. Minocqu, Wis.: Northwood Press, 1989.

Davids, Richard C. *Lords of the Arctic*. New York: Macmillan, 1982.

Domico, Terry. *Bears of the World*. New York: Facts on File, 1988.

Koch, Thomas J. *The Year of the Polar Bear*. New York: Macmillan, 1975.

"Polar Bear's First Swim." *Frank Schaffer's School Days*. November-December-January 1988-1989.

"Polar Bears in Phoenix." *Project Wild*. Harrisburg, Pa.: 1986.

Scott, Peter. *World of the Polar Bear*. Secaucus, N.J.: Book Sales, 1986.

Steiner, Barbara. *Biography of a Polar Bear*. New York: G. P. Putnam's Sons, 1972.

Stirling, Ian, and Dan Guravich. *Polar Bears*. Ann Arbor, Mich.: University of Michigan Press, 1988.

"What Bear Goes Where?" *Project Wild*. Harrisburg, Pa.: 1986.

Magazine Articles

Bruemmer, F. "Diary of a Bear-Watcher." *International Wildlife* (September-October 1989): 46.

Larson, Thor. "Polar Bear: Lonely Nomad of the North." *National Geographic* (April 1971): 574-590.

Milkius, S. "Land of the Giants." *National Wildlife* 28, no. 4 (June-July 1990): 44.

Osgood, Wilfred H. "The Big Game of Alaska." *National Geographic* (July 1990): 624-636.

"Polar Bear Alert." *National Geographic* (March 1982): 395.

"Polar Bears—Conservation and Restoration." *International Wildlife* (July-August 1984): 4.

"Polar Bears—Social Aspects." *Smithsonian* (March 1989): 40.

Richards, Bill. Photos by Hiser. "Henry Hudson's Changing Bay." *National Geographic* (March 1982): 380-405.

"Sleeping Giants." *Natural History* (January 1989): 34.

Annotated Bibliography
for Polar Bears
and the Study of Life Science

Children's Books

Bailey, Bernadine. Illustrated with photographs. *Wonders of the World of Bears*. New York: Dodd, Mead, 1975.
The author extensively researched bears from all over the world. When combined with photographs taken in remote areas, one gets an in-depth opportunity to look at the polar bear. Nonfiction.

Beard, Isobel. Illustrated by Isobel Beard. *Bears*. New York: Wonder Books, 1974.
The reader learns about characteristics, habitats, and behavior of bears, including the polar bear, Malayan, sloth, brown, black, and panda bears. New words associated with each kind of bear have picture explanations in the starter dictionary at the end. Nonfiction.

Biel, Timothy. *Polar Bears*. San Diego, Calif.: Wildlife Education, 1985. May 1985, Volume One, Number Eight. Zoobooks 2.
This is a wonderful, detailed, colorful book about the polar bear. Nonfiction.

Brockman, Alfred. Illustrated by Philip Craven. *Bears*. Vero Beach, Fla.: Rourke Enterprises, 1986.
The book describes the characteristics, habitats, and behavior of bears, including the black, brown, and polar bears. Nonfiction.

Crow, Sandra Lee. *Penguins and Polar Bears*. Washington, D.C.: National Geographic Society, 1985.
Colorful photographs combined with a story line about animals that live on the ice and snow. Nonfiction.

Davids, Richard C. Photographs by Dan Guravich. *Lords of the Arctic: A Journey Among the Polar Bears*. New York: Macmillan, 1982.
Detailed look at the polar bear of the Arctic. Nonfiction.

de Beer, Hans. Illustrated by de Beer. *Ahoy There, Little Polar Bear*. New York: North-South Books, 1988.
While swimming in the ocean, a young polar bear gets caught in a fishing net that takes him to the city where the friendly ship's cat helps him to return home. Fiction.

Elish, Dan. Illustrated by John Stadler. *Jason and the Baseball Bear*. New York: Orchard Books, 1990.
Jason, the only member of his Little League team who can talk with animals, improves his team's chances to win the championship with the help of an elderly polar bear, Whitney. Fiction.

Harrison, Virginia, and Martin Banks. Photographs by Oxford Scientific Films. *The World of Polar Bears*. Milwaukee, Wis.: Gareth Steven, 1989.
This book is part of a series, Where Animals Live. Nonfiction.

Johnston, Ginny, and Judy Cutchins. Photographs by Constance Noble. *Andy Bear*. New York: Scholastic, 1985.
Andy Bear is born at the Atlanta Zoo. He is the size of a guinea pig and very cute, but sickly. His zookeeper takes him home to her apartment. You'll learn a lot of things about polar bears and see how Andy grows strong and healthy. Nonfiction.

Kalas, Sybille. *The Polar Bear Family Book*. Saxonville, Maine: Picture Book Studio, 1990.
Beautiful photographs of polar bears and Alaska. Nonfiction.

Matthews, Downs. *Polar Bear Cubs*. New York: Simon & Schuster, 1989.
This book follows a female polar bear and her two cubs through the Arctic summer as the cubs learn to survive in the harsh northern world. Beautiful color photographs give the reader a glimpse into the life of a magnificent wild animal. Nonfiction.

McDearmon, Kay. Illustrated with photographs. *Polar Bear*. New York: Dodd, Mead, 1976.
Details the life cycle of the polar bear, "undisputed animal ruler of the Arctic ice." Nonfiction.

Moore, Tara. *The Endangered Species Polar Bears*. Champaign, Ill.: Garrard, 1982.
The author seeks to bring to young readers a real appreciation of the polar bear, its fascinating habitat, needs, and timeless way of life. Nonfiction.

Steiner, Barbara A. Illustrated by St. Tamara. *Biography of a Polar Bear*. New York: Putnam, 1972.
Traces the life of a polar bear from birth to maturity. Nonfiction.

Wexo, John Bonnett. *Bears*. Mankato, Minn.: Creative Education, 1989.
A factual pictorial book about many kinds of bears that details a story of their lives. Nonfiction.

Whitehead, Robert. Illustrated by James Teason. *The First Book of Bears*. New York: Franklin Watts, 1966.
This book presents in-depth information about black, Alaskan brown, Kodiak, polar, brown, sloth, sun, and spectacled bears, and it discusses their history, characteristics, habitats, and behavior. Nonfiction.

Magazine Articles

Binderup, D. B. "Six Slick Tricks to Keep Warm." *Ranger Rick* (January 1990): 28.

   Information on the ways that many animals keep warm in the winter. The habits of furry animals are discussed, including warming tricks used by the polar bears.

Churchman, D. "Let's Take a Snooz-z-z." *Ranger Rick* (December 1990): 32.

   A photo essay of sleeping animals. Included are the red fox, polar bear, leopard, red squirrel, and walrus. The reader learns where, when, and why animals sleep.

"When the Bears Come to Town." *National Geographic World* (January 1991): 3.

   Describes the Canadian town of Churchill, Manitoba, the polar bear capital of the world. Included are bear-watching tourists and methods for protecting bears and people.

2

The North American Black Bear

Overview of Learning Experiences for the North American Black Bear

The North American Black Bear chapter presents methods and learning experiences designed to stimulate the young, inquiring mind in the areas of life science, social studies, language arts, and art. These methods and experiences, designed for use in the classroom, maximize creative, divergent thinking by the students and are structured to apply to individual students and team activities. The following is an overview of the specific experiences addressed in this chapter.

Life Science

- identifying the physical characteristics of the North American black bear

- investigating the black bear's food needs, its food supply, and how food supplies affect its survival

- reviewing the other animals that share the black bear's habitats

- comparing the different relationships between the North American black bear and other animals and between the black bear and humans

- employing facts about the North American black bear in the Black Bear Game as a tool for studying this bear

Social Studies

- locating the areas in North America and Canada where the North American black bear can be found

- locating on a map of the United States the states in which the black bear can be found

- reviewing and describing the geographical terrain in the states in which the black bear is found

- developing strategies for use by families to protect themselves from black bears living near their homes

Language Arts

- reading magazines, library books, and national park literature to acquire information about the black bear

- employing student research skills to gain needed information for participating in the Black Bear Game

- collecting supplemental information about the North American black bear through the use of films and videos

Art

- creating in the classroom a black bear's habitat by using a large appliance box as its centerpiece

- creating props and scenery around the habitat to simulate a forest containing trees, flowers, grasses, bushes, and so on

North American Black Bear Facts Pack

The North American black bear is the largest bear species in number on the continent. It is estimated that between 400,000 and 750,000 black bears live in 28 states of the United States. In Canada they are found in all provinces and territories.

This bear is quite familiar to people living in wooded areas and on farms. Sometimes they wander into towns—even into large cities. Because it appears that the North American black bear is at ease with humans, most people think they are harmless. Quite the opposite is true. Although the North American black bear is the smallest North American bear, it is still dangerous.

In the following pages you will learn many interesting facts about this bear. A North American black bear's fur can be one of many different colors. Why are there so many different colors of fur? Why do people have such a difficult time telling the difference between a black bear and a grizzly? How do scientists learn more about the North American black bear? This chapter helps you to answer these and many more questions about this bear.

The Life of a North American Black Bear

What's in a Name? Scientists have special names for the animals they study. These names are written in Latin. The black bear found on the North American continent is known as *Ursus americanus*. The name means "American bear." *Ursus* is its genus name, and *americanus* names its species.

The North American Black Bear Family. Adult North American black bears mate during the spring of the year. Two or three days may be spent together at this time. After mating, the male leaves. He may even mate with other females. When the cubs are born, the father bear does not help to care for them. For the first year and a half of the cubs' lives they live with their mother.

North American Black Bear Hierarchy. Every North American black bear has a place in the social hierarchy of its home range. The strongest males fight to be at the top of the social order. This is very important at feeding time, because the bears at the top of the order get the best spots to eat. The female with cubs is usually second in this order, because she is very aggressive when raising cubs. Most males will not come near them. The third place in the social order is held by the rest of the strong males. Females without cubs follow. Older, sickly, male bears and young males are at the bottom of the order.

North American Black Bear Cubs

North American black bear cubs are born in the winter months while their mother is having her winter's sleep. At birth the cubs are born blind. Their ears have not developed. They have what is known as ear buds. The cubs cannot smell. Their little bodies are covered with 1/10 inch (.25 centimeters) of hair. Weighing between 6 and 16 ounces (170-454 grams), their weight will increase 280 times by the time they become an adult.

Usually two or three cubs are born in a litter. After the cubs are born, they crawl into their mother's warm fur and drink her milk. As they grow larger, their fur gets longer and darker. Their eyes open, and their sense of smell develops. Soon the young cubs are moving around the den. Lots of whining and crying sounds can be heard.

At the beginning of April the North American black bear family leaves their winter home. The cubs weigh between 5 and 6 pounds (2.3-2.7 kilograms) each. Mother bear builds a nest for them at the base of a tree. She stays very close to her cubs at all times. If she is gathering food or nesting material, a cry from a cub will bring her to its side.

North American black bear cubs begin to play while they are still in their den. This play continues as they grow. Quietly, they will wrestle with one another. Swatting back and forth with their forepaws is great fun. As they grow older, the cubs begin play fighting. Using their forepaws the cubs try to knock one another over. Biting at the neck is also part of the action. Play fighting can go on for hours.

By the time the cubs are several months old they are climbing trees. From the very beginning the young cubs are able to move up and down trees with little difficulty. In a time of danger as well as during playtime, cubs can scurry up a tree's trunk. The mother bear often uses a tree as a baby-sitter when she needs to hunt for food. She knows that the cubs will be safe until she returns.

The mother bear and her cubs communicate with one another by making several different sounds. Cubs are very noisy. A lot of crying and whining takes place during the day. At feeding time the cubs are happy and make a purring sound. When the mother bear senses danger, she warns her cubs by making loud woofing and huffing sounds. When the danger is past, she signals her cubs with a series of grunts.

By July the cubs are able to feed themselves. They have been growing very fast. Their bodies are long and slender. The cubs' ears are so large that they really stick out of their heads. After a summer of eating, the cubs look just like their mother.

Throughout the summer mother bear teaches her cubs how to take care of themselves. Keeping young cubs from harm can be a difficult job. Occasionally, an adult male will attack a cub and kill it. Since North American black bears are always eating, learning to find food is another important lesson to be learned.

By the time fall arrives, cubs are able to help their mother build a den for the long winter's sleep. Mother bear and cubs spend the winter together—though the den is crowded! Each cub weighs between 30 and 90 pounds (13.6-40.9 kilograms).

The Yearling

As the young bears leave their den after the second winter, they prepare to live on their own. By midsummer, the mother bear drives her yearlings away. It is time for her to mate again. All of a sudden the yearlings are on their own.

Life is not easy for the yearlings. Mother bear is no longer there to protect them and to see that they get fed. As the young males move from their mothers' home range in search of a new one, they may get themselves into a lot of trouble. Many will be killed while crossing highways or raiding humans' food supplies.

As in other bear species, the young male North American black bear has difficulty understanding bear social hierarchy. Many males travel into the territories of older and stronger males. Since they are not welcomed by the adults, problems often start. This may be the first time a young male has a real fight. More male North American black bears are killed at this age than any other time.

Young adult females do not have as many problems as their brothers. Most females do not travel great distances to find a new territory. Often they will stay near their birthplace. Researchers have noticed that many females will build their dens near their mother. Even though mother is close by, rarely do the bears become a family again.

From *Investigating Science Through Bears,* ©1994. Teacher Ideas Press, P.O. Box 6633, Englewood, CO 80155-6633.

Adult North American
Black Bears

A male North American black bear is known as a boar. He can father his first litter of cubs by the time he is three or four years old. Females may have their first litter by this age. Usually a young female will have two cubs in her first litter. As she gets older, it is not unusual for her to have a litter of four cubs. The female North American black bear—better known as a sow—has a litter of cubs every other year.

The female outlives the male. The average age for a female is about 30 years. Because the male travels more and is more aggressive than the female, his life span is shorter. Hunters usually kill the males, because the males are larger and the hunting season is longer for the male black bear.

The North American black bear male lives by himself most of his adult life. Once in a while, two males will share the same territory. Females often live with other females in the same area. If a territory is small and there are many bears living in the area, two or more females may share it with a male.

Hibernation

Scientists consider the North American black bear an animal that takes a long winter's sleep. It is not a true hibernator. Animals that hibernate have a change in body temperature, as well as breathing and heart rates. The North American black bear's body does not have as great a change in body functions. While it's sleeping, the North American black bear does not eat, urinate, or defecate. Bears that are in poor health or that have not eaten enough food will have difficulty sleeping through the entire winter. On warm days they will be out of their dens looking for food or just wandering around.

The location of the North American black bear's habitat controls the time when it begins to hibernate. Some black bears start hibernating in October; others wait until December. The colder the climate, the longer the bear will sleep. The North American black bears in Alaska sleep for seven months. The black bears in California sleep for only four. Mother black bears with cubs enter their dens before males.

Some researchers believe that black bears start looking for future dens in the spring. Others feel that the search begins in the early fall. Dens are usually found within the North American black bear's territory. The bear may be miles away feeding, but it will return to its own territory for its winter sleep. Dens used the year before are rarely used again by the same black bear. Sometimes another bear will use the den next year.

Where are these North American black bears' dens? They are found in many places. Once again, it depends on where they are living. Dens are built in piles of brush, in between tree roots, in rock caves, under a pile of fallen trees, in drainage pipes, and in hollow trees. Sometimes black bears build what seems like a nest on top of the ground, or they dig a den in the ground. Underneath front porches and house foundations are sometimes ideal spots for a den. In some areas female North American black bears may den high up in a tall tree.

Dens are built so that they are hidden from prying eyes. Protection from blowing snow and cold winds is important. Females often line their dens with tree boughs, grass, and leaves. This is often done if the birth of cubs will occur during hibernation.

Geographic Location

More than 1 million North American black bears are found in the United States and Canada. Hunters, who kill more than 7,000 black bears during hunting season, are surprised that the species is doing so well. In most places the black bear population is growing larger. The North American black bear has adapted well to the changes in its environment.

North American black bears can be found living in forests, meadows, and wetlands. These areas provide them with a good food supply, as well as protection from predators. Black bears do not like to stray far from the forest cover.

North American black bears live in many different types of forests. Some forests are filled with conifers; others have deciduous trees. The wetlands are great habitats for the black bears because these bears are good swimmers. It also provides a wonderful escape from predators.

Physical Characteristics

The North American black bear is the smallest bear found in North America. It has similar body characteristics and is often mistaken for a grizzly. Even though it is called the North American black bear, its coat comes in 18 different colors.

Body Shape. Many people have difficulty in distinguishing between a grizzly and a North American black bear. Just looking at the color of their coats can cause problems. One must check the shape of the body. The North American black bear's shoulders do not have the hump found on a grizzly. Also, the black bear has a long, narrow face, but the grizzly's is shaped like a dish.

Size. An average adult male black bear weighs between 140 and 400 pounds (63.6-181.8 kilograms), compared to the average grizzly weight of between 400 and 600 pounds (181.8-272.7 kilograms). Yearling black bears weigh about 100 pounds (35.5 kilograms). Two-year-olds gain an extra 50 pounds (22.7 kilograms). In rare cases, a 600-pound (272.7-kilogram) male black bear can be found.

From nose to tail, an adult male black bear measures between 50 and 85 inches (127-216 centimeters) in length. The shoulder height is between 26 and 30 inches (66-76.2 centimeters). When standing on its hind legs, the North American black bear is at least 6 feet (1.83 meters) tall.

Feet. The foot of a North American black bear is similar to the human foot. Its foot has five toes and a pad of leather. Because the black bear walks flat-footed, the hind footprint almost looks human. The

North American black bear has a plantigrade foot—a sole and heel that touch the ground at the same time. This type of foot allows it to stand. When walking, a black bear shuffles its feet.

Claws are found on all four of the black bear's feet. These claws, which are sharp and curved, allow a full-size black bear to quickly climb a tree. Whether digging for food or building a den, these claws come in handy.

Skin and Fur. Under the black bear's skin is a thick layer of fat. Place layers of hair on top of this, and you have a round-shaped animal. The black bear has two kinds of hair covering its body. Next to its skin is a layer of soft, thick fur. This is known as the underfur. It keeps the bear warm and dry. On top of the underfur is the guard fur. Much thicker than the underfur, the guard fur also protects the black bear from cold and dampness and acts as camouflage. In the late spring the North American black bear begins to shed. All summer long, the black bear looks rather shaggy. By late fall, a new coat has grown in.

Eighty percent of the North American black bears have black fur coats. The other 20 percent of these bears come in 18 different colors. The coat of no other mammal in North America has so many different colors. Black bears can have coats that are cinnamon (reddish brown), beige, and brown. Sometimes they can be white or blue. Many times the bear's habitat will decide the bear's coloring. For example, black bears living in the most eastern part of the United States have the darkest coats. Cubs in a litter may be differently colored, but are most often the same color.

As a black bear gets older, the hair around its muzzle, chest, and legs begins to grizzle. People think they are looking at a grizzly bear.

No matter the color of the black bear's fur, its muzzle is always tan. This is another way of telling a black bear from a grizzly.

Sense of Smell. A North American black bear's sense of smell is excellent. Its ability to smell has been compared to that of a dog. Because of its well-developed nose, a black bear is able to smell predators and food that are miles away.

Sense of Hearing. The ears on a North American black bear are the largest ears of any bear species. Researchers will often check a bear's head to see the size of its ears. Ears often tell the age of the bear. Large ears and a small head are an example of a younger bear. As the bear gets older, its head becomes larger and the ears appear smaller.

Eyesight. Researchers are never quite sure about the black bears' ability to see. There are many different opinions. Since their noses are so sensitive, they may not make good use of their eyesight.

Most of the time black bears are nocturnal, but they also travel during the day. The ability to do this well usually shows that the animal has good eyesight.

Research has shown that black bears notice movement at a distance. When they are eating side by side at a garbage dump, black bears know where the other bears are. Scientists believe that black bears make good use of their side vision. This is known as peripheral vision.

Testing done on black bear eyesight at the University of Tennessee shows that black bears can see shape and color. This allows the black bear to find food—especially small pieces.

Speed. People who come face-to-face with a black bear should not try to run to escape from it. Black bears are powerful runners. They can run up to speeds of 30 miles per hour over a short distance. Black bears also swim well.

Intelligence. It is well known that bears are intelligent mammals and are shy by nature. The North American black bear is the only bear that has been able to live successfully near people.

As are all bears, North American black bears are curious. Sometimes this gets them into trouble. Usually, though, black bears use this curiosity to find themselves new sources of food.

Black bears remember where there are good food supplies. When hungry, they will return to these spots.

Many times black bears have what is called a sixth sense about traps. They know how to set them off without getting caught. Researchers trying to study these animals are often fooled by these clever tricks.

Habitat Requirements

North American Black Bears share habitats with many other animals throughout the United States and Canada. Their habitats are found in forests, meadows, and wetlands. They adapt well to their habitats as long as there is a good supply of food, water, shelter, and space to live. But each year humans move farther into the black bears' habitat. Learning to live together is a problem that people must work out now.

Home Range. The home range is the area in which a black bear usually travels throughout the year. As a cub, the black bear travels in its mother's home range. Once a black bear becomes an adult, it may choose a new home range or remain in the area of its birth.

The size of a black bear's home range depends on where its habitat is located, how many bears are living in the area, and how much food is available. Male black bears have larger home ranges than females. Males have a home range of between 10 and 50 square miles (26-132 square kilometers). Females have smaller home ranges, usually between 2.5 and 10 square miles (6.4-26 square kilometers).

In many areas where black bears are living, there just isn't enough room for each bear to have its own home range. If there is plenty of food available, many black bears will overlap their home ranges. Home ranges often change if there is a severe food problem. If food is scarce, black bears may travel miles in search of something to eat. Once their stomachs are full, they return to their old home range.

Territory. Within a North American black bear's home range is its territory. This is the area that the black bear calls home. Although territories are shared with other animals, the black bear does not like to share its territory with another bear. Females, though, share a territory with other females when it is necessary. Black bears have a difficult time trying to move into another black bear's territory. Both male and female black bears defend their territory.

Adult bears know that other bears are in their territory by smelling their scent or markings. During the summer, the male bear will place his scent on what is called a bear tree. Standing on his hind legs, he rubs his back against the tree trunk. As he is rubbing his back, he lifts his forepaws over his head and scrapes large bits of bark off the tree. Bits of his coat are often left on the tree. Other bears repeat this marking. Over the years a lot of claw marks and fur will be left behind.

From *Investigating Science Through Bears,* ©1994. Teacher Ideas Press, P.O. Box 6633, Englewood, CO 80155-6633.

Food Supply. North American black bears eat almost anything. They have been called furry garbage disposals. By using their strong sense of smell, black bears can easily pick up the scent of food. Bears are carnivorous by nature, but black bears do not eat a steady diet of meat as the polar bears do. Black bears' diets are usually made up of plant matter—and meat when it can be found. They are known as omnivores.

The location of the black bears' habitat controls the type of food they eat. Because they live in forests, meadows, and wetlands, there is usually plenty of food. North American black bears enjoy fruit—especially berries—nuts, leaves, grasses, plant roots, and, of course, honey. Insects, small reptiles, mammals, carrion, and fish provide meat for them.

If food is scarce, black bears may become a nuisance and raid farmers' livestock. Pigs, goats, and sheep make delicious eating. Crops, especially corn, also provide food for hungry black bears. Beekeepers have a difficult time keeping black bears away from their beehives.

Black bears have learned that where there are people there is food. Black bears will raid a camper's tent or cabin in search of food. People must learn to store their food properly. Sometimes when no food can be found, black bears may travel into populated areas and raid vegetable gardens.

The North American Black Bear and Man

The North American black bear is the least aggressive of all the bear species. Because of this trait, black bears have been able to adapt to the changes in its habitat. Humans have moved into the territory that once belonged to the animals. Many of the creatures living in these areas have not survived. Black bears have been one of the survivors.

Being shy, black bears try to avoid people. When black bears meet humans, they try to leave. If the humans do not walk away from the bear, the bear may show its anger by making low woofing and popping sounds. It may run toward the people. If this action does not work, the black bear takes its paw and swats at the people. The bear is then making blowing sounds with its jaws and lips. Black bears rarely charge toward people. They try to bluff their way out of the problem. If after all these warnings the people do not move, the black bear may charge. With its head lowered and ears flattened, the black bear moves quickly toward the people. Using its forepaws, the black bear can knock the people to the ground. The black bear may snap and bite at their bodies. Occasionally, it will use its paws.

Over the years there have been few reports of black bears attacking humans for unknown reasons. When this has occurred, game wardens have felt that it was because of the lack of food. Most bear attacks are caused by human error.

Although the black bear has adapted well to the presence of humans, it has not done well with the logging industry. When they awaken from their winter's sleep, black bears are hungry. The outside layers of certain trees used for timber are prize food for the bears. Found in these layers is a juicy liquid that black bears love. At night the bears strip the bark from the tree. Without this protective bark, the trees soon die. Records show that a hungry bear can strip the bark from 50 trees a night. Logging companies in California, Oregon, Washington, and southern British Columbia hired hunters to kill the black bears in these areas because black bears can destroy whole crops of trees.

Researchers have worked over the years to find ways to get rid of this problem. Ralph Flowers, who hunted these bears for almost 40 years, came up with the answer. He invented a mixture of fruit pulp and other ingredients. This mixture was placed near the damaged trees. When the black bear returned to feed upon the new crop of trees, they ate the mixture instead. The Washington State Department of Fish and Game supported his work and encouraged him to continue testing his mixture. More and more logging companies used his procedure. It is much more reasonable financially to use Flowers' mixture to save a tree than hunt a bear. Not only are trees saved, so are the black bears. The mixture was a success, and the trees went untouched. Not all logging companies use Ralph Flowers' method of tree preservation. Many use the mixture, some do not.

Black Bear as Prey

The North American black bear has few predators to worry about in the wild. But when black bears share a home range with grizzlies or Kodiaks, they can become their victims. Young bears, especially cubs, sometimes are eaten. Even black bears will eat their own cubs. A wolf may also attack a black bear. Since a wolf is large and powerful, young and old bears have trouble defending themselves from its attack.

Black bears have also become easy prey for humans. This is because farmers, not knowing what to do if black bears raid their crops or livestock or beehives, will shoot the bears. And because North American black bears destroy thousands of trees in areas where the logging industry is important, hunters are hired to shoot the bears.

Each year, usually during the fall, hunting is permitted by the government in areas where the black bears are plentiful. During a period of several weeks, thousands of bears are killed. Hunting seasons are generally instituted to help control the population of a specie, including the bear.

The Garbage-Dump Problem

Garbage is one of the black bears' favorite foods. Years ago national parks had large garbage dumps for the campers' trash. For black bears this was the ideal place to find a meal. No longer did they have to search for food. But these garbage dumps attracted tourists as well as bears. Some parks even set up bleachers and spotlights so that the tourists could watch the nightly feeding, and, unfortunately, many tourists were injured by the bears. Bears were not only visiting the dumps, they were begging for food.

Today the garbage dumps are closed, and people are told how to bear proof their food. Though the black bears' contact with humans has decreased, black bears may still be a nuisance. Backpackers are often bothered by them and raids on the campers' food supplies still occasionally occur. Because black bears are intelligent animals, they continually try to get at a food supply.

North American
Black Bear Research

Game commissioners—the people who take care of our parks—must learn how to manage the animal populations that live within the parks. They use the information given to them from scientists who study the parks' animals. This information is known as research. From this research, game commissioners are able to help the animal populations stay healthy and to keep them from outgrowing their habitats.

Trapping Black Bears

There are several ways of trapping black bears for research. A barrel-type trap is the best way to trap them. Bait is placed inside a large barrel. When the bear takes the bait, the door slams shut. The bear is caught inside.

A snare is another way of trapping. As a black bear walks through the woods, its foot gets caught in the snare. Sometimes the bear will harm itself in trying to escape.

Large dogs can also be used to chase a black bear. They chase the bear into a corner, where it is unable to escape from the researchers.

Studying the Black Bear

Once the black bear is captured, it must be drugged before the scientists can examine it. The drugs are measured exactly for the size of bear they have captured. Too much of a drug will harm the bear, and too little of the drug will not work. Although drugs can be given to a black bear by using a syringe, it is safest to place the drug in a syringelike cylinder. The cylinder is shot from the barrel of the "capture gun" into the bear. The gun permits the user to be a safe distance from the bear.

Once the bear is asleep the scientists begin their work. They check the bear's teeth, which tell its age. Weighing and measuring the bear is also important. Its fur and skin are also checked. Blood and stool samples are recorded. The bear's eye color is written down. Scientists also check for parasites. Scars tell that a black bear has been in fights.

When all of the examining is finished, an ear tag and a tattoo or sometimes a radio collar may be put on the bear. These devices help keep track of the bear in its habitat.

The tag has important information on it. It is placed in the bear's ear. If a hunter shoots the bear, the tag is returned to the game commission. Research information is collected from these returned tags.

Tattoos are placed inside the upper and lower lips of the bear. These are used as backups in case the tag is lost.

Some bears receive radio collars. These collars are used for tracking the bears in their habitat. A transmitter inside the collar sends out signals. These collars work well as long as the bear travels in the radio's receiving range.

Successful North American black bear research takes many years, and the people who do the research work devote their lives to it. They work and live among the bears. These scientists from all over North America sometimes get together and discuss the results of their studies. Working together helps solve the black bears' problems of adapting to life in an ever-changing environment.

The Future of the North American Black Bear

The North American Black Bear is doing well in the United States and Canada. Except for a few areas, the North American black bear population is growing. Under the careful management of the game commissions, the black bear should continue to be a strong species. There is little danger of them becoming extinct.

There are several reasons why the North American black bear has been able to adapt to the change in its environment. Important to its survival is that black bears can live in several different types of habitats. They can live in the wetlands as well as in the forests. As long as there are trees, they will be able to easily escape from danger. Also, because they are less aggressive than other bears, black bears shy away from people.

Poaching, though, is still a problem for the black bear. The gallbladder of the black bear is in great demand in the Orient. Bear body parts always bring a high price. Even though fines and jail terms are given to poachers, poaching is a serious problem in states with large black bear populations, such as Pennsylvania, Washington, and Oregon.

With people moving into the black bears' environment, in the future black bears may have no place to go. Bears and other animals may have to live their lives on protected lands. Millions of acres of government-owned land is waiting if this becomes a problem. But before the black bears lose their environment, the public needs to be educated. It has been proved that the black bear can adapt to a human environment. Can people live with black bears in their environment?

From *Investigating Science Through Bears,* ©1994. Teacher Ideas Press, P.O. Box 6633, Englewood, CO 80155-6633.

Black Bear Activities

Activity No. 1
A Black Bear Game—
Become a Park Ranger

The introduction to the black bear consists of playing the game titled A Black Bear Game—Become a Park Ranger. This game was created to investigate the black bear and its place in the animal kingdom. The game may be given to the students as their first encounter with information needed to have a basic knowledge of the black bear. Using the game card questions as study-guide questions, the students are able to investigate the black bear by reading the preceding Black Bear chapter. The students should then draw conclusions and evaluate the answers. The black bear investigation is concluded by playing A Black Bear Game—Become a Park Ranger. The students will have the appropriate information for a successful conclusion.

Background Information

The American black bears inhabit a widespread area of the North American continent's forested areas. They represent the greatest bear population in North America. Black bears prefer forests with meadows that provide them with adequate food. It is estimated that the black bear population in North America is between 400,000 and 750,000. Coloration of the black bear varies depending on the climatic environment of their home. Physical structure—not the color of the black bear—determines family membership. The black bear is a plantigrade, climbs trees easily, and swims well. The black bear's acute sense of smell helps it find food.

Black bears' habitats are shrinking as humans take over more of the forests. However, where the logging industry occurs, black bears are considered a problem. Black bears strip bark from trees, and this eventually kills the trees. But black bears are learning to live with humans—they often wander into populated areas and raid campsites looking for food.

Efforts at black bear management are paying off in many regions of the country. A balance between people's needs and the black bears' survival needs is being achieved: Bears have their food and trees, and humans protect the environment and the bear.

Park Ranger Game

In learning about black bears and their place in the animal kingdom, students will:

- discuss the black bear information needed for A Black Bear Game—Become a Park Ranger after reading the Black Bear chapter;

- investigate the black bear facts in order to recognize true and false statements found on game question cards;

- organize facts into categories that are related to the black bears' environment, physical characteristics, food supply, and family;

- evaluate the black bears' future as it relates to their food supply, habitat changes, human intervention, and population control.

Materials
- game boards
- game-board question cards
- game-board pieces (teddy bear miniature cookies, miniature animal crackers, or oaktag paper bears)
- dice

Preparation
1. Duplicate four game boards and four sets of game question cards. This count is for a class of 20 with 5 members on a team.

2. Select game pieces such as miniature teddy bear cookies, animal crackers, miniature marshmallows, or oaktag paper bears.

3. Duplicate parts of the Black Bear chapter and make them available to the students for investigative reading and class discussion.

4. Prepare game boards and game question cards.

   - game boards may be enlarged during the duplicating process.

   - cut out game boards and game question cards.

   - glue game boards to poster board or cardboard.

   - laminate all game boards and game question cards.

5. Provide the following items for A Black Bear Game—Become a Park Ranger activity:

   - two or more players

   - one pair of dice for each game board

   - game boards

   - game question cards

   - game playing pieces

6. Game Rules for A Black Bear Game—Become a Park Ranger:

   - Roll the dice to see who goes first (highest roll wins).

   - The first player draws a game question card from the stack of cards. The student should read the game question aloud, and then answer the question either true or false. After answering, the student must tell why the statement is true or why the statement is false. (True statements can be proved but false statements cannot.) The majority of group members must agree with the answer given by the player. The Black Bear chapter is the source of information for the answers to the questions. (The teacher should settle any disputes.)

   - Roll the dice once if a question is answered correctly. The number on the rolled dice is the number of spaces moved forward.

   - Note: If a game question is answered incorrectly, the student must move back two spaces on the game board.

   - The first player to reach the finish line wins!

Procedure

1. Introduce the black bear by grouping the young park-ranger students into groups of four to six for cooperative learning experiences. Rangers need to know facts about the black bear. Use this game as an introduction to the facts about this bear. As the game begins, the new park rangers may find that they are lacking necessary information to answer the questions correctly. When this occurs, the students must go to the Black Bear chapter for information before answering the question correctly.

2. After the facts have been researched and the question answered correctly, a discussion should take place within the group.

3. If students initially answer the question correctly, they get to take their turn rolling the dice. If they answer incorrectly, they do not roll the dice but move their marker back two spaces.

4. Players take their turns, and the one to the finish line on the game board is ready for the park-ranger job first.

5. After the completion of the initial round of game playing, each member of the group is asked to record the game question card answers in categories such as bears' environment, physical characteristics, food supply, family structure, and past and future.

6. Each group should first discuss and then write a summary paragraph of the most important black bear facts. This is presented to the class.

7. As a conclusion for the Black Bear Game activity, the students should be regrouped. Each group then plays the game in its entirety without stopping to review the Black Bear chapter.

Bear Extensions

1. Students can become park rangers and plan tours that include observing the black bears in the wild. The student park ranger can prepare a spoken text that a visitor would understand when visiting a national park.

2. Because the black bear is the bear found living the closest to populated areas in the United States, what would students do to protect their families and the bear if they saw one coming into their yard and eating at the family's bird feeder (an actual happening!)?

Vocabulary Word

- park ranger

Black Bear Game Board

START

FINISH

Name one food a black bear might eat

Move one space forward

Eat one leftover game piece

Does a black bear shuffle walk?

Move back one space

Shake hands with one game partner

Eat one leftover game piece

Walk a plantigrade walk

Move one space forward

Give a mother bear warning to her cubs

Eat one leftover game piece

Move back two spaces

You are ready to be a park ranger

—1—
Questions and Answers for
Black Bear Game Question Cards
—2—
Additional Study Questions

Teacher Guide

Questions and Answers

For each question listed on the game question cards, complete in-depth answers can be found in the Black Bear chapter. The following questions and answers can be used as a simple outline guide for the teacher to use as support information.

1. Black bears walk in a shuffling, flat-footed manner. (**True**)

2. Black bears are found in the Arctic region. (**False**. Only polar bears are found in this region.)

3. Black bears are found only in Pennsylvania. (**False**. They are found from Mexico to Canada to Florida.)

4. Black bears climb easily and swim well. (**True**)

5. Top speed for black bears is 30 miles per hour (50 kilometers per hour). (**True**)

6. Black bears have an acute sense of smell. (**True**)

7. Mother bears warn their cubs of danger by making woofing and huffing sounds. (**True**)

8. Black bears run and play all day and forget about eating. (**False**. They are mainly nocturnal.)

9. Black bears find food mainly by scent. (**True**)

10. Common foods for black bears include bananas, carrots, rats, and pineapples. (**False**. Their food includes acorns, leaves, insects, grass, fish, and honey.)

11. Black bears are camp raiders, destroy honeybee colonies, and get into people's garbage. (**True**)

12. First-year cubs den with their mother. (**True**)

13. Black bears may be roused from their deep sleep while they are in the dormant state. (**True**)

14. Black bears go to the bathroom many times while in their winter sleep. (**False**. They do not go to the bathroom while they are asleep.)

15. Black bears must eat lots of food before going into their den for their winter sleep. (**True**)

16. Black bears have the largest ears of all the species of bears. (**True**)

17. When the cubs are born, their eyes are closed and have no sense of smell. (**True**)

18. Birth weight of a black bear cub is 6 pounds (2.7 kilograms). (**False**. Cubs at birth weigh 6 to 16 ounces [170-454 grams].)

19. After one year, the cubs can weigh as much as 30 to 90 pounds (13.6-40.9 kilograms). (**True**)

From *Investigating Science Through Bears,* ©1994. Teacher Ideas Press, P.O. Box 6633, Englewood, CO 80155-6633.

20. Adult male black bears sometime kill and eat cubs. (**True**)

21. The mother black bear protects her cubs by sending them down to the river. (**False**. She sends them up a tree.)

22. The estimated black bear population in the North American continent is 400,000 to 750,000. (**True**)

23. Black bears are the smallest of the North American bears. (**True**)

24. Black bears travel from 10 to 52 miles (17-86 kilometers) looking for food. (**True**)

25. Black bears hibernate in hollow logs or caves in rock formations. (**True**)

26. Black bears may wander into populated areas and raid campsites looking for food. (**True**)

27. The logging industry has difficulty with black bears because they strip the bark and kill the trees. (**True**)

28. One hungry black bear can peel 50 trees in one night, destroying the trees. (**True**)

29. Black bear habitats are growing each year, so there is lots of room for bears and people. (**False**. Bear habitats are shrinking because people are moving into bear lands.)

30. Black bears are found in every state in the United States. (**False**. About half the states have black bears.)

Supplemental Questions

The following list of questions gives the student an opportunity to develop and integrate thinking skills. These questions may be discussed during whole class discussions.

1. Why are black bears the least common bear found on the Great Plains of the United States? What factors contributed to this situation?

2. Why do black bears come in about 18 different colors? What environmental or climatic conditions might have influenced this coloring?

3. Food is a frequent cause of trouble between black bears and humans. Why?

4. Describe a bear-proof container. Where and when would you use this kind of container?

5. Why do U.S. park rangers tell park visitors not to feed the black bears or any bears? What problems are occurring for park visitors, bears, and park rangers?

6. Smokey the Bear is a famous symbol for the national parks of the United States. What is the story that makes Smokey the Bear famous?

7. Consider how much food you would need to survive for three months of hibernation. Would hibernation be possible for humans? Why or why not?

8. Are black bears getting along with people better than the grizzly bears? Why or why not?

9. Black bears do wander into populated areas. How would you remove a black bear from your backyard without killing it?

10. Consider the future of the black bear. List factors and considerations that will influence the relationship between humans and the black bear.

Black Bear Game Question Cards

1. Black bears walk in a shuffling, flat-footed manner.	2. Black bears are found in the Arctic region.
3. Black bears are found only in Pennsylvania.	4. Black bears climb easily and swim well.
5. Top speed for black bears is 30 miles per hour (50 kilometers per hour).	6. Black bears have an acute sense of smell.
7. Mother bears warn their cubs of danger by making woofing and huffing sounds.	8. Black bears run and play all day and forget about eating.
9. Black bears find food mainly by scent.	10. Common foods for black bears include bananas, carrots, rats, and pineapples.

From *Investigating Science Through Bears,* ©1994. Teacher Ideas Press, P.O. Box 6633, Englewood, CO 80155-6633.

Black Bear Game Question Cards

11. Black bears are camp raiders, destroy honeybee colonies, and get into people's garbage.	12. First-year cubs den with their mother.
13. Black bears may be roused from their deep sleep while they are in the dormant state.	14. Black bears go to the bathroom many times while in their winter sleep.
15. Black bears must eat lots of food before going into their den for their winter sleep.	16. Black bears have the largest ears of all the species of bears.
17. When the cubs are born, their eyes and ears are closed.	18. Birth weight of a black bear cub is about 6 pounds (2.72 kilograms).
19. In the period of a year, the cubs can weigh as much as 30 to 90 pounds (13.6-40.9 kilograms).	20. Adult male black bears sometimes kill and eat cubs.

From *Investigating Science Through Bears,* ©1994. Teacher Ideas Press, P.O. Box 6633, Englewood, CO 80155-6633.

Black Bear Game Question Cards

21. The mother black bear protects the cubs by sending them down to the river.	22. The estimated black bear population in the North American continent is 400,000 to 750,000.
23. Black bears are the smallest of the North American bears.	24. Black bears travel 10 to 52 miles (17-86 kilometers) looking for food.
25. Black bears hibernate in hollow logs or caves in rock formations.	26. Black bears may wander into populated areas and raid campsites looking for food.
27. The logging industry has difficulty with black bears because they strip the bark and kill the trees.	28. One hungry black bear can peel 50 trees in one night, destroying the trees.
29. Black bear habitats are growing each year, so there is lots of room for bears and people.	30. Black bears are found in every state in the United States.

From *Investigating Science Through Bears,* ©1994. Teacher Ideas Press, P.O. Box 6633, Englewood, CO 80155-6633.

Activity No. 2
Outdoors-Indoors with the
Black Bear

The black bear is the most common bear found in North America. Because these bears are so numerous, the students should become familiar with the world that surrounds the bears. To investigate the bears' habitat, food supplies, family structure, and wildlife neighbors, the students may create the outdoor environment of the black bear in the classroom. The classroom then becomes a live-in environmental setting as the study of the black bear is presented. This activity may be a follow-up to A Black Bear Game—Become a Park Ranger in activity 1, because all park rangers must know the total park story of the black bears' environment.

Background Information

The classroom becomes a stage for a life-science experience with the black bear as the main character. Different areas of the classroom may be developed into environmental settings that represent the black bear's habitat, food supply, family structure, and wildlife neighbors. Scenery and props may be created after studying the vegetation and plant life in the bears' environment.

By bringing the outdoors into the classroom through the application of tree branches, plants, and other outdoor materials, the students have the opportunity to experience a simulated environment of the black bear. By employing this simulated environment, the students can expand their wildlife studies to investigate other living creatures that share the neighborhood with the black bear. The park ranger concept is an important feature of this activity because the rangers and wildlife conservationists are important in the management of the black bears' environment, control of the bear population, and evaluation of the vegetation of the black bears' habitat.

Black Bear Habitats

In learning about the black bear's world, students will:

* become familiar with the environment and habitat of the black bear;

* discuss the family structure of the black bear and the relationships of mothers to cubs, fathers to cubs, and yearlings to other members of the family group;

* discuss the food supplies for the black bear, and establish how they relate to the bear's survival when roaming from area to area;

* become familiar with the other animals that share the environment with the black bear.

Materials
* North American map
* world map
* Black Bear Classroom Habitat Guide
* one large box (such as an appliance box)
* throwaway or recycled items (such as cardboard boxes, shoe boxes, and so on) for props and scenery
* pictures of black bears in their natural habitat

From *Investigating Science Through Bears,* ©1994. Teacher Ideas Press, P.O. Box 6633, Englewood, CO 80155-6633.

- small tree branches (optional)
- paints and crayons
- construction paper
- stones, potted plants, and flowers (optional)
- stuffed wildlife animals and birds from wildlife organizations and private individuals
- learning sheet:
  No. 1. Black Bear Investigation Chart

Preparation

1. Duplicate the Black Bear Facts Pack for each student for his/her reading and discussion.

2. Collect materials (tree branches, flowers, and so on) necessary for the students to create the classroom natural habitat.

3. Select a large box (such as an appliance box) for the bears' den.

4. Collect materials for construction of the scenery and the related props.

5. Select books from the library that present the black bear story. Have these books available for leisure reading.

6. Collect information that explains the responsibilities of a park ranger and describes the ranger's relationship to black bear management.

7. Write to the following address in Washington, D.C., for information relating to park rangers and black bear conservation and management: National Park Service, U.S. Department of the Interior, P.O. Box 37127, Washington, DC 20013-7127.

Procedure

1. Begin the black bear study by reviewing the Black Bear Facts Pack as a follow-up to playing A Black Bear Game—Become a Park Ranger.

2. Review the activity 1 game question cards for use as a study guide for black bear information.

3. Use the Black Bear Investigation Chart as a guide for the students to use as they select items for the various props and simulations to be used in their outdoors-indoors environmental scenes.

4. Discuss the black bear information that has been selected for the environmental scenes, and discuss the importance of the life cycle and ecological factors as they relate to the black bear.

5. Discuss the Black Bear Classroom Habitat Guide and how to use the information in it for the selection of props and scenes.

6. Assign groups of students to make props, scenery, and items that will complete each area discussed in the habitat guide.

7. Ask students to design, create, and assemble props, scenery, and other items that will make up the natural environment of the black bear. The goal is to bring the outdoors inside for students to experience.

8. Encourage students to act out or role-play the behaviors of animals living together in the wild after they have researched the life cycles of the black bear and other animals that live in the bear's environment.

9. Emphasize the role of the park ranger by focusing on the ranger's responsibilities. Then discuss the ranger's job responsibilities and list them on a chart. Also discuss the overall responsibilities that person has to preserve the natural environment of the black bear on the North American continent.

10. Invite other classrooms to experience the outdoor environment constructed in the classroom, and select students to be park rangers who are available to present to these other classes the information related to each of the topic areas identified in the habitat guide.

Bear Extensions

1. Use the outdoors-indoors environment that has been created in the classroom as a large game board for playing the park ranger game of activity 1. Place paper squares with labels on the floor as stepping-stones. The squares for the game can be used by the students as they progress from start to finish. The stepping-stones can be placed so that they go into each of the areas of the black bear's environment, including the den area, the animal neighborhood, and the food supply area.

2. Retain the classroom habitat for further discussions. If other animals are going to be studied as part of the curriculum in life science, select animals or vegetation that share the black bear's environment. Use the existing scenery and props to expand the learning experiences by investigating such things as the plants, flowers, trees, and birds that make up the total environmental picture.

Vocabulary Words
- habitat
- terrain
- yearling
- environment
- vegetation

Learning Sheet No. 1
Black Bear Investigation Chart

Student Copy

Name_____

Date_____

Read the Black Bear Facts Pack. Select information that belongs in each category listed below. This information will help with the design, item selection, and creation of the scenery and props in the black bear's environment.

Black Bear Home	Black Bear Food Supply	Black Bear Family	Black Bear Neighbors

Black Bear
Investigation Chart

Teacher Reference Sheet

The items provided below are a general guide for the teacher to aid the students with their investigation. Many additional items may be included in this list.

Black Bear Home (answer key)	Black Bear Food Supply (answer key)	Black Bear Family (answer key)	Black Bear Neighbors (answer key)
1. mountainous terrain	1. berries	1. mother	1. white-tailed deer
2. wooded areas (birch, oak, cedar, and sassafras)	2. beehives	2. baby cubs	2. bats
3. rocks and twigs	3. fish streams	3. 1½-year-old cubs	3. osprey
4. caves	4. acorns	4. father bear eats small cubs	4. screech owl
5. rock ledges	5. beechnuts		5. praying mantis
6. fallen trees	6. leaves of hardwood trees		6. blue jay
7. wildflowers	7. grasses		7. green frogs
	8. insects		8. garter snake
	9. plant roots		9. copperhead snake
	10. fish		10. raccoon
	11. small animals		11. turkey
	12. human garbage		12. fox

Black Bear Classroom Habitat
Activity Guide

Teacher Reference Sheet

Choose areas of the classroom for the following activities when planning for a classroom habitat:

1. Bear's den (large appliance box).

2. Props and scenery around the den to simulate a forest containing trees, flowers, grasses, berry bushes, and so on.

3. Bear's food supply, including a stream with fish in it.

4. Bear's wildlife neighbors that are found in the forest.

5. Bear family members (father bears will not be included but will be in another area away from the mother, cubs, and yearlings).

6. People-populated areas (city and town areas with garbage cans, bird feeders, and beehives).

From *Investigating Science Through Bears,* ©1994. Teacher Ideas Press, P.O. Box 6633, Englewood, CO 80155-6633.

Vocabulary for
Black Bear Chapter

ability—a skill or talent.

aggressive—forceful; energetic.

barrel—a container with a round, flat top and bottom and with sides that curve out slightly.

bough—one of the main branches of a tree.

camouflage—a disguise or appearance that makes a person or animal look much like its surroundings.

carcass—the dead body of an animal.

carnivore—meat-eating animal; feeding mainly on flesh.

carrion—dead and decaying flesh.

cementum—the external bony layer of the part of the tooth normally within the gum.

commissions—government agencies.

conifer—a tree or shrub that has cones. The pine, spruce, and hemlock are conifers.

curious—eager to know.

deciduous—a tree that loses its leaves at the end of the growing season. The maple and elm are deciduous.

defecate—to void feces from the bowels.

drainage pipes—pipes that collect running water.

environment—all of the surroundings that influence the growth, development, and well-being of a living thing.

foundation—a part on which other parts rest or depend; the base.

grizzled—grayish; gray.

habitat—a place where a living thing is naturally found.

hierarchy—an order.

hind—back, rear.

hollow—having nothing or only air; a low place between two hills; a valley.

industry—any form of business, manufacturing, or trade.

ingredients—parts of a mixture.

intruders—ones that force themselves into where they are not wanted.

mammal—one of a group of warm-blooded animals with a backbone and usually having hair. Mammals feed their young with milk from the mother's breast. Human beings, cattle, bears, cats, and whales are all mammals.

management—control; handling; direction.

muzzle—the part of an animal's head that extends forward and includes the nose, mouth, and jaws.

nocturnal—of the night.

nuisance—a thing or person that annoys, troubles, offends, or is disagreeable.

omnivore—an animal that eats meat and vegetable substances.

Orient—the East; eastern countries; China and Japan are the most important countries of the Orient.

parasite—a living thing that spends its life on or in another and from which it gets its food—often harming the other in the process.

peripheral—things not in the center; located on the sidelines.

poaching—to kill or capture without permission.

population—all the living things of one kind living in a single place.

predator—an animal that lives by killing and eating other animals.

premolar—the tooth that comes in before the molar.

pulp—the soft, fleshy part of any fruit, vegetable, or tree.

sensitive—easily affected or influenced.

sheen—brightness; luster.

shuffle—to scrape or drag the feet when walking.

snare—a trap used for catching animals.

social—living or liking to live with a group.

species—a group of related living things that have certain basic characteristics in common.

stool—a bowel movement.

subspecies—an animal classification category that ranks immediately below a species.

syringe—long, needlelike tube; used to inject a liquid into the body.

tattoo—to mark the skin with designs or patterns by pricking the skin and putting in colors.

Tennessee—one of the south-central states of the United States.

territory—land; region; an area such as a nesting ground in which an animal lives and from which it keeps out others of its kind.

transmitter—the part of a radio device that gives off signals; it sends messages.

wetlands—land with wet and spongy soil, such as a marsh, swamp, or bog.

yearling—a one-year-old animal.

Teacher Educational Resources

Books

"Bears." *The American Peoples Encyclopedia*. 1969 ed., Vol. 2, 9-11.

"Bears." *Compton's Encyclopedia*. 1989 ed., Vol. 3, 116-118.

"Bears." *The New Encyclopaedia Britannica*. 1991 ed.

"Bears." *The World Book Encyclopedia*. 1987 ed., Vol. 2, 137-141.

Burk, Dale. *The Black Bear in Modern North America*. Clinton, N.J.: Amwell Press, 1979.

Cramond, Mike. *Of Bears and Man*. Norman, Okla.: University of Oklahoma Press, 1986.

Domico, Terry. *Bears of the World*. New York: Facts on File, 1988.

Fergus, Chuck. *Black Bear*. Harrisburg, Pa.: Pennsylvania Game Commission, Bureau of Information and Education, 1991.

Gilchrist, Duncan. *Black Bear Hunting*. Stevensville, Mont.: Stoneydale, 1988.

Hoagland, Edward. *Red Wolves and Black Bears*. New York: Random House, 1976.

Matson, J. R. *The Adaptable Black Bear*. Philadelphia, Pa.: Dorrance, 1967.

Stehsel, Donald. *Hunting the California Black Bear*. Arcadia, Calif.: Stehsel, 1965.

Walker, Ernest P. *Mammals of the World*. Baltimore, Md.: Johns Hopkins University Press, 1975.

Magazine Articles

Ballard, S. "Man Versus Ursus." *Sports Illustrated* (August 15, 1988): 14.

Bashin, B. J. "Please Don't Eat the Trees." *Sierra* (July-August 1989): 22.

"Bear Care." *Alaska* 57, no. 7 (July 1991): 10.

"Bears Chow Down on Tons of Corn." *Current Science* 76, no. 1 (November 1990): 3.

"Bears Invade Western Cities." *Current Events* (November 3, 1989): 3.

"Black Bears—Habits and Behavior." *Boys' Life* (January 1986): 22.

"Black Bears—Habits and Behavior." *National Geographic World* (November 1986): 10.

"Black Bears." *Mother Earth News* (May-June 1986): 46.

"Black Bears." *Outdoor Life* (December 1986): 50.

"Black Bears." *Outside* (May 1985): 46.

"Black Bears—Massachusetts." *New England Monthly* (March 1985): 46.

"Black Bears—Pennsylvania." *Philadelphia* (November 1984): 135.

Dagget, D. "Bear Hunting the Hard Way." *Arizona Highways* (May 1988): 36.

Giddings, T. "Massachusetts Bear Take Down Slightly." *Outdoor Life* 187, no. 1 (January 1991): 8.

Grossmann, J., and G. L. Alt. "Learning to Live with Bears." *National Wildlife* 28, no. 3 (April-May 1990): 4.

Hanley, P. "Suburbs Are Wary of Bears' Wanderlust." *New York Times* 139, no. 48289 (July 7, 1990): 25.

Kerr, P. "Instead of Nuts, Bears Gather Foes in Trenton." *New York Times* 140, no. 48376 (October 2, 1990): B1.

Kinney, Paul B. "Once in a Lifetime: Blacks Rarely Have Quadruplets, but Goofy Did—And the Camera Caught Her Nursing Her Remarkable Family." *National Geographic* (August 1941): 249.

Negri, C. "Bear Fever." *Arizona Highways* (May 1988): 18.

Peterson, R. W. "Comeback of the Bears." *Boys' Life* (June 1990): 9.

"Poaching Persists Despite Stings." *National Parks* 64, no. 5-6 (May-June 1990): 14.

Rennicke, J. "The Long Sleep of the Bear." *Backpacker* (November 1988): 18.

Revkin, A. C. "Sleeping Beauties." *Discover* (April 1989): 62.

Reynolds, J. "New Brunswick Black Bear Management." *Field and Stream* 96, no. 1 (May 1991): 59.

Schwartz, Charles C., and Albert W. Franzmann. "Interrelationship of Black Bears to Moose and Forest Succession in the Northern Coniferous Forest." *Journal of Wild Life Management* 55 (January 1991): 1.

Smith, B. S. "The Bear Facts of Zero-G." *Odyssey* 12, no. 3 (March 1990): 16.

Stiak, J. "Cone-Fleeing Bears." *Backpacker* (March 1989): 8.

Wilkengren, I. "Bone Loss and the Three Bears." *Science News* (December 24, 1988, 18; December 31, 1988): 424.

Annotated Bibliography
for North American Black Bears
and the Study of Life Science

Children's Books

Bailey, Bernadine. *Wonders of the World of Bears*. New York: Dodd, Mead, 1975.
　　This book summarizes and describes the characteristics and the habits of various species of bears. Nonfiction.

Brenner, Barbara, and May Garelick. Illustrated by Erika Kors. *Two Orphan Cubs*. New York: Walker, 1989.
　　The true story of the plight of orphan twin bear cubs rescued by a wildlife biologist and placed with a surrogate mother bear. Nonfiction.

Charman, Andrew. Illustrated by Chris Forsey. *The Book of Bears*. New York: Gallery Books, 1989.
　　The contents of this book include information about true bears, endangered bears, and the barely bears. The book is very readable for elementary students. Nonfiction.

Eberle, Irmengarde. *Bears Live Here*. New York: Doubleday, 1966.
    A nature study tracing one year in the life of a family of black bears, from the birth of the cubs in February to the bears' hibernation the following winter. Nonfiction.

Eberle, Irmengarde. *Bears Live Here*. Garden City, N.Y.: Doubleday, 1966.
    The complete story of the black bear, from the cub stage through adulthood. The book describes the characteristics, habitats, and behaviors of the black bear. Nonfiction.

Freschet, Berniece. Illustrated by Glen Rounes. *Little Black Bear Goes for a Walk*. New York: Scribner, 1977.
    While a mother bear sleeps, a little black bear steals away for his first solo adventure. Fiction.

George, Jean Craighead. Illustrated by Mac Shepard. *The Moon of the Bears*. New York: Thomas Y. Crowell, 1967.
    The book describes the seasonal changes of many animals. A black bear in the Tennessee range of the Smoky Mountains plays the main role as she goes through one year of her life. Nonfiction.

Laycock, George. *Big Nick: The Story of a Remarkable Black Bear*. New York: Norton, 1967.
    An account of the largest and shrewdest black bear in the Great Smoky Mountains National Park. Nonfiction.

Liers, Emil. Illustrated by Ray Sherin. *A Black Bear's Story*. New York: Viking, 1962.
    The mother bear shows her devotion to her cubs, teaching them to live in the forest with the other animals. This training begins in Minnesota in April after their long winter sleep, and it lasts for about a year. This is a mature study as well as an animal storybook for youngsters. Nonfiction.

Parker, Nancy. *The Ordeal of Byron B. Blackbear*. New York: Dodd, Mead, 1979.
    In his attempt to discover the secret of hibernation, Dr. Alfred Clothears rudely awakens the sleeping Byron B. Blackbear to attach complicated scientific equipment to a very disgruntled Byron. Fiction.

Pringle, Laurence. Photographs by L. Rogers. *Bearman: Exploring the World of Black Bears*. New York: Scribner, 1989.
    An absorbing look at the black bear by the wildlife biologist who spent 20 years studying them. Nonfiction.

Turkle, Brinton. *Deep in the Forest*. New York: Dutton, 1976.
    A small black bear strays into a frontier cabin, eats the porridge left on the table, breaks the smallest chair, and falls asleep on a small bed. Fiction.

Whitehead, Robert. Illustrated by James Teason. *The First Book of Bears*. New York: Franklin Watts, 1966.
    The history and habits of bears in general and of the grizzly, black, brown, Kodiak, polar, sloth, and spectacled bears in particular. Nonfiction.

Films and Videos

Bear Country. 16 mm, 33 min., color, 1991. Walt Disney Films, Cranford, N.J.
Black bears in the Rocky Mountains are featured. Nonfiction.

Bears: Kings of the Wild. 16 mm, 23 min., 1991. Distributed by Britannica, Chicago.
This fascinating look at bears—their life cycles, behavioral patterns, and physical characteristics—invites viewers to closely examine several varieties of bears, including the North American *black bear*, the polar bear of the Arctic region, and the spectacled bear of the Andes. The film also describes the historical importance of bears to early human tribes and cultures, and it contrasts the appealing zoo dweller with the dangerously unpredictable inhabitant of the world. The film is available in video. Nonfiction.

Sleeping Bears. 16 mm, 8 min., color, 1982. Bull Frog Films, Inc., Oley, Pa.
Research biologists track radio-collared black bears as part of a 5-year program to learn more about their habits. The film is available in video. Nonfiction.

3

The Brown Bear

Overview of Learning Experiences for the Brown Bear (Including the Grizzly and Kodiak Bears)

The Brown Bear chapter, which focuses on the grizzly and Kodiak bears, presents methods and learning experiences designed to stimulate the young, inquiring mind in the areas of life science, social studies, and language arts. These methods and experiences, designed for use in the classroom, maximize creative, divergent thinking by the students and are structured to apply to the individual student and team activities. The following is an overview of the specific experiences addressed in this chapter.

Life Science

- identifying the physical characteristics of the brown bears, with emphasis on the special body features of the grizzly and Kodiak bears

- identifying the environments in which the brown bears live

- determining the foods, vegetation, and terrain that are necessary for the brown bears' survival

- evaluating the relationship between the brown bear and other animals that share the same environment

- describing the variations in the fur coats of the brown bears, including the grizzly and Kodiak bears

- comparing the behaviors and living styles of the brown bear and its Alaskan neighbor, the polar bear

Social Studies

- locating the areas of the world where the brown bears, including the grizzly and Kodiak, are found

- identifying the specific parks and areas where grizzly and Kodiak bears are located in the United States

- locating the specific areas, such as rivers and mountainous areas, that support the life cycle and food chain of the brown bears

- reviewing and discussing why man has destroyed large numbers of brown bears and identifying the conservation methods man must now use to preserve the grizzly, Kodiak, and other brown bears

Language Arts

- reading the Brown Bear Facts Pack included in the chapter, plus magazines, library books, travel brochures, and national park literature to gain information about the grizzly, Kodiak, and other brown bears

- practicing communication skills by writing to national parks for information about brown bears

- reading folklore about bears and their relationships with people to help students assess the differences between fact and fiction

- employing the time-line concept as it applies to the brown bear in explaining long periods of time

Grizzly Bear Facts Pack

Say the name grizzly bear to yourself. What picture comes to your mind? Most people think of a huge, ferocious, man-eating animal. History has not been kind to this shy and peaceful bear. Horror stories have been written about the few yearly attacks by the grizzly on man. Learning about the grizzly should teach people to view them from a safe distance.

Fewer than 600 grizzlies live in the lower 48 states. This has caused the U.S. Fish and Wildlife Service to place the grizzly bear on its threatened-animal list. There are many questions among researchers and the government about the best way to deal with the shrinking grizzly population. Fortunately, the grizzly bear population is healthy and growing in Alaska and Canada.

From *Investigating Science Through Bears,* ©1994. Teacher Ideas Press, P.O. Box 6633, Englewood, CO 80155-6633.

The Life of a Grizzly Bear

What's in a Name? Scientists have special names for the animals that they study. These names are written in Latin, and for the grizzly bear it is *Ursus horribilis.* What does the name *grizzly* mean? Many people think that *grizzly* means dreadful, full of fear, and large. The dictionary tells us that *grizzly* deals with the color of the bear's fur coat. The grizzly's coat is often a mixture of several different colors, or grizzled (i.e., gray).

The Grizzly Bear Family. Male and female grizzly bears do not live together. During the late spring and early summer, male grizzlies seek out females for mating. Once mating is over, the males return to their territories. Sometimes males stay to defend females from other interested male bears.

The mother and her cubs live together for at least two winters. Once in a while a mother grizzly—known as a sow—cares for her cubs during a third winter season. By the time the cubs are four years old, they are adults.

Grizzly Bear Cubs

Usually two grizzly bear cubs are born while the mother is in her winter den. The cubs—sightless, hairless, and helpless—weigh a little more than 1 pound (454 grams) at birth.

The mother bear's rich milk is the only food the cubs have until they leave the den in the late spring. Because the cubs are so tiny, the mother grizzly, who is not eating at the time of their birth, does not have a difficult time giving them enough rich milk.

During the time the grizzly bear is taking care of her cubs, she may quietly move around her den. Sometimes when the winter weather becomes warmer, the mother bear will wander outside her den. She does not go far, because she must protect her cubs.

By the time the cubs leave their birthplace in late April or early May, they have grown to be between 4 and 5 pounds (1.8-2.3 kilograms). Their eyes are open, and their chubby little bodies are covered with thick fur. The cubs are ready to explore life outside of their den. Mother grizzly is close behind.

It takes the sow and the cubs a few days to get used to living outside of their winter home. The sow may be thin and shaggy, but she slowly moves her family in search of food. Luckily for the sow, she is able to live off her stored body fat. Food may be in short supply because it is spring.

Grizzly cubs may have a slow start finding food, but by summer they have gained a lot of weight and have found plenty of food to eat. The well-fed cubs are then very active. Their days are filled with playful games. Much time is spent running and chasing through the meadows and up and down trees. Young male cubs can be seen standing on their hind legs and boxing with one another.

Sows spend a lot of time teaching their young to climb trees, because climbing a tree quickly is a matter of life and death for a young cub. The top of a tree is a safe place for a small cub when danger is nearby. During playtime, tree climbing becomes a game.

By the end of summer the bear cubs are many times the weight they were when they were born. Their mother has taught them to find food, dig dens, and protect themselves from danger, and they have learned how to deal with other grizzlies that also live in their territory. This means that young cubs can begin to fend for themselves. But mother is still close by.

In the fall, the mother grizzly returns to the area of her winter den. The cubs share their mother's den. Sometimes another young bear may also share the den. This bear is one of the cubs born to the sow two years earlier. The older cub, known as a youngster, will help the sow care for the young cubs.

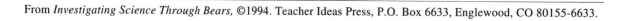

From *Investigating Science Through Bears,* ©1994. Teacher Ideas Press, P.O. Box 6633, Englewood, CO 80155-6633.

Most grizzlies live on their own after the third summer. Some travel many miles to stake out a new home but many stay in the territory where they were raised. A few grizzlies build their winter den close to their birthplace. All the skills the mother grizzly taught them are put to use. In a year or so, the grown cubs will start their own families.

The Male Grizzly

When the young male grizzly leaves his mother, he weighs at least 200 pounds (90.9 kilograms). Looking for a place to live is his first job. Some males choose to live in their mother's territory but most look for a new habitat. Because male grizzlies grow to be large, powerful animals, they must have a territory that has plenty of food and space.

Although male grizzlies live alone most of their adult lives, they still have other grizzlies close by. They often share these home ranges.

As in other bear species, the grizzlies live their lives within a social hierarchy. This social order is important, especially to male bears. Grizzlies seldom fight. But when they do fight, it is over food, territory, or a mate. The strongest and most ferocious males will claw, bite, and swipe at each other. It is quite a sight to see these large animals standing on their hind legs battling. The winner may fight with other strong males until one becomes the leader. Losers often leave the area to look for a new territory. Other grizzlies will show respect to the leader by allowing him to have first choice of a feeding area, territory, or mate. Once the leader has made his choice, the other bears get to choose from the remains. The leader is in power as long as he is strong. Once he begins to lose his strength, a new leader is waiting to take over his place. Young bears must wait until they are mature before they try to take over a leadership role. Most male grizzlies, young and old, must be satisfied to be followers.

When the male is four years old, he is old enough to father cubs. Males may have several mates during the mating season. Like many animals, the grizzly does not mate for life nor does he help to care for the cubs when they are young. Mother grizzlies do not allow the males around the cubs because the males may harm them.

The Female Grizzly

By the end of the third summer most female grizzlies are ready to leave their mother's care. The young female is able to begin her own family when she is three years old. Many times she will be a year or two older. A female will usually have between one and three cubs. Sometimes four cubs are born. Although females can have a litter every year, litters are usually born every other year. As the female grows older, she has fewer litters.

Female grizzlies make excellent mothers and teach their cubs well. Even though they may share a feeding spot with other grizzlies, the mother always keeps a watchful eye on her young. The female is usually less aggressive than the male, but she is fearless when the safety of her cubs is threatened.

As you have read, the grizzlies live in a social hierarchy. During her life the female moves up and down the scale of power in her world. When a female has small cubs to protect, she is considered dangerous by the other bears. Within the grizzly bear community, mother grizzlies are given great respect by the males. They are almost as powerful and as dangerous as the leader. But once her cubs are raised, the female loses her power and returns to the bottom of the social order.

From *Investigating Science Through Bears,* ©1994. Teacher Ideas Press, P.O. Box 6633, Englewood, CO 80155-6633.

Hibernation

The first sign of cold weather tells grizzlies that it is time to hibernate. Grizzlies spend from five to six months each year in a deep sleep. This sleep takes place during the coldest time of the year. Grizzlies, though, are not true hibernators. Their body temperature drops a few degrees, and their heartbeat slows slightly. The food stored in their bodies feeds them while they sleep. Many calories are burned. During this time the grizzlies do not eat, drink, urinate, or have bowel movements. Within the bears' bodies the usual body poisons are made harmless.

Sometimes a grizzly will awaken during its winter sleep. Outside noises bother the bear. And if the bear did not eat enough food before it went to sleep, it will awaken and look for food outside of its den. Warm weather will cause a grizzly to end its rest early.

Geographic Location

Two hundred years ago, grizzlies could be found in the mountains and on the plains west of the Mississippi River. Today, few of these bears can be found in the lower 48 states. The largest grizzly population in the United States can be found in Wyoming, Montana, and Idaho. About 300 grizzlies make their home in and around Yellowstone National Park. More than 600 grizzlies live in the northwestern Rockies. Alaska and Canada have large grizzly populations.

From *Investigating Science Through Bears,* ©1994. Teacher Ideas Press, P.O. Box 6633, Englewood, CO 80155-6633.

Grizzlies live in the wilderness of these areas. They have always been there, but have disappeared from other parts of the United States because farmers thought they were a threat to their livestock.

People have long been fearful of the grizzly. Many grizzlies were killed just for that reason. Of course, the grizzly made very tasty eating. And once hunters realized that the grizzly was a great trophy for their hunting collection, the grizzly became the target of many a sportsman's gun. By the beginning of this century, there were few grizzlies left.

Physical Characteristics

People are often confused when looking at a grizzly. Are they looking at a grizzly or a black bear? Because black bears can have the same color coat as a grizzly, one must check the shoulders on the bear. The grizzly has high, humped shoulders with large muscles covering the shoulder blades. Many times people are so frightened when they see a bear, they never bother to check for the humped shoulders.

Body Shape. The body of a grizzly is large and strong. It has a broad head with a narrow jaw. Unlike other bears, the grizzly has a face shaped like a dish, and it slopes inward. The broad chest of a male grizzly bear may measure 70½ inches (1.8 meters) with a neck of 47 inches (1.2 meters). Because a grizzly is always walking, its legs are muscular and well developed. On the hind end of the grizzly is an unseen stubby tail.

Size. An adult male grizzly is a large bear. He weighs between 200 and 600 pounds (90.9-181.8 kilograms). Records show that there have been male grizzlies weighing as much as 1,000 pounds (453 kilograms). Females are much smaller.

Feet. Grizzlies, like most bears, have feet similar to humans'—called plantigrade. This means that grizzlies walk with their feet flat on the ground. Their feet allow them to stand up straight, but grizzlies do not stand up on their hind legs unless they are boxing, fighting, or searching for food.

The grizzlies' feet have a heavy pad on their sole. The toes also have pads. There is no fur between the grizzlies' toes. When they walk, their feet leave a heavy print on the ground.

Claws are important to grizzlies. The front claws are much longer than the claws on the hind legs. Sometimes the front claws are as long as 6 inches (15.2 centimeters)—especially after a long winter's sleep. A grizzly cub has short, curved claws that are no longer than 2 inches (5.1 centimeters). This allows the cub to climb trees. As the cub matures, its claws become longer, straighter, and sharper—which ends the cub's tree-climbing days. Claws allow the grizzlies to dig for food, hold the food in their paws, and defend themselves.

Fur. One cannot always tell a grizzly by the color of its fur. The range of colors goes from black to almost white. It is not uncommon to have three or four colors mixed together. This mixture is known as grizzled. The color of the grizzly's coat can change with the season. Many times during the winter, for example, the grizzly's coat becomes grayer and is tipped with silver.

The grizzly bear has a long, thick fur coat. Over certain parts of the bear's body, the fur is much thicker. Underneath the outer layer of fur, known as the guard fur, there is a layer of soft fur. When the temperatures begin to warm up, the grizzly begins to shed its fur coat. The grizzly looks very shaggy until the new coat has grown in. By the time the weather turns cold again, the grizzly will have a new, darker fur coat.

From *Investigating Science Through Bears*, ©1994. Teacher Ideas Press, P.O. Box 6633, Englewood, CO 80155-6633.

Grizzly Bear Senses. The grizzly has small, dark eyes. Researchers are not quite sure how well it can see, but the grizzly's ability to see is not that important, because it does not have natural predators. A grizzly is able to hear fairly well, however. Its ears are round and small and close to its furry head.

It is the grizzly's keen sense of smell that helps it protect itself and find food. Prey as well as humans can be smelled for miles before they can be seen.

The grizzly also has a good sense of taste. This permits the grizzly to enjoy the bitterness of roots as well as the sweetness of honey.

Intelligence. The National Park Service can tell you that grizzly bears are intelligent animals, able to learn quickly, and have a good memory. A grizzly learns to like human food after just one taste. It remembers where the food was found and will return to find more. Often these bears lose their fear of humans and become dangerous.

Usually grizzlies are peaceful animals. They are loners and do not like to be disturbed. They do not hunt for people. Unfortunately, though, people journey into the grizzlies' habitat. Grizzlies do not attack unless they are suddenly surprised, their cubs are in danger, or their food supply is bothered. But one never knows how grizzlies are going to react.

Strength. Grizzlies often look clumsy when they are walking. Some people think grizzlies move slowly. They would be surprised to know that an adult male grizzly is able to run 35 miles per hour (58.1 kilometers per hour) in a chase. It can outrun a horse. Yes, a grizzly can run fast—but only for a short period of time.

When grizzlies awake from their winter sleep, they do not have a lot of energy. As they begin to eat again, they grow stronger and stronger. In the grizzlies' daily life, they can wander for hours looking for food. Their strong legs enable them to walk without tiring. Hours can be spent digging for food with their powerful claws busily sending dirt into the air.

Life Span. Grizzlies live between 15 and 20 years. The bears that live in zoos usually live longer, because zoos protect grizzlies from humans—especially hunters.

Habitat Requirements

As with all animals, grizzly bears must have a habitat that gives them a good supply of food, water, shelter, and space. They can be found wandering through large meadows, along river valleys, and in the mountains. Since grizzlies are large animals, they need miles of land in their habitats.

Home Range. The home range is the area in which a grizzly bear usually travels throughout the year. Male grizzlies usually choose home ranges that are different from those of their childhood. Females will often share a home range with their mother.

Within the home range, grizzlies are able to move freely, hunting for food. If one food source becomes scarce, they move to another part of the range. Researchers have noted that some of the large male grizzlies have home ranges more than 1,000 square miles (2,778 square kilometers). Females have smaller home ranges.

Grizzlies often share home ranges. Because these home ranges are so large, there is usually plenty of food, water, and space for all of the grizzlies. Grizzlies living in national parks often share a feeding area.

Home—Grizzly Bear Style. Male grizzlies sleep anywhere they wish during the spring and summer months. Mother grizzlies, however, must be careful where they rest with their cubs. Their safety is very important.

Because the grizzlies spend from five to six months sleeping during the winter, they must have a safe resting place. Grizzlies build their dens, or lairs, in their home range. These resting places are built long before the cold winds of winter blow. Grizzlies usually travel high into the hills or mountains to find the ideal spot to build their dens. This spot can be found under rocks, trees, or shrubs. Sometimes a cave is used.

Grizzlies know to build their dens on a slope so that there is good drainage for the rain or melting snow. The entrance faces away from the wind. A tunnel is built from the den to the entrance. Snow protects the entrance from humans and other animals.

Researchers have watched grizzlies build their dens in seven or eight days. The grizzlies' sharp claws are wonderful digging tools. The dens are about 3 feet (91 centimeters) high by 4 feet (122 centimeters) deep. The size depends on how many bears are using the den. Males and females without litters line their dens with tree boughs. Sows expecting cubs add grass to cover the floor.

Dens are used year after year, so the den of an older grizzly is larger and more comfortable than the den of a young bear. Female family members often built their lairs near one another. Sometimes a male grizzly, better known as a boar, will build a den near his mate.

Food Supply. *Hungry as a bear* describes the huge appetite of the grizzly. From the time the grizzly awakens from its long winter sleep until it returns to its winter den five or six months later, it is always eating. The grizzly must eat a year's worth of food in six months' time.

Grizzlies are omnivores, which means they eat plants as well as animals and fish. Researchers tell us that grizzlies know where to find certain foods in their home range. They also know what time of year to find it.

When their winter sleep is over, grizzlies are able to eat fresh green grass, tender leaves, and roots of young plants. Insects—found by digging with their long claws—will also add to the grizzlies' menu. During the summer, fruits and wild berries become a part of the diet, and honey, of course, is a favorite grizzly treat. And then in autumn, as the leaves begin to fall, grizzlies are able to feast upon many different kinds of nuts.

Although plants and insects are a large part of the grizzlies' diet, fish and animals help to fill the stomachs of these large mammals. Grizzlies will hunt small animals, such as ground squirrels, gophers, and mice. Larger animals are difficult for grizzlies to catch. Slow-moving farm animals, however, are easy prey for hungry grizzlies. In the spring, baby animals can also be a tasty treat.

Grizzlies often eat carrion and the kill of other animals. They are scavengers. Carcasses of animals that did not make it through the winter often make a meal for grizzlies. It is not uncommon for two or more grizzlies to share a dead carcass.

Grizzlies have also learned to enjoy human food—provided by the campers at national parks. Through the years bears were known to raid garbage dumps. When the dumps were closed, the bears traveled to the campsites. Accidents began to happen between the grizzlies and humans. Today, the people in charge of the parks take great care to instruct campers how to bear proof their food and garbage. Getting food from human sources is not the safe way for a grizzly to eat.

Salmon—A Grizzly Bear Favorite. In some wilderness areas the grizzly is close to water, which provides fish. Salmon is a bear favorite, and grizzlies will travel miles to enjoy this yearly feast. One never knows how the grizzly is going to catch the fish. A grizzly may stand in the water and lunge at the salmon as it swims by. Visitors have seen a grizzly take its paw and swipe at the fish. Quickly the grizzly picks up the fish in its mouth and eats. Sows will pick up a salmon, take a small bite, and fling it to their cubs standing on the shore.

Some grizzlies put their heads underwater to catch a fish. When a fish is spotted, the bears open their jaws and catch it. This method of fishing is known as snorkeling.

When the salmon are swimming upstream in the rivers, the grizzlies fish until the salmon have moved out of the area. Although grizzlies like to be alone, during salmon-running time, they gather together in large numbers. This gathering is not always peaceful. But after the leader picks its favorite fishing spot, the rest of the grizzlies fish with few problems. Grizzlies can catch as many as 20 salmon an hour on a good day.

The Grizzly Bear and Man

Today, many grizzlies live on protected land. They are safe from hunters. People visiting the areas in which the grizzlies live are often eager to see them. Sometimes this is not a pleasant meeting.

From *Investigating Science Through Bears,* ©1994. Teacher Ideas Press, P.O. Box 6633, Englewood, CO 80155-6633.

Visiting in the Grizzlies' Territory

Now that humans have more free time to enjoy life, they are spending this time in the wilderness hiking and camping. Occasionally people and grizzly meet. A surprised or frightened grizzly will often attack a human. Usually the human is badly injured—sometimes killed. The National Park Service will track down that grizzly so that it cannot harm others. If someone is killed, the grizzly is usually destroyed.

When families began to camp, grizzlies soon learned that where there were people there was food. Grizzlies followed the scent right to the campsite or the garbage dumps. After a time the grizzlies were no longer afraid of people. The park rangers had a real problem on their hands.

Great care is taken by the National Park Service to keep humans and grizzlies safely apart. Rules and regulations are given to the visitors of national parks to help them avoid life-and-death meetings with the grizzlies. There are several simple things to remember when traveling in grizzly country.

> Food and odors attract bears.
> Bears don't like surprises.
> Bears are wild animals.
>
> —Yellowstone Guide, 1992

If visitors remember these statements, they have a good chance of being safe. You must be sure to keep your eyes open and to be on the lookout for signs that a grizzly is close by. Always remember: One never knows what the grizzly is going to do.

The Grizzly Bear as Prey

Over the years, the grizzly bear population has been slowly disappearing. The grizzly has no animal as its enemy, though occasionally male grizzlies will attack each other. Humans are the real enemy of the grizzly.

For hundreds of years the grizzly ruled the Great Plains of the United States. There were thousands of them throughout the western part of this country. They lived peacefully among themselves, knowing that they were safe from other animals.

Native Americans and early explorers respected the grizzly. They knew that it was a great and powerful animal. At that time, humans and the grizzly were able to live in the same habitat.

But soon the settlers, along with their guns, moved west. Farms and towns were built where the grizzly lived, and hunting the grizzly became a great sport. The grizzly began to disappear from certain areas of its habitat.

Hunting the Grizzly

Today, many states will not permit hunting of the grizzly. Some states, such as Montana, and parts of Canada, will permit hunting during a limited time. If too many grizzlies have been killed during the year—as the result of raiding farmers' livestock, for example, when their own food supplies are gone—the hunting season is canceled.

If a hunting season is permitted, young grizzlies are at great risk. They are much smaller than an adult grizzly and, therefore, are often mistaken for a black bear.

Poaching and the Grizzly Bear

There is a market for grizzly bear body parts throughout the world. Since there is limited legal hunting of the grizzly allowed, illegal hunting often takes place. This is known as poaching. Many times it is difficult for the National Park Service to know that poaching is taking place, and hunters are careful because they are well paid for certain body parts. A grizzly bear skin, for example, sells for more than $10,000. Medicines made in the Orient use dried grizzly gallbladder—at $700 an ounce. A perfectly shaped claw is priced at $200. Of course, some believe that a grizzly's head is a perfect trophy for a game room.

More park rangers patrolling the areas of poaching activities would help to reduce the problem. Unfortunately, this is a difficult task, because the grizzly lives in a large area of wilderness. In addition, it is expensive to protect millions of square miles. But stopping the demand for animals as decoration or medicine would take away the poachers' job.

Grizzly Bear Research

Research is a way to help save the grizzly bear. The National Park Service and the U.S. Forest Service have scientists studying the habits of grizzlies. Even people who do not work with the government spend hundreds of hours studying these animals. Experts feel that the more people there are researching the grizzly, the better the chance the grizzly population will be saved.

What do the researchers do when they study the grizzly? If the grizzlies are living in a territory with few trees and little ground cover, researchers can sit and observe them for hours. But most of the time, studying the grizzly is a difficult task. Their mountainous and heavily wooded habitats make it almost impossible to see them. Radio collars are the best way for the scientists to study the daily routine of the grizzly. By listening to the signals from the collar, scientists are able to track the bear and record its travel throughout its home range.

How do the scientists place the collars on the grizzlies? Grizzlies are usually caught by using traps that are placed in areas where grizzlies have been seen. Each day the scientists check the trap. If the grizzly has been caught, a tranquilizer gun is used to put it to sleep. When the scientists are sure that the grizzly is unconscious, they examine the bear. A tooth is removed to check the bear's age. The length and weight of the grizzly's body is measured. Blood samples are taken. Scientists check to see if the bear is male or female. The bear's fur and feet are also checked. When the examination is finished, a radio collar is placed around the grizzly's neck.

Trapping bears for research is not always a safe project. Scientists must be careful when handling the animal. A trapped animal is scared as well as angry. It can easily harm itself. Tranquilizer guns can also harm the animal if they are not used correctly. There is always a great risk to people and the bear during this research.

Many scientists spend years studying the grizzlies. John and Frank Craighead were two well-known animal researchers who studied the grizzly bear problem in Yellowstone National Park from 1959 to 1971. The bears' daily habits were watched and recorded. The Craigheads even crawled into their dens to get firsthand information about the grizzlies' winter sleeping conditions. They recommended that the grizzly bears be slowly removed from feeding at the garbage dumps. The National Park Service did not follow their advice. Serious problems resulted from the National Park Service's decision. Their work for this agency ended at this time. Because of their efforts, many researchers have continued to study bears. Along with other scientists, the Craigheads made many suggestions on how we can help save the grizzly population.

The Future
of the Grizzly Bear

Today the grizzly bear is considered a threatened species by the U.S. Fish and Wildlife Service. Research has shown that the grizzly will become endangered if man does not learn how to live with the grizzly peacefully.

Thousands of acres of land in Yellowstone and Glacier national parks in the United States have been made into protected areas for many different types of wildlife. Because the grizzly is a threatened species, it can enjoy the freedom of living in this area under the protection of government agencies. Fewer than 600 grizzlies live in Wyoming, Montana, and Idaho. Once there were thousands. Officials of Yellowstone National Park, a safe home for many grizzlies, spotted about 200 grizzlies within the park's borders last year.

What about the wilderness that is not protected by the law? Some of America's human population has moved into the territory of the grizzly. Businesses such as logging and land development have greatly changed the forests where the grizzly live. Humans must limit their expansion into the wilderness, otherwise the grizzly will lose its natural home.

Education—
The Key to Understanding

To some people the grizzly bear is a nuisance and should be destroyed. Fortunately, the majority of the population wants to protect the grizzly and its habitat. By learning how the grizzly lives, following rules and regulations while visiting its habitat, and limiting the development of the land in the grizzlies' habitat, there is a good chance that people can help to rebuild the grizzly population.

The Kodiak Brown Bear

The brown bear can be found throughout the United States, Canada, Europe, and Asia. A grizzly is a brown bear that lives in the mountains and plains west of the Mississippi River. It is larger than the regular brown and has a grizzle-colored coat. Its cousin, the Kodiak bear, is a grizzly that lives on Kodiak Island in Alaska.

The Kodiak brown bear (*Ursus arctos middendorfii*) is the largest land carnivore in North America. It lives in the coastal areas of Kodiak Island. The main food in a Kodiak's diet is fish. Because fish contains lots of protein, the Kodiak grows larger than the grizzly. Although grizzlies do eat meat, they do so in much smaller amounts than Kodiaks.

Although the Kodiak looks much like its cousin, the grizzly, there are differences. Besides the differences in weight, there are two body differences. The Kodiak has a wider face and a larger skull than the grizzly.

The way the two bears live are very similar. Although they both live on protected land, the Kodiak population is larger. Fifty years ago the Kodiak almost disappeared from the island. As time went on, however, the people living there realized that tourists were visiting Kodiak Island to see the bears. A lot of money was being spent by the tourists. The Alaska Department of Fish and Game made Kodiak Island a protected habitat for the Kodiaks. Photographers from around the world go to the island to take pictures of these bears salmon fishing every year, and hunters travel there for a chance to hunt a limited number of Kodiaks. In part because scientists spend hours studying the Kodiaks' habits, the Kodiak population is growing larger every year.

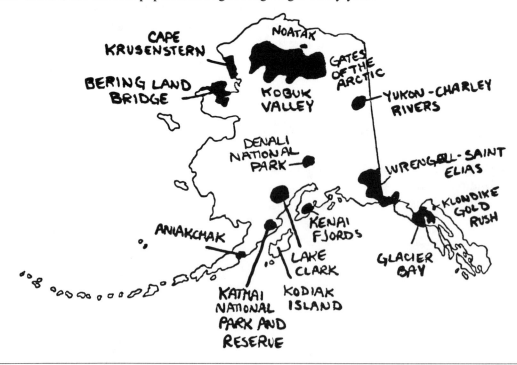

Brown Bear Activities

Activity No. 1
Going Fishing

The brown bear found in Alaska eats large amounts of food to fuel its large body. The students may investigate the brown bear's special needs for salmon as a food source. The bear's fishing techniques demonstrate unique food-gathering methods for an animal. The students may build a model of the bear's fishing environment to demonstrate these methods.

Background Information

The salmon migration in the streams of Alaska is a grand spectacle. The brown bears feast daily as the millions of fish fight their way upstream. Each bear develops its own style of fishing. To see the bears "fishing" for salmon is a fascinating event each year. The students may build a model illustrating the salmon migration and the bears' fishing activities.

Bear Food

In learning about the brown bear's need for salmon as a food source, students will:

- locate the rivers in Alaska where the salmon run;
- calculate the amount of salmon eaten by the Alaskan brown bear in a summer season;
- study the techniques the brown bear uses to catch salmon;
- investigate the migration process used by the salmon each year;
- build an environmental model to simulate the bear's activities at the streams while it is catching salmon.

Materials
- Brown Bear Facts Pack
- Teacher Reference Sheet: Suggested Review for the River Model Activity
- Teacher Reference Sheet: Assignment Guide—River Model Activity
- 3-x-5-inch (7.6-x-12.7-centimeter) cards
- sand
- rocks and soil
- pine tree sticks
- box (lid of appliance box)
- fish-shaped crackers
- card stock
- blue plastic wrapping material
- brass clips
- Christmas tree "icicles"

- modeling clay
- learning sheet:
  No. 1. Brown Bear Facts About Fishing

Preparation
1. Select books from the library for discussion of salmon migration in Alaskan waters.

2. Collect materials for building the river model.

3. Prepare 3-x-5-inch (7.6-x-12.7-centimeter) cards with project assignments from those suggested in the attached Teacher Reference Sheet.

Procedure
1. The Brown Bear Facts Pack and Brown Bear Learning Sheet No. 1 are available to provide information for discussions relating to the brown bear and its fishing habits and techniques.

2. Discuss the brown bear's food supply, its need for fish in its diet, and how salmon meets this need.

3. Assign the students supplemental materials to read about salmon migration, and discuss how this phenomenon can help the brown bear's preparation for its winter sleep.

4. Divide the students into groups of twos for the building of a river model of the fishing area of the brown bear. Have the student pairs each draw a card to determine their specific assignment in this activity.

5. Initiate a classroom discussion after the students have researched the areas given on their cards.

6. Follow the above discussions on all topics identified on the cards by asking the students to build that portion of the salmon migration-bear fishing river model as identified on their specific 3-x-5-inch (7.6-x-12.7-centimeter) card.

7. Assemble all the assigned parts of the project on a large table for viewing by parents and other classes.

8. Identify students who will be assigned to answer questions from parents and other students on specific parts of the river model.

Vocabulary Words
- salmon
- migration
- spawning

Brown Bear Learning Sheet No. 1
Brown Bear Facts About Fishing

Fishing Techniques

Each bear has its individual style. Some of these include:

- plunging headlong into the river and grabbing the fish in its jaws;

- waiting quietly for the salmon to come by, and then quickly pinning it with a forepaw;

- throwing itself into a pool of fish with a belly flop (young, inexperienced bears often use this technique);

- standing at one place in the river where the salmon jump high enough to clear the rocks, and then grabbing the fish out of the air;

- climbing into a pool below the rocks, stretching its paws out into the current, and when a salmon brushes against a paw, pinning it with the other paw (as if the bear is clapping its hands!);

- standing in a river the bear takes a deep breath, puts its head underwater (with its ears sticking out), and wades upstream. When it sees a fish, it just open its jaws and grabs it!

Brown Bear Trivia

- Bears do not like to get their ears wet and will try to "snorkel" with their ears above water—just as they do in the last fishing technique above.

- When not salmon fishing in the river, the bear's main diet consists of plants and berries.

- The brown bear has a shaggy fur coat whose colors can be black, cinnamon, red, blond, or a mixture of all these colors.

Food Facts

- Bears catch, partly eat, and discard as many as 20 salmon each hour!

- Brown bears consume as much as 80 or 90 pounds (36.4-41 kilograms) of fish each day when the salmon are running. Bears can gain between 3 and 6 pounds (1.4-2.7 kilograms) of fat in 24 hours.

From *Investigating Science Through Bears,* ©1994. Teacher Ideas Press, P.O. Box 6633, Englewood, CO 80155-6633.

Suggested Review
for the River Model Activity

Teacher Guide

Prior to starting the River Model Activity it is suggested that the following questions be reviewed to provide a base of knowledge for the students' activities.

1. What are the shapes and sizes of the rivers and streams that are located in those Alaskan areas where the salmon do their spawning?

2. Locate the sources of the above streams and rivers. How and where does a stream begin?

3. What factors are needed to create waterfalls?

4. The streambeds and riverbeds are created because what natural factors take place? List materials that make up a streambed or riverbed.

5. What will the shorelines of the Alaskan rivers and streams look like where the salmon spawn? List what vegetation might be found in the wilderness.

6. What will the mountains look like in the spring and summer? List items and environmental conditions that will exist on the mountains and mountain peaks.

7. Investigate the salmon story. How many fish will attempt to return to their spawning ground, and what percentage will be successful? What are the unique characteristics of the salmon that take them back to their spawning grounds?

8. What do the streams and rivers of Alaska look like since pollution is not a problem? Analyze what would happen if humans were to begin polluting these streams and rivers. How would this affect the salmon, the bears, and other wildlife?

9. Review how the brown bears catch the big salmon. What techniques do the brown bears demonstrate when fishing? List the bear movements or positions that are used as the bears catch the salmon.

10. List the animals and birds that are part of the brown bear's environment.

An Assignment Guide—
River Model Activity

Teacher Guide

The following items are suggested assignment guides for the 3-x-5-inch (7.6-x-12.7-centimeter) cards to be given to the students prior to their building activities. A total of 10 guides are given (for a class size of 20 students with 10 two-student teams). Larger classes require additional guides or larger teams. Prior to the construction of the river model, the teacher should place a large cardboard box with low sides on a solid base such as a table.

1. Outline with a pencil on the bottom of the large cardboard box the shapes of possible rivers and streams as they come from the mountains. Outline with the pencil where the mountains are to be placed. Build the mountains from brown grocery bags stuffed with crumpled newspapers. Glue the mountains in place.

2. Determine where the waterfalls will be placed in the rivers and streams. Build the waterfalls with rocks and tinsel.

3. Outline the rivers and streams, and locate the waterfalls. Then create the riverbeds and streambeds with sand and rocks.

4. Determine where the river and stream shorelines are to be placed. Use sand, soil, and small rocks to build the shorelines that would be found in the wilderness.

5. List the items and climatic conditions of spring and summer in Alaska, then cover the shorelines and mountains with vegetation. Use pine tree sticks, branches, and small leaves along with other outdoor vegetation to simulate what might be found in an Alaskan wilderness.

6. Place salmon in the streams and rivers as they would be when they are traveling to their spawning areas. Fish crackers make great salmon!

7. Note that because our pollution has not reached the Alaskan wilderness, the streams and rivers should have a blue, clear look. Carefully place the blue plastic wrap in the streams and rivers. It will appear as if you are looking down into the clear, blue waters and watching the fish swim upstream.

8. Color many of the card-stock patterns. Put together the bear pieces with the brass fasteners. This makes movable parts for the bears. They are now ready for the model.

9. Move the bear parts as if the bears were catching fish in the streams and rivers. Mount the bear models in small pieces of modeling clay so that they will stand up on the model. Place the bears in the streams and rivers and along the shorelines.

10. Use oaktag paper to make animals and birds that share the brown bear's environment. Color the animals and birds, and then cut them out. Mount them in modeling clay also, and place them in their environment along the streams and rivers and shorelines.

Making Bears
for the River Model

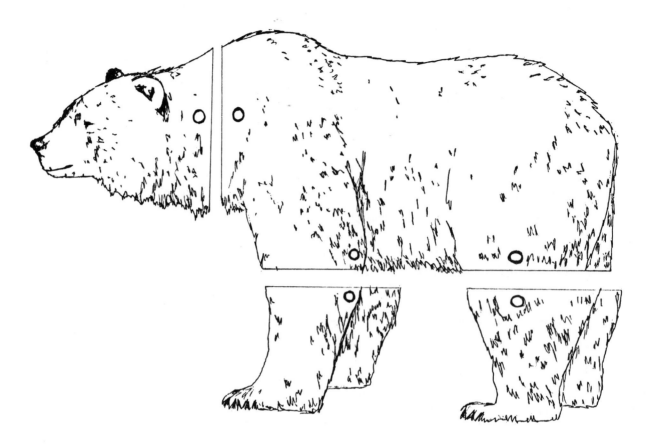

- Each student should make two bears.
- Color the brown bear parts.
- Cut out the pieces.
- Join the bear parts together with brass fasteners.

Your bears are now ready to "go fishing" in the streams and rivers.

Activity No. 2
Nosing Around with the
Grizzly Bear

The grizzly bear, a member of the brown bear family, is found only on the North American continent. As with the other members of the brown bear family, the grizzly uses its excellent sense of smell to hunt for its food. Exploring the olfactory senses in both human beings and the grizzly bear allows the students to investigate the need for the sense of smell in both humans and other mammals such as the grizzly bear. This activity gives students an opportunity to understand how the grizzly bear relies on its superior sense of smell in 1) searching for proper food for its diet, and 2) staying aware of its surroundings. A comparison is made between the students' olfactory sense and the grizzly bear's olfactory sense as the students go through the activity of "nosing around with the grizzly bear."

Background Information

The sense of smell is of great importance to the grizzly bear in its search for the food necessary for survival. In addition, the grizzly bear's keen sense of smell keeps it aware of its environment, helping it to gather information on its neighbors and predators. In this activity, discussions address the grizzly bear's olfactory system and the human's olfactory system. Comparisons are made between the human's need for food and the sense of smell that enhances the desire to eat. The distances over which certain smells can be identified are also discussed and demonstrated.

The Grizzly's Sense of Smell

In learning about the grizzly bear's keen sense of smell, students will:

- study the physical construction of the grizzly bear's nose;

- analyze the need for proper diet as it relates to the bear's hibernation needs;

- discuss the distances traveled by the grizzly bear as it meets its nutritional needs;

- determine how the grizzly bear's keen sense of smell can alert it to danger.

Nose to Nose—Comparing the Human
and the Grizzly Bear Noses

In comparing the human olfactory system with that of the grizzly bear, students will:

- study the human body's olfactory system;

- discuss humans' sense of smell as it relates to their diet and appetite;

- analyze how humans might determine danger through their sense of smell.

Materials
- Brown Bear Facts Pack—grizzly bear facts section
- pictures of noses of humans, bears, and other mammals
- drawings of the internal structure of the human nose
- pictures of food eaten by humans
- pictures of dangerous situations (those with fire, smoke, and so on) that affect people's safety
- chart paper
- crockpot
- jar of unsweetened applesauce
- sugar and spices from the kitchen
- wooden spoons
- graham crackers
- learning sheets:
  No. 1. The Human Nose
  No. 2. The Bear Nose
  No. 3. As Far as a Country Mile

Preparation
1. Collect pictures of bear noses, human noses, and noses of other mammals for a general discussion of noses.

2. Prepare the following learning sheets and supplemental materials for discussion:

   - pictures of the construction of the human nose

   - learning sheets:
     No. 1. The Human Nose
     No. 2. The Bear Nose
     No. 3. As Far as a Country Mile

   - maps and additional information about national parks in the United States and Canada. These can be obtained free from the following sources:

     - United States Department of the Interior
       National Park Service
       Denali National Park
       P.O. Box 9
       Denali National Park, AK 99755

     - United States Department of the Interior
       National Park Service
       Glacier National Park
       West Glacier, MT 59936

     - United States Department of the Interior
       National Park Service
       P.O. Box 168
       Yellowstone National Park, WY 82190

     - The Canadian Parks Service
       Ottawa, Ontario, Canada
       KIA OH3

From *Investigating Science Through Bears,* ©1994. Teacher Ideas Press, P.O. Box 6633, Englewood, CO 80155-6633.

3. Hang chart paper on wall in preparation for composing a list of foods that grizzly bears might feed on.

4. Provide a picture of the internal construction of the human nose as reinforcement for classroom discussion.

5. Collect pictures of foods that create in humans the desire to eat.

6. Assemble necessary ingredients and crockpot in preparation for cooking apple butter.

7. Have available napkins, graham crackers, and spoons for serving the apple butter.

Procedures

1. Ask the students to provide what they know about the grizzly bear's sense of smell. Record their responses on the chart. Provide pictures of various human and animal noses, and discuss the differences.

2. Using the grizzly bear section of the Brown Bear Facts Pack as a reference, have the students look for facts about how the bear uses his nose. How does his sense of smell help the bear's survival when looking for food, watching for predators, and sensing danger? Record the information on the wall chart.

3. Give each student learning sheets on the human nose and the bear nose. Initiate discussions with grizzly bear facts that relate to its nose, and compare the grizzly bear's nose with those of other bears.

4. Begin discussions on the human nose and how it relates to a person's sense of smell.

5. Analyze the structure of the human nose and how it affects a person's desire to eat. Discuss pictures of various foods and how the students feel about eating them.

6. Explore the odors or smells that are related to bad smells, and discuss their effects on our appetites.

7. Discuss and analyze the importance of a human's sense of smell in alerting the person to danger.

8. Provide a copy of learning sheet 3, "As Far as a Country Mile," for each student, and discuss what the findings might be. Discuss how the smell of cooking apple butter will be strong, weak, or not detectable in various parts of the school building.

9. Continue the lesson on the next day by starting the day with the cooking of apple butter with spices. Use learning sheet 3 to record the strengths of the smells at 10:00 A.M., 1:00 P.M., and 3:00 P.M. in different parts of the school building.

10. At the conclusion of this cooking activity, discuss the findings that have been recorded on the learning sheet chart. Analyze the findings, and discuss how distances affect the sense of smell in both bears and humans.

11. Conclude the activity by eating the apple butter on the graham crackers!

12. Pass out the following apple butter recipe for a take-home item.

From *Investigating Science Through Bears*, ©1994. Teacher Ideas Press, P.O. Box 6633, Englewood, CO 80155-6633.

Apple Butter—
Bears' Way

This is a modern way of making apple butter that can be done at home in 30 min. in a heavy saucepan. A crockpot does not get as hot as it does if made in a saucepan, and it can be placed in the classroom with ease and safety.

Ingredients
- 2 cups (470 cubic centimeters) of unsweetened applesauce (a 1-pound, 9-ounce [710 grams] jar of unsweetened applesauce)

- ¼ to ½ cup (59-118 cubic centimeters) of white sugar

- 1 teaspoon (4.8 cubic centimeters) of cinnamon

- ¼ teaspoon (1.2 cubic centimeters) of allspice

- ⅛ teaspoon (0.6 cubic centimeter) of ginger

- ⅛ teaspoon (0.6 cubic centimeter) of ground cloves

Utensils
- crockpot

- wooden spoon

- pot holders

- measuring spoons

- glass measuring cup (optional)

Makes
- 1¼ cups (294 cubic centimeters) of apple butter

Preparation Time
- 5 minutes

Cooking Time
- 4 hours

Follow the Bear Tracks
- Combine unsweetened applesauce, sugar, cinnamon, allspice, ginger, and cloves in the crockpot.

- Bring to a boil, then lower temperature and simmer until the mixture thickens. Stir often. (You are evaporating some of the liquid from the applesauce.)

- Let mixture simmer for 3 to 4 hours, stirring frequently. The aroma is pleasant while cooking the apple butter. You will find many "bear neighbors" wanting to help your class eat the apple butter!

- Note: All ingredients are combined in a saucepan, and cooked for 30 minutes at a medium-low temperature for top-of-the-stove preparation.

Bear Extensions

1. Visiting a national park where bears live requires special behavior on the part of humans. Campers and hikers have to take special precautions with the handling of their foods. Grizzlies like humans' food. What can campers do to prevent being bothered by the bears? What precautions are taken by the National Park Service to protect both bears and people?

2. Find out from a zookeeper at a local zoo what grizzly bears in captivity are fed. Is their menu there different from what they eat in the wild? What foods are served to the grizzlies in captivity? How much does it cost to feed a grizzly per day, per week, and per month at the zoo?

Vocabulary Words
- olfactory
- senses
- appetite
- Yellowstone National Park
- Denali National Park
- Glacier National Park
- Grand Teton National Park
- British Columbia, Canada

Learning Sheet No. 1

Student Copy

Name:_____

Date:_____

The Human Nose

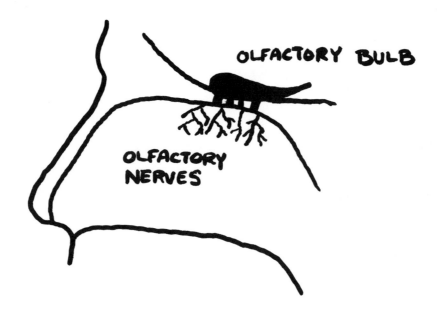

  The human structure called the nose has two functions. The first is to provide a pathway for the air that is taken into the lungs. The second is to provide a location for the olfactory nerve endings that detect smells.

  The nose has two cavities that are separated by a wall of cartilage. The cartilage on each side of the nose bone gives the nose its shape. In general, the lower part of the nasal cavity is called the respiratory area; the upper part, the olfactory region. The respiratory area filters, warms, and moistens incoming air on its way to the lungs. The olfactory nerves lead to the undersurface of the brain. The nerve endings, or receptors, in the olfactory region that are used for smelling cover a limited area in the upper part of the nasal cavities.

  Sense of smell is aroused by chemical substances coming in contact with these nerve endings. Substances smelled must be in the form of a gas. Gases diffuse through the air, permitting people to recognize things at a distance by their odor. Examples of this include an apple pie baking in the oven and a turkey roasting in the oven at Thanksgiving.

- What happens to people's sense of smell when they have a cold?

- How are taste and smell related in humans? Which comes first—the sense of smell or the sense of taste? Can humans smell and taste something at the same time?

- Can humans' sense of smell be compared with that of bears? How would the sense of smell be the same, and how would it be different?

Learning Sheet No. 2

Student Copy

Name:_____

Date:_____

The Bear Nose

The sense of smell for bears allows them to survive in the environment in which they live. The nose provides a means for air to be taken into lung-breathing animals, and it has developed in bears to look like those shown on this page. Bears need the sense of smell to search for food, to detect predators, and to obtain information on their neighbors.

The shape of bears' noses is different for each bear family. However, the shape of the nose does not interfere with the olfactory senses. A faint odor stimulates the nerve endings in the nasal passages of all the bears.

Researchers have found that bears use their sensitive noses to do lots of sniffing. Bears can learn about humans or predators by sniffing odors. A bear's sense of smell is as good as a bloodhound's sense of smell.

A grizzly bear's sense of smell is regarded as excellent—making up for the bear's average hearing and sight.

The polar bear's nose is so incredibly sensitive that it can detect a seal more than 20 miles (32 kilometers) away. Researchers in Alaska have watched a male polar bear walk in a straight line for 40 miles (64 kilometers) to reach food that it had detected. Polar bears can sniff out a seal den covered by 3 feet (1 meter) of ice and snow. Eskimo hunters have seen polar bears cover their black noses with a paw to keep the seals from seeing them while the bears stalked the seals on the open ice.

The black bear's sense of smell is also excellent. Its ability to smell has been compared to that of a dog. Black bears can also smell food and predators from miles away.

- Does the shape of the bear's nose affect its smelling ability?

- How can a bear's excellent sense of smell protect it from predators, including humans?

- Compare the different prey each bear sniffs when it hunts for food.

- If a bear were to get its nose hurt in a fight, how might that affect its chances for survival?

BROWN BEAR

BLACK BEAR

POLAR BEAR

KODIAK BEAR

GRIZZLY BEAR

Learning Sheet No. 3

Student Copy

Name:_____

Date:_____

As Far as a Country Mile

    This activity is to be carried out as part of the study of the olfactory system in humans and the grizzly bear. While the apple butter is cooking in the crockpot, go to the areas shown below and record the smells your olfactory system is sending back to you. Record the words *strong*, *weak*, or *none* for each of the items below the time at which the investigation is done.

10:00 A.M.   **1:00 P.M.**   **3:00 P.M.**

1.   the classroom next door

2.   the gym

3.   the cafeteria

4.   by the principal's office

5.   by the student health service room

6.   outdoors by the front door

7.   just inside the school's front door

8.   on the playground

9.   in the hallway

10. in a classroom that is the farthest
      from your classroom

Activity No. 3
The North American Grizzly

The grizzly bear is a member of the brown bear family and is only found on the North American continent. The students are introduced to the grizzly bear and its environment through a variety of learning experiences, including A Pre-Grizzly Teaser question-and-answer sheet. The grizzly bear's life and life-style are depicted through the use of the Grizzly Question Wheel. The grizzly's past, present, and future are addressed by using a student-constructed wall mural containing a time line of events in the life of the grizzly. For a concluding event, the students may develop a simulated television game in which facts about the grizzly bear are covered.

Background Information

Two hundred years ago grizzly bears populated the mountains and plains of what is now the United States in the area west of the Mississippi River. Native Americans and early explorers had great respect for the large, powerful grizzlies. The westward movement of settlers with guns, the development of farms and towns, and the presence of trophy hunters brought on the decline of the grizzly bear. Today, the largest population of grizzlies is found in Alaska and Canada. Wildlife managers estimate that there are about 3,000 grizzlies left in North America.

A study of the grizzly bear allows students to study not only this continent's geography but its animal and human population and the interaction between the two. The grizzly bear also has several unique body-structure characteristics that make it different from other bears.

Students may work individually or in a cooperative group to accumulate information about the grizzly bear. The past, present, and future of the grizzly bear is illustrated on a time line project that the students may construct.

Grizzly Bear Characteristics

In learning about the grizzly bears, students will:

- locate on maps and globes the continent, countries, and states where grizzly bears are found;

- discuss the unique characteristics of the grizzly bear's body structure;

- recognize animals that live with the grizzly bears in the mountainous regions of the North American continent;

- identify the foods needed by grizzly bears for their continued survival;

- analyze the problems that humans and grizzly bears share as they attempt to survive together;

- investigate the facts illustrated on the time line of the grizzly bear's life about how discoverers found the bear and how people today coexist with it.

Materials
- the grizzly bear section of the Brown Bear Facts Pack
- pictures of grizzly bears and their environment for posting in the classroom
- maps of the United States, Canada, and the North American continent, plus a globe of the Earth

From *Investigating Science Through Bears,* ©1994. Teacher Ideas Press, P.O. Box 6633, Englewood, CO 80155-6633.

- butcher paper and poster paper
- magazines with bear stories, such as *National Geographic* and *Field and Stream*
- library books with stories of bears and Native Americans
- national park information from libraries, travel bureaus, and individual national parks
- opaque projector
- learning sheets:
  1. The Grizzly Question Wheel
  2. A Pre-Grizzly Teaser
  3. Television Game Instructions
- park addresses:
  - U.S. Department of the Interior
    National Park Service
    P.O. Box 168
    Yellowstone National Park, WY 82190

  - U.S. Department of the Interior
    National Park Service
    Glacier National Park
    West Glacier, MT 59936

  - U.S. Department of the Interior
    National Park Service
    P.O. Box 9
    Denali National Park
    Denali National Park, AK 99755

  - U.S. Department of the Interior
    Katmai National Park
    P.O. Box 7
    King Salmon, AK 99613

  - The Canadian Parks Service
    Ottawa, Ontario, Canada
    KIA OH3

Preparation

1. Display a world map, a North American map, a United States map, a map of Canada, and a world globe for the students to study.

2. Collect and post pictures of the grizzly bear, its environment, its neighbors, and the North American mountain terrain in which the grizzly lives. These can be found in *National Geographic*, *Field and Stream*, and other outdoor magazines.

3. Prepare butcher paper for drawing. Use an opaque projector to create a large outline of the North American continent, and then outline the continent on the paper with a marking pen.

4. Represent the western mountainous regions of the North American continent by crinkling some additional butcher paper. Glue or tape these "mountains" onto the outline of the North American continent. Post the mural map on a chalkboard, convenient wall, or school bulletin board for further discussion.

From *Investigating Science Through Bears*, ©1994. Teacher Ideas Press, P.O. Box 6633, Englewood, CO 80155-6633.

5. Draw a time-line outline at the top of the butcher-paper map. Label the time line with dates of every 50 years, beginning with the 1600s and ending with 1993.

6. Prepare copies of the grizzly bear section of the Brown Bear Facts Pack for students as study guides.

7. Collect United States and Canadian national park information. Be sure to include Yellowstone, Glacier, and Katmai National Parks, which are home to the grizzlies.

8. Duplicate learning sheets for classroom activities.

9. Display books from your library that relate to the grizzly bear, Native Americans living in the grizzly bear home areas, and legendary stories of early explorers who traveled in the grizzly home areas.

Procedures

1. Begin by quizzing the students about their knowledge of grizzly bears. Questions should include where grizzlies live, what they look like, and what they eat. Use the Pre-Grizzly Teaser learning sheet as an opening activity.

2. Introduce the grizzly bear section of the Brown Bear Facts Pack to the class. The booklet will state facts about the physical characteristics, eating habits, growth patterns, environmental neighbors, and so on.

3. Use the Grizzly Question Wheel (see p. 100) as a study guide. Students will search for information in the Facts Pack and record answers on the answer wheel in the matching numbered space.

4. Discuss the questions and answers on the question wheel. This includes information about the grizzly bears' life cycle, food supplies, neighbors and enemies, environment, and so on.

5. Continue the discussion of the history of the grizzly bears and the vast numbers of grizzly bears that lived in the 1800s. Discuss why many bears were lost to settlers and trophy seekers.

6. Track the grizzly bear's history on the time line on the mural map. Students should label the significant events in the history of the grizzly bears as they occurred throughout the years.

7. Have the students draw or collect magazine pictures, label them correctly, and place them on the map mural. These pictures and labels should depict the bears' neighbors, vegetation, food supply, and so on, and will present a pictorial story.

8. Give the Pre-Grizzly Teaser exercise again before the final exercise of creating the television game. All students should score 100 percent.

9. Ask students for a final exercise to create the "Jeopardy!" game by developing the questions and answers, setting up a simulated television stage, and then playing the game. The "Jeopardy!" Game instruction sheet is to be used as a guide for this event.

From *Investigating Science Through Bears,* ©1994. Teacher Ideas Press, P.O. Box 6633, Englewood, CO 80155-6633.

Bear Extensions

1. Folklore that deals with bears and their interaction with such people as Davy Crockett, Daniel Boone, and Native Americans will help the students to assess the difference between fact and fiction as it pertains to the grizzly bear.

2. The United States and Canadian national park services have factual information that discusses the grizzly bears in the various national parks. This information is readily available upon request. Use the addresses given above in this activity. After the students investigate the grizzly bear story in national parks, they should write and illustrate a pamphlet containing safety rules and explanations on how to backpack and camp in parks where grizzly bears live.

Vocabulary Words

- Canada
- Rocky Mountains
- North America
- Alaska
- yearling
- carnivores
- salmon
- omnivores
- bighorn sheep
- carcasses
- Yellowstone National Park
- Denali National Park

- grizzled
- elk
- arctic ground squirrel
- caribou
- bison
- moose
- metabolism
- mountain goats
- digestion
- mule deer
- cougar
- wolves

Learning Sheet No. 1

Teacher Guide

A Pre-Grizzly Teaser

Pre-Grizzly Teaser Directions

Ask the students to answer the questions on the Pre-Grizzly Teaser sheet *before* they read the grizzly section of the Brown Bear Facts Pack. Students should be given an opportunity to read each "teaser" on the Pre-Grizzly Teaser sheet, decide whether the question is true or false, and record their answers in the appropriate spaces on the question sheet. Discuss with the students why they chose their answers. Then give them an opportunity to read about the grizzly bear. At the conclusion of all grizzly bear activities, have the students go over the teasers again and record whether they have changed their minds about the truth of each question.

Pre-Grizzly Teaser Answers

The following are general answers for the teacher to use as a guide for discussion of the Pre-Grizzly Teaser.

1. These massive creatures are rarely fortunate enough to find meat to fulfill all their food needs. They spend much of their time eating on plants, digging for roots, and stripping berries from low-lying bushes.

2. Grizzly bears' eyesight is considered equal to humans'. However, they have a sense of smell rivaling that of a bloodhound.

3. Grizzly bears are omnivores—they feed on plant and animal food, so their teeth and intestines can handle both. Their intestines are long, and their teeth are flattened for crushing and chewing.

4. Grizzly bears—with the exception of a mother bear and her cubs—are normally quite solitary animals. However, when fishing for salmon, bears gather together and risk serious injury from the claws and jaws of other bears just to get a favorite fishing spot.

5. Bears put their feet down flat on the ground when they walk—the same as humans do. This flat-footed walk is called a plantigrade walk. Bears can stand straight up as humans do, but they rarely walk when standing up. Most other large animals such as dogs and horses walk on their toes.

6. Male grizzly bears weigh up to 900 pounds (409.1 kilograms).

7. Grizzly bears are most commonly brown or blond. The name *grizzly* comes from the light tips on the long hair (called guard hairs) of the bear's coat. These colors often give the animal a frosted or grizzled look.

From *Investigating Science Through Bears,* ©1994. Teacher Ideas Press, P.O. Box 6633, Englewood, CO 80155-6633.

8. The number of fish eaten by one bear was counted by scientists. The bear was actually seen eating more than 300 fish (salmon, of course) during one day! He probably ate 200 more fish when no one was around! This would mean that grizzly bears eat three and one half times their own weight in fish in about six weeks! Fish weigh about 10 pounds (4.5 kilograms) each. The total number of pounds of fish eaten could be as much as 10 pounds (4.5 kilograms) per fish or 500 fish = 5,000 pounds (2,273 kilograms) of fish eaten!

9. If a warm spell occur during the winter months, bears come out to walk around. If they did not eat enough food before hibernation, they are hungry bears looking for food!

10. Humans are the enemies of the grizzly bear. But people try to save the bear from the dangers of encounters with humans through park management in the national parks. Without this help the grizzly is in peril of poachers and ranchers—angered when the bears stray onto their ranches—and people themselves when grizzlies eat from garbage dumps close to towns or stray into populated areas.

11. Grizzly bears live near streams and where grasses are abundant. Dens are very different for grizzly bears. They like a steep slope where there is enough soil, rock, and plants to make cover for a roof that will not collapse, but they also seek a place shallow enough that snow can cover the entrance. Dens are dug in the mountains—at heights above 6,000 feet (1,829 meters) in Yellowstone National Park.

12. Grizzly bears spend most of their time feeding on plants, digging roots, and stripping berries. They do eat meat, but mainly they feed on dead animals that they find. Salmon are their favorite food.

13. Cubs stay with their mother until she is ready to have another set of cubs. Everything the cubs learn is from their mother. Cubs obey their mothers! If a cub does something its mother does not like, she may slap the cub roughly with her paw to let it know its behavior is not acceptable.

14. The areas where grizzly bears are most abundant on the North American continent are Alaska, Canada, and the Rocky Mountains of the United States. Montana and Wyoming are other states where the grizzly bears make their homes.

15. The grizzly bears were killed by the hundreds at the beginning of the 1900s. Today, a single claw sells for $200. A grizzly bear hide might bring as much as $10,000! In other parts of the world, a dried grizzly gallbladder is used for medicines and might bring as much as $700 an ounce! The grizzly bear is an endangered animal today, so parks such as Yellowstone National Park are managing the species to save them.

From *Investigating Science Through Bears,* ©1994. Teacher Ideas Press, P.O. Box 6633, Englewood, CO 80155-6633.

Learning Sheet No. 1

Student Copy

Name:_____

Date:_____

Pre-Grizzly Teasers

	Before Reading		After Reading	
	T	F	T	F
1. Grizzly bears are popularly portrayed as meat-hungry hunters.				
2. Grizzly bears rely on their superior noses for finding food.				
3. Bears are omnivores.				
4. Grizzlies like to have their families around them all the time.				
5. Bears walk like people.				
6. A male grizzly bear can weigh no more than 300 pounds.				
7. The grizzly's coat has frosted-colored tips that give the grizzly its name.				
8. A grizzly bear has been seen eating more than 300 fish in one summer.				
9. Grizzly bears cannot be disturbed when they are hibernating.				
10. Grizzly bears are endangered animals.				
11. The environment of the grizzly bear is the same as that of the polar bear.				
12. Grizzly bears dig roots and bulbs in Montana and Alaska.				
13. Mother grizzly bears take care of their cubs for two years, and the cubs obey her wishes.				
14. Pennsylvania, Iowa, and New Mexico are states where grizzly bears can be found.				
15. Grizzly bear body parts are valuable, which creates the temptation for poaching.				

From *Investigating Science Through Bears,* ©1994. Teacher Ideas Press, P.O. Box 6633, Englewood, CO 80155-6633.

Learning Sheet No. 2

Student Copy

Name:_____

Date:_____

The Grizzly Question Wheel

1. Grizzly bears live in what kind of environment?

2. What kind of animals share the mountain region with the grizzly bear?

3. What kind of food does the grizzly bear eat?

4. Where do the grizzly bears live on the North American continent?

5. How does the grizzly bear survive with humans?

6. Who are the grizzly bears' friends and enemies?

7. Are there any unusual facts about the grizzly bear that make it unique?

Learning Sheet No. 3
Game Instructions

Teacher Reference

As a concluding exercise, the students may create a television-like game. The students may work individually, in pairs, or in cooperative groups to develop the questions and answers for the game.

As with a popular television game, the students should first write the answers, and then match them with questions. All the questions should be related to the grizzly bear. The Question Wheel and the related answer sheets will contain the information for both questions and answers. The questions and answers should be written on cards and used by the program master of ceremonies.

Select a program master of ceremonies, program director, question-and-answer directors (they categorize the questions and answers and put a dollar value on each), contestants, and an audience. Rotate the assignments so that contestants and audience get equal time to play the game.

Grizzly Bear
Time Line

Teacher Guide

The time-line drawing above depicts the grizzly bear's survival. Enlarge the drawings and use them on the bulletin board in conjunction with the drawn time line. The events depicted are as follows:

1. The Native Americans lived in harmony with the grizzly bear.

2. The early explorers respected the grizzly bear, but the explorers carried guns.

3. The settlers traveled west, building farms and towns.

4. The movement westward brought more people and guns. Killing buffalo and grizzly bears became a popular hunting sport.

5. The farmers and loggers found the grizzly bears to be a nuisance. Killing grizzly bears became the answer.

6. Today, the grizzly bear population is so small that the bears are protected by the National Park Service.

Vocabulary for
Brown Bear Chapter

Alaska—one of the Pacific states of the United States, in the northwest part of North America.

Aleutian Islands—islands located in the western part of the Alaskan peninsula.

algae—a group of plant or plantlike organisms that are usually found in water and that can make their own food.

Asia—the largest continent, east of Europe and west of the Pacific Ocean. China, India, and Israel are countries in Asia.

assets—a valuable quality or possession; things of value.

beaver—an animal with soft fur, a broad, flat tail and webbed hind feet for swimming, and large, front teeth. The animal lives in water and on land.

bison—a wild animal of North America, related to cattle, with a shaggy head and a hump above the shoulders; buffalo.

bluff—something said or done to fool or mislead others.

boar—a male pig or hog; the name of a male bear.

bough—one of the main branches of a tree.

Canada—a country in North America, north of the United States.

carcass—the dead body of an animal.

carnivore—meat-eating; feeding chiefly on flesh.

carrion—dead and decaying flesh.

clumsy—awkward in movement.

coastal—at the coast; along a coast; near a coast.

Colorado—one of the western states of the United States.

community—all the people living in the same place; neighborhood; all the living things in any one place.

corm—a rounded, thick, underground stem, covered with membranes or scaly leaves; similar to a bulb.

crab—a shellfish with eight legs, two claws, and a broad, flat shell covering.

defecate—to void feces from the bowel.

disturb—to bother someone by talking or by being noisy; interrupt.

dread—to fear greatly what is to come; dislike to experience.

elderberries—the berries from the elder bush.

endangered—liable to become extinct.

energy—the power to work or act; force.

enormous—very, very large; huge.

Europe—the continent west of Asia and east of the Atlantic Ocean.

extinct—no longer existing.

ferocious—fierce; savage; very cruel.

genus—a category of organisms ranking below a family and above a species.

gopher—a ratlike animal with large cheek pouches living in North America.

graze—to feed on growing grass.

grizzled—grayish; gray.

habitat—a place where a living thing is naturally found.

herring—a small food fish of the northern Atlantic Ocean.

hibernators—animals that pass the winter in a dormant state; to be in an inactive or a dormant state.

hierarchical—in order of importance.

hind—back; rear.

home range—the place where a thing is especially common; the land used for grazing.

Idaho—one of the western states of the United States.

identify—to recognize as being a particular person or thing.

intelligent—having or showing understanding; able to learn and know; quick at learning.

Juneau—the capital city of Alaska.

keen—able to do its work quickly and exactly; quickly aware.

Kodiak—name for the islands off the west coast of Alaska.

lair—a den or resting place of a wild animal.

litter—the young animals produced at one time.

Montana—one of the western states of the United States.

nourish—to make grow; keep alive and well with food.

omnivore—an animal that eats both meat and plant life.

permanent—lasting; intended to last; not for only a short time.

photograph—a picture made with a camera.

photographer—a person who takes pictures.

physically—in a physical manner.

predator—an animal that lives by killing and eating other animals.

prehistoric—of or belonging to times before histories were written.

protein—one of the substances containing nitrogen; a necessary part of the cells of plants and animals; contained in foods such as meat, milk, cheese, eggs, and beans.

respect—honor; esteem; care for.

salmon—a large food fish with silvery scales and yellowish pink flesh.

Scandinavia—a region of northwestern Europe that includes Norway, Denmark, Sweden, and sometimes Finland and Iceland.

scavengers—animals that feed on dead or decaying matter.

shortage—not enough of something.

slaughter—brutal killing; much or needless killing.

snorkeling—to dive underwater just beneath the surface.

sow—a fully grown female pig; also the name of a female bear.

Spain—a country in southwestern Europe.

species—a group of related living things that have certain basic common characteristics.

stench—a strong, foul odor.

subspecies—a taxonomic category that ranks immediately below a species.

survive—to live longer than; to continue to exist or live; to remain.

swat—to hit sharply or violently.

tension—a strain.

territory—land; region; an area such as a nesting ground in which an animal lives and from which it keeps out others of its kind.

Tibet—a mountainous country in Asia.

tourist—a person traveling for pleasure.

tracking—keeping track of; following with electronic equipment to observe or monitor a trail that a bear follows.

tranquilizer—a drug used to calm.

trespass—to go onto someone's property without any right.

tundra—a vast, level, treeless plain in the Arctic regions; the ground beneath its surface is frozen even in summer. Much of Alaska and northern Canada is tundra.

unconscious—not able to feel or think.

unpredictable—uncertain; not known in advance.

urinate—to discharge liquid waste from the body.

wilderness—a wild place; a region with no people living in it.

yearling—a one-year-old animal.

Teacher Educational Resources

Books

"Bears." *The American Peoples Encyclopedia.* 1969 ed., Vol. 2, 9-11.

"Bears." *Compton's Encyclopedia.* 1986 ed., Vol. 3, 116-118.

"Bears." *The New Encyclopaedia Britannica.* 1991 ed., Vol. 2, 11.

"Bears." *The World Book Encyclopedia.* 1987 ed., Vol. 2, 137-141.

Brown, David E., *The Grizzly in the Southwest: Documentation of an Extinction.* Norman, Okla.: University of Oklahoma, 1985.

Brown, David E., and John Murray. *The Lost Grizzly and Other Southwestern Bear Stories.* Tempe, Ariz.: University of Arizona Press, 1988.

Cherry, Lynne. *Grizzly Bears.* World Wildlife Fund Books. New York: Dutton, 1987.

Craighead, Frank C., Jr. *Track of the Grizzly.* Sierra Club Paperback Library. San Francisco: Sierra Club, 1988.

Cramond, Mike. *Of Bears and Man.* Norman, Okla.: University of Oklahoma, 1986.

Domico, Terry. *Bears of the World.* New York: Facts on File, 1988.

Grzimek, Bernhard. G*rzimek's Animal Life Encyclopedia.* New York: Van Nostrand Reinhold, 1975.

Hanna, Warren L. *The Grizzlies of Glacier.* Missoula, Mont.: Mountain Press, 1988.

Haynes, Bessie, and Edgar Haynes. *The Grizzly Bear Portraits from Life.* Norman, Okla.: University of Oklahoma, 1979.

Holzworth, John Michael. *The Wild Grizzlies of Alaska.* New York: G. P. Putnam's Sons, 1930.

Hoshino, Michio. *Grizzly.* Bedford, N.Y.: Chronicle Books, 1987.

Jones, William. *Monarch: The Big Bear of Tallac.* Golden, Colo.: Outbooks, 1978.

Keating, Bern. Illustrated by G. F. Mobley. *Alaska.* Washington, D.C.: National Geographic Society, 1969.

Mills, Enos A. *The Grizzly.* Sausalito, Calif.: Comstock Editions, 1976.

Milotte, Alfred, and Edna Milotte. *The Story of an Alaskan Grizzly Bear.* Edmunds, Wash.: Alaska Northwest, 1987.

Nentle, Jerolyn. *The Grizzly.* Riverside, N.J.: Crestwood House, 1984.

Our National Parks, America's Spectacular Wilderness Heritage. Pleasantville, N.Y.: Reader's Digest, 1989.

Patent, Dorthy H. *The Way of the Grizzly.* New York: Ticknor and Fields, 1987.

Peacock, Doug. *The Grizzly Years: Encounters with the Wilderness.* New York: Henry Holt, 1990.

Phelps, John, and Gilbert Phelps. *Animals Tame and Wild.* New York: Topaz Publishing, 1979.

Russell, Andy. *Grizzly Country.* Clinton, Iowa: Lyons and Burford, 1986.

Sarage, Candace. *Grizzly Bears.* San Francisco: Sierra Club, 1990.

Seton, Ernest T. *The Biography of a Grizzly*. Lincoln, Nebr.: University of Nebraska, 1987.

Stevens, Montague. *Meet Mr. Grizzly: A Saga on the Passing of the Grizzly Bear*. San Lorenzo, New Mex.: High Lonesome, 1988.

Storer, Tracy, and Lloyd Tevis. *California Grizzly*. Lincoln, Nebr.: University of Nebraska, 1978.

Thomas, Bill. *Talking with the Animals*. New York: William Morrow, 1985.

Walker, Ernest P. *Mammals of the World*. Baltimore, Md.: Johns Hopkins University Press, 1975.

Wright, William H. *The Grizzly Bear: The Narrative of a Hunter-Naturalist*. Lincoln, Nebr.: University of Nebraska, 1978.

Young, Ralph W. *Grizzlies Don't Come Easy*. Hermosa Beach, Calif.: Winchester Press, 1981.

Magazine Articles

Bear Handling Seen to Shift at Yellowstone." *National Parks* 64 (November-December 1990): 12.

"Bears Chow Down on Tons of Corn." *Current Science* 76 (November 16, 1990): 3.

"Brown Bears—Alaska." *Alaska* (May 1986): 34.

"Brown Bears—Alaska." *Natural History* (May 1985): 30.

Budiansky, S. "Sawdust and Mirrors." *U.S News & World Report* 3 (July 1, 1991): 55.

Chadwick, Douglas. " 'Grizz'—Of Men and the Great Bear." *National Geographic* (February 1986): 148-158.

Cherry, B. "Bear Scares." *Outdoor Life* 187, Issue 2 (February 1991): 64.

Clarke, J. "Grizzlies and Tourists." *Society* 27, Issue 2 (January-February 1990): 23.

Craighead, Frank, Jr., and John Craighead. "Grizzly! 639A-639B, Trailing Yellowstone's Grizzlies by Radio." *National Geographic* (August 1966): 252-267.

Craighead, Frank, Jr., and John Craighead. "Knocking Out Grizzly Bears for Their Own Good." *National Geographic* (August 1960): 276-291.

"Easy Catch." *National Geographic World* (February 1991): 18.

Eberhardt, L. L. "Survival Rates Required to Sustain Bear Populations." *Journal of Wildlife Management* 54 (October 1990): 587.

Egbert, Allan, and Michael H. Lugue. "Among Alaska's Brown Bears." *National Geographic* (September 1975): 428.

French, Steve, and Marilyn French. "Yellowstone Grizzlies." *National Parks* (November-December 1989): 24.

"Grizzly Bears." *Field and Stream* (February 1987): 52.

"Grizzly Bears." *National History* (January 1987): 50.

"Grizzly Bears." *New York Times Magazine* (August 31, 1986): 22.

"Grizzly Bears." *Outdoor Life* (November 1986): 50.

"Grizzly Bears—Conservation and Restoration." *Outdoor Life* (July 1986): 56.

"Grizzly Bears—Environmental Aspects." *Outside* (January 1986): 28.

"Grizzly Bears—Habits and Behavior." *Outdoor Life* (January 1986): 56.

"Grizzly Bears—Habits and Behavior—Montana." *New Yorker* (September 9, 1985): 76.

"Grizzly Bears—Habits and Behaviors." *Field and Stream* (August 1986): 58.

Jans, N., and K. Marsh. "My Last Grizzly." *Alaska* 56 (May 1990): 18.

Kostyal, K. M. "Katmai National Park: Land of the Great Bear." *National Geographic Traveler* (May-June 1989): 96.

Little, C. "Urus Arctos Horribilis: Origins of an Idea." *Wilderness* (Winter 1987): 20.

Luoma, J. "New Approaches Bring Predators Back to the Wild." *New York Times* (March 7, 1989): C1.

Merritt, J., and S. Catalano. "Theodore Roosevelt—Western Sportsman." *Field and Stream* 95, Issue 5 (September 1990): 42.

Milstein, M. "The Quiet Kill." *National Parks* (May-June 1989): 18.

Norton, B. "It's a Good Thing McNeil's Big Bears Get Plenty to Eat." *Smithsonian* (April 1989): 56.

"Odd Bears Out." *Alaska* 57 (April 1991): 29.

Prothero, W. L. "A Season of Grizzlies." *Outdoor Life* 186 (November 1990): 74.

Reiss, M., and L. Mueller. "Bulldozer Bears." *Outdoor Life* 185, Issue 1 (January 1990): 64.

Robbins, J. "Grizzly and Man: When Species Collide." *National Wildlife* (February-March 1988): 20.

Shepard, P., B. Sanders, A. Smith, and D. Peacock. "A Practical Guide to Grizzly Country." *Backpacker* 18, no. 6 (October 1990): 80.

Walker, T. "Of Bears and Men." *Alaska* 56 (September 1990): 38.

Annotated Bibliography for Brown Bears and the Study of Life Science

Children's Books

America's Wonderlands—The Scenic National Park and Monuments of the United States. Washington, D.C.: National Geographic Society, 1966.
This book presents the Rocky Mountains, the Great Plateau, the Southwest, the Golden West, the East, Alaska, Hawaii, and the Virgin Islands, with travel tips for visiting the national parks located in these parts of the United States. Nonfiction.

Bailey, Bernadine. *Wonders of the World of Bears.* New York: Dodd, Mead, 1975.
This book summarizes and describes the characteristics and habits of various species of bears. Nonfiction.

Burton, Jane. Photographs by the National Geographic Society. *Baby Bears and How They Grow.* Washington, D.C.: National Geographic Society, 1986.

Text and photographs presented on several bears—including polar, grizzly, and black bears—engaged in a variety of activities. Nonfiction.

Charman, Andrew. Illustrated by Chris Forsey. *The Book of Bears.* New York: Gallery Books, 1989.

This book includes a discussion of all true bears, endangered bears, and the "barely" bears. Each bear is discussed in depth. The source is a very readable book for elementary students. Nonfiction.

Dixon, Paige. Illustrated by Grambs Miller. *The Young Grizzly.* New York: Atheneum, 1974.

An insight into the behavior and character of the grizzly bear through a sensitive narrative describing the first three years in the life of a male cub. Nonfiction.

Freschet, Berniece. Illustrated by Donald Carrick. *Grizzly Bear.* New York: Scribner, 1975.

The story of a year in the life of a grizzly and her cubs as they fight for survival in mountainous terrain. Fiction.

George, Jean Craighead. Illustrated by Tom Catania. *The Grizzly Bear with the Golden Ears.* New York: Harper & Row, 1982.

A grizzly bear who bluffs rather than hunts for her food learns an important lesson. Fiction.

Nentl, Jerolyn Ann. *The Grizzly.* Mankato, Minn.: Crestwood House, 1984.

Discusses the powerful North American bears: where and how they live, what they look like, and what is to become of them. Nonfiction.

Patent, Dorthy. Photographs by William Munoz. *The Way of the Grizzly.* New York: Houghton Mifflin, 1987.

This book describes, in text and illustrations, the physical characteristics, habits, and natural environment of the grizzly bear. It also discusses the threats that humans pose to the grizzly's survival. Nonfiction.

Radlauer, Ruth. Photographs by R. McIntyre, E. Radlauer, and R. Radlauer. *Denali National Park and Preserve.* Chicago: Children's Press, 1988.

This book presents the geography, plant and animal life, and distinctive features of this national park located in an area south of the Arctic Circle in the state of Alaska. Nonfiction.

Radlauer, Ruth. Photographs by Rolf Zillmer. *Glacier National Park.* Chicago: Children's Press, 1977.

An introduction is given to Glacier National Park, which includes nearly 50 small glaciers. Also included are discussions of the bighorn sheep, and hiking and camping within the Park. Nonfiction.

Radlauer, Ruth. Photographs by Rolf Zillmer. *Yellowstone National Park.* Chicago: Children's Press, 1985.

A brief text and photographs present the geographic features, plant and animal life, and other attractions of the first national park. Nonfiction.

Spanjian, Beth. Illustrated by John Butler. *Baby Grizzly.* New York: Angel Entertainment, 1988.

This book explains how the mother grizzly takes care of her cubs. Data on grizzly bears also included. Nonfiction.

Stonehouse, Bernard. Illustrated with photographs. *Bears*. New York: Raintree, 1980.
    Text and photographs introduce the characteristics, habits, and environments of grizzly, polar, and other bears. Nonfiction.

Weaver, John L. *Grizzly Bears*. New York: Dodd, Mead, 1982.
    The text follows the life of three Rocky Mountain grizzly bear cubs with their mother during the first 15 months after their birth. Nonfiction.

Wexo, John Bonnett. *Bears—Zoo Books*. Mankato, Minn.: Creative Education, 1989.
    This book is a colorful, descriptive, photographic presentation of bears. The contents include descriptions of the Kodiak, black, brown, and polar bears and of the three smallest bears. The future of bears is discussed. Nonfiction.

Whitehead, Robert. Illustrated by James Teason. *The First Book of Bears*. New York: Franklin Watts, 1966.
    The history and habits of bears in general are discussed, with special emphasis on the grizzly, brown, Kodiak, polar, sloth, sun, and spectacled bears. Nonfiction.

Films and Videos

Autumn with Grizzlies. Film, 16 mm, 16 min., color. Distributed by Beacon Films, Norwood, Mass., 1991.
    A female grizzly and her yearling cub return to a remote valley of the Rockies after a summer of ranging far for food. They become part of a hierarchy among grizzlies for sharing a food source—a means of avoiding endless clashes. Autumn is over, and it is time for the long winter sleep of the monarch of the Rockies. The film is also available in video. Nonfiction.

The Grizzlies. Film, 16 mm, 59 min., color. National Geographic Society Educational Services, Washington, D.C., 1991.
    This informative film about the grizzly bear is also available in a 59-minute color video in three languages—English, Spanish, and French. Nonfiction.

Grizzly! Video, 52 min., color. National Geographic Society Educational Services, Washington, D.C., 1991.
    Case study of the grizzly bear. Two scientist brothers roam Yellowstone National Park armed with drug-filled darts. Using electronic devices, they follow the bears to winter dens. Working with drugged bears, they risk their lives to find out how the bears live and to check their vital life systems for information that might have scientific and medical application. Nonfiction.

4

The Giant Panda Bear

Overview of Learning Experiences for the Giant Panda Bear

The Giant Panda Bear chapter presents methods and learning experiences designed to stimulate the young, inquiring mind in the areas of life science, social studies, and language arts. These methods and experiences, designed for use in the classroom, maximize creative, divergent thinking by the students and are structured to apply to individual students and students working in teams. The following is an overview of the specific experiences addressed in this chapter.

Life Science

- identifying the physical characteristics of the giant panda bear

- investigating the environment of the giant panda bear in the wild, including a study of its habitat and food supply

- determining the importance of the giant panda bear's thumb and its role in helping the bear to survive

- identifying the giant panda bear's living needs and developing a simulated habitat for the bear that would support its need for bamboo in the wild

- designing a habitat for the giant panda bear in captivity that would simulate its natural environment in the wild

Social Studies

- locating the People's Republic of China on a world map

- locating on the map of the People's Republic of China the cities of Peking and Ch'eng-tu where zoos have giant panda bears in captivity

- recognizing and evaluating the cultural differences between the people living in the People's Republic of China and those living in the United States and Canada

- identifying the documents needed by United States citizens when traveling throughout the world

- investigating long-distance airline travel by simulating an airline trip from the United States to the People's Republic of China to study the giant panda bear

Language Arts

- reading the Giant Panda Bear Facts Pack included in the chapter, plus library books, travel brochures, and so on to gain information about the giant panda bear and the People's Republic of China

- planning, designing, and constructing a poster that tells the story of the giant panda bear as an endangered species

- developing, designing, and writing an illustrated short story that makes use of the Chinese art of calligraphy

- collecting background information from filmstrips and videos to develop a comprehensive picture of the Chinese people, their country, and their culture

Giant Panda Bear
Facts Pack

What do you know about a giant panda bear? For more than 100 years scientists have studied this animal, trying to figure out whether it is a bear or a raccoon. Although the giant panda had the word *bear* after its name, many researchers said it belonged to the raccoon family. This discussion continued until 1987. Steven O'Brian, a researcher at the National Cancer Institute in Bethesda, Maryland, used a process known as DNA (deoxyribonucleic acid) genetic fingerprinting to prove that the giant panda was a member of the bear species. Finally the question had been answered.

The Life of the
Giant Panda Bear

What's in a Name? Scientists have special names for the animals they study. The names tell which family, genus, and species each animal belongs to. For many years the giant panda had a species and genus but no family. Today the family has been added to giant panda's name. The giant panda belongs to the family *Ursidae*. Its genus name is *Ailuropoda*, and *melanoleuca* is its species. The Chinese call their beloved national symbol, *Daxiong-Mao*. The name means "large bear cat." They chose this name because the pupil of the giant panda's eye is slit like a cat's eye.

The Giant Panda Bear Family. As with most bears, the giant panda male and female do not live together as a family. They do seek each other out during the spring mating season, but when mating is finished, the male leaves the female's territory. The young giant panda cub usually stays with its mother until it is a year and a half old. Sometimes it stays longer.

Giant Panda Bear Cubs

When giant pandas are born, they are very small. Five ounces (141 grams) is the most they can weigh at birth. Sometimes twins or triplets are born, but only the healthiest cub survives. The mother giant panda spends all of her time caring for the helpless cub.

Giant pandas are usually born in a hollow tree. This is known as a den. A cub stays in the den until it is able to walk by itself. This takes between four and six months. During this time the mother giant panda is always close by if she is not keeping the cub warm with her body heat.

At the time of birth, the cub is held close to the mother's chest under her arm. The mother holds her cub as she nurses it. As mother and cub travel through the forest, the mother giant panda carefully carries the cub in her mouth.

When born, giant pandas are blind. They are able to see after several months. Their bodies are covered with a fine white hair, but as the cub grows, the hair becomes long and coarse. Soon the black coloring begins to show through.

Food is important to the young cub. By the time the cub becomes an adult bear, its weight is 800 times what it was at birth. The cub lives off of its mother's milk for the first seven months of its life. The mother giant panda shows the young cub how to drink water. Slowly, bamboo is introduced into the diet. At seven months, the cub is able to eat bamboo by itself and is beginning to take care of itself.

As the cub is growing, it is learning how to survive in the bamboo forests. Mother giant panda teaches her cub how to climb trees. Although learning to climb trees is the way a young cub protects itself from danger, it is also a great way to have fun. The young panda builds its strength by sliding up and down its mother's back. A cub often nips and wrestles with its mother's legs. Giant pandas enjoy playing until they are three years old.

By the time the young giant panda is a year and a half old, it weighs about 120 pounds (54.5 kilograms) and is ready to leave home. The young adult begins to look for its own home range. Usually the young panda finds a home range close to its mother. Researchers have observed that giant pandas do not like to travel great distances.

Adult
Giant Panda Bears

As giant pandas become adults, they learn to live alone. They do not live in groups. Many giant pandas may share a home range, but seldom are they seen together.

Silently, the giant panda travels through thick bamboo forests, which protect it from predators— as well as researchers. Most of its day is spent eating and resting, however, because this is an animal with a limited amount of energy. After eating, a favorite resting place might be beds of bamboo leaves and branches, hollow trees, and rock crevices.

By the time a male giant panda is fully grown, he weighs more than 200 pounds (90.9 kilograms) and measures between $5\frac{1}{2}$ and 6 feet (1.667-1.83 meters) in length. Female giant pandas are somewhat smaller than males. Even though the giant pandas eat most of their day, they do not grow into large bears like the polar or the grizzly.

When the female reaches her sixth or seventh birthday, she has her first litter of cubs. Females usually have their litters between $3\frac{1}{2}$ and $5\frac{1}{2}$ months after mating. Litters are born every two years.

From *Investigating Science Through Bears*, ©1994. Teacher Ideas Press, P.O. Box 6633, Englewood, CO 80155-6633.

Hibernation

Giant pandas do not hibernate. Animals that hibernate sleep through the coldest months of the year and live off stored body fat. The giant panda's diet does not allow it to store fat. Because the giant panda does not have this stored fat, it must constantly eat to survive.

Geographic Location

Wild giant pandas are found in the Kansu, Szechwan, and Shensi provinces in the People's Republic of China. High in the mountains—at elevations between 4,000 and 11,000 feet (1.26-3.46 kilometers)—the giant panda makes its home. Covered with thousands of miles (kilometers) of coniferous forest, this area of China is cold, wet, and snowy. These forests are so thick that it is almost impossible to see the giant pandas that live in them.

Fourteen reserves have been set aside by the People's Republic of China for the giant pandas. Researchers feel that more than half of the giant panda bear population live on the reserves. The Chinese government, along with scientists from around the world, watch and study the giant pandas. These reserves are shared, however, with the local farmers. As more and more people move into the area, the giant pandas are forced to move their habitats higher into the mountains. There they live in small pockets of the forest.

Physical Characteristics

Scientists have had difficulty deciding whether the giant panda is a bear or a raccoon. It has many characteristics of each family. Although it was eventually decided that the giant panda belongs to the bear family, the animal does have several unique body characteristics that set it apart from the rest of the world's bears.

Body Shape. The body of a giant panda bear is similar to that of other bears. Giant pandas are muscular across the front of their body. Though their front legs are strong, their back legs do not have as much strength. When the giant panda moves, it moves very slowly. But when the giant panda is scared, it runs quickly.

The head of the giant panda is very round compared to the heads of other bears. Underneath the black and white fur, the giant panda has extra muscles and strong jaws for crushing bamboo. The wide teeth of a giant panda help it to chew bamboo.

If you were to look at a giant panda's face closely, you would notice that its eyes look more like cat's eyes than the eyes of a bear. The pupils in bears' eyes are round, but the pupils in the giant panda's eyes are like slits.

Fur and Skin. If you were to ask several people the color of a giant panda, they would tell you that it is black and white. But in 1986, researchers found that the giant panda could have a light brown period in its life. In the wild, the black coloring on a giant panda often looks more brown or red than black. Dust and dirt often discolor the white fur. The fur on an adult giant panda is about 2 inches (5.08 centimeters) long. It looks soft but is actually thick and coarse to touch. This coat is great protection for the giant panda during the winter months in the mountains of China.

Underneath the giant panda's fur are different colors of skin. The skin is pink under the white fur, and dark skin can be found underneath the black fur.

Senses. All bears depend on their senses to survive in the wild, and the giant panda is no different. The sense of smell and the ability to hear are excellent in the giant panda. Unfortunately, it cannot see well, especially at night.

The Sounds of the Giant Panda Bear. Noise is not characteristic of a giant panda. Seldom does it make noise. Though most bears roar, giant pandas—at the time of mating and at birth—bleat, chirp, honk, growl, and bark. Dr. George Schaller, a well-known giant panda expert, tells of hearing "a medley of squeals, yips, chirps, moans, and barks" when giant pandas meet each other in the wild.

The Giant Panda Thumb. The giant panda's forepaw allows it to grasp food—just as a human does. On each forepaw there is an extra long wristbone attached to five claws. This wristbone is covered with a pad of leathery skin. When the giant panda grasps food, it wraps its claws around the object, pushes the object against the wristbone, and holds the food in place. The wristbone is known as a radial sesamoid bone. Since the giant panda has this special thumb, it is able to grasp and bring food to its mouth better than other bears.

 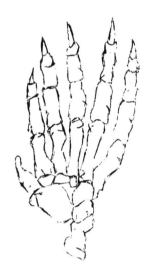

Splinterproof Esophagus. The esophagus is the pipe in the giant panda's throat through which food travels to its stomach. Bamboo is the main food in a giant panda's diet. But bamboo is difficult to digest and is full of splinters. The giant panda's esophagus has thick walls to protect itself from splinters.

Intelligence. Little is known about the intelligence of the giant panda in the wild. Researchers know that giant pandas in captivity are able to be taught tricks. At one of the Chinese zoos, keepers have been able to teach them to do many tricks, such as riding a bicycle and throwing a basketball through a hoop. Some of the Chinese zoos lend their trained giant pandas to other zoos so that thousands of people can view them.

Because the giant panda has few enemies to worry about, it does not need to be constantly concerned about being attacked. When the giant panda's food supply is used up, it is able to search for a new feeding ground.

Life Span. No one knows how long giant pandas survive in the wild. In the Washington National Zoo in Washington, D.C., the two pandas, Ling-Ling and Hsing-Hsing, have lived healthy lives for more than 20 years.

From *Investigating Science Through Bears,* ©1994. Teacher Ideas Press, P.O. Box 6633, Englewood, CO 80155-6633.

Habitat Requirements

As with all animals, the giant panda must have a food supply, water, shelter, space, and a safe place to live. Researchers have had a difficult time studying the giant panda in its natural habitat, because thick trees and plants make it almost impossible to see into its environment. Most of the research on the giant panda has been done at the nature reserves in China and at zoos throughout the world.

The Food Supply of the Giant Panda. Living in the mountains of China has not been easy for the giant panda. The main food supply is often only a few types of bamboo, which grows throughout the panda habitat. As time passes, the bamboo supply is getting smaller or dying out entirely. Giant pandas are being forced to move higher into the mountains to find enough food to eat. As humans move into the habitats, they destroy many of the bamboo trees for houses and farm buildings. These villages also cut off the panda from its food supply.

Ninety-nine percent of the giant pandas' food supply comes from bamboo. Bamboo is a grass that can grow as tall as trees. There are more than 700 different kinds of bamboo that grow throughout the world. Many kinds grow in the reserves, but the giant pandas favor just 25 types. Giant pandas are fussy eaters.

Bamboo grows well in the area in which the reserves are located. Water and moisture must be plentiful to grow a healthy crop. These reserves receive more than 50 inches (127 centimeters) of rain and snow a year.

Bamboo stays green all year-round. Giant pandas eat the leaves, shoots, and stalks. The leaves and shoots are their favorite parts. The giant pandas only eat certain parts of the bamboo at certain times of the year. Scientists think there is a taste change during the different seasons.

Occasionally the giant panda is faced with a bamboo shortage. The lifetime of a certain type of bamboo ranges between 40 and 120 years. At the end of the bamboo's life cycle, they flower, drop seeds, and die. All the bamboo in a given area dies at one time. It can take years for a new crop to grow. Hopefully, another type of bamboo will be in the same area. Giant pandas cannot always move into new areas in the reserve because people are living there.

During the past 20 years, two of the giant pandas' favorite types of bamboo—arrow and umbrella—died. In 1975, as many as 138 giant pandas starved to death. By the time the next bamboo life cycle ended in 1983, the Chinese government and the World Wildlife Fund had learned more about the effect of the bamboo life cycle on the giant panda and were prepared to take care of the problem. Thousands of volunteers took bamboo into the reserves, thus saving most of the giant pandas.

The Giant Panda's Diet. Like most bears, giant pandas are carnivores. Their short digestive systems are made for animals that regularly have meat in their diet. Unfortunately, there is little meat available for them to eat. Researchers have, however, recorded giant pandas raiding the researchers' camps in search of meat. Rodents, pikas, and carrion are rare taste treats. Over the centuries, the giant pandas' digestive system has adapted to eat bamboo.

Mix a little meat, flowers, vines, roots, different grasses, a touch of honey, and lots of bamboo. What do you have? The giant pandas' diet. Sixteen hours a day the giant pandas are eating. Most of the time bamboo is the food. Why does the giant panda spend so much time eating? Because its body does not digest bamboo well and because the bamboo gives the giant pandas few nutritious ingredients and little energy. The foodstuff travels through the giant pandas' digestive system quickly. When they are finished eating, it is time to take a nap. When they awake, it is time to eat once more.

Bamboo is everywhere in the giant pandas' habitat. The giant pandas' radial sesamoid thumb and wide teeth allow them to eat hundreds of stalks of bamboo daily with little effort. Sitting on the forest's floor, the giant pandas grab stalks of bamboo with their forepaws. The leaves, stems, and shoots are easily eaten. By peeling the outer covering off the bamboo, the giant pandas get to the pith. Crushing jaws and wide teeth chew the pith into small pieces. Within a day's feeding time, giant pandas eat more than 30 pounds of bamboo.

Giant Pandas in Captivity

Giant pandas are the most loved and sought after zoo animals in the world. Requests for them far outnumber the supply. Zoos that are fortunate to have giant pandas in their collection are always a major tourist attraction, and the giant pandas become great money-makers. But zoos are also a good place to research animals. By studying the giant pandas in the zoo setting, researchers are able to understand how they live. Scientists record their behavior, hoping to find answers that will prevent the giant panda from becoming extinct. Unfortunately, giant pandas have a difficult time giving birth to live cubs in captivity. Researchers are studying this problem carefully.

Life in the Washington National Zoo. Life in the zoo is much different for the giant pandas from their life in the wild. Housed in an air-conditioned paddock and surrounded by giant pandaproof glass, Ling-Ling and Hsing-Hsing spend their days eating and sleeping. Supplying them with food is not a problem for zookeepers. Bamboo, which is still an important part of their diet, is grown in many different gardens around Washington, D.C. After mixing it all together, the zookeepers feed the following diet to Ling-Ling and Hsing-Hsing twice a day:

> cooked rice, 2 pounds (.91 kilograms)
> powdered cottage cheese, ½ cup (118 cubic centimeters)
> vitamin mix, 2 tablespoons (29.2 cubic centimeters)
> mineral mix, 2 tablespoons (29.2 cubic centimeters)
> soybean oil, 1 tablespoon (14.6 cubic centimeters)
> honey, 2 tablespoons (29.2 cubic centimeters)
> water, 2 cups (170 cubic centimeters)
> carrots, ½ pound (.23 kilograms)
> apples, 2 pounds (.91 kilograms)
> bamboo, 15 pounds (6.8 kilograms)

> —Washington National Zoo, 1992

From *Investigating Science Through Bears,* ©1994. Teacher Ideas Press, P.O. Box 6633, Englewood, CO 80155-6633.

The giant pandas are fed at 11:00 A.M. and 3:00 P.M. Healthy snacks of fruit and vegetables are also a part of the diet. For visitors, feeding time is an excellent time to view the giant pandas because it is much easier to coax them out of their dens. Food is used as a reward to move the giant pandas from their resting spot. Ling-Ling and Hsing-Hsing know their keepers and come when called. They are always looking forward to a snack or a meal.

Giant pandas are not as playful in captivity as they are in the wild. Throughout the day the giant pandas, each in its own play area, do somersaults, headstands, and rolls. Tubs of water help to cool off the giant pandas during the heat of Washington's summers. Toys have been a problem. It is difficult to find a toy that will take the hard blows from their strong forepaws. Zookeepers work hard to keep them active and give them exercise.

Ling-Ling and Hsing-Hsing have attracted millions of visitors to the Washington National Zoo for the past 20 years. It was hoped that they would mate and have cubs. Over the years, Ling-Ling has given birth to five cubs. Unfortunately, they did not live. Eight newborn giant pandas have survived in zoos outside of China. Researchers had hoped that the births in zoos would have greatly increased after years of study. Although the increase has been slow, each year more births occur.

Giant Panda Bear Research

In 1957, the Chinese realized the giant panda population was rapidly decreasing. Research projects were started. Twelve reserves were set up in the Shensi, Kansu, and Szechwan provinces. The World Wildlife Fund joined the research efforts in the late 1970s. Laboratories and nurseries were built to study bamboo growth as well as the giant panda.

Research Methods. Studying giant pandas is very similar to studying other types of bears. One must become a part of their habitat. Since the bamboo forests are so thick, it is difficult to spot the giant pandas.

A trap is set for the giant panda. After capturing it, the bear is given a shot to put it to sleep. The giant panda is weighed and measured. A blood sample is taken. Researchers carefully check over the giant panda's entire body. They even look at the teeth carefully.

A radio collar is placed around the giant panda's neck. In this collar there is a transmitter that gives off radio signals. As the giant panda travels throughout its habitat, researchers are able to track and record its activities. The giant panda can travel miles from the researchers, but signals from its collar will continue to be received loud and clear.

Good scientists are able to observe the giant panda without letting the animal know that they are there. By following the radio signals, scientists can observe the area through which the giant panda has traveled. A giant panda leaves large amounts of undigested bamboo in its droppings. Scientists collect and study these droppings to check on the amount of bamboo eaten by the giant panda on that day.

The radio signals have also allowed the scientists to travel to the area in which mating or birth is taking place. Then the scientists are able to watch from a distance the actual activity in the wild.

Most of the giant pandas living on the reserves are living in the wild. At Wolong Natural Reserve, a number of them live in captivity. They are observed by researchers just as if they were in a zoo. This allows researchers to spend time on breeding problems. Several giant pandas have been born at Wolong. If giant pandas are to survive, scientists must learn how to successfully breed them in captivity.

The Future
of the Giant Panda

Most scientists agree that fewer than 1,000 giant pandas live in the wild today. Millions of dollars need to be spent researching the giant panda and its food supply, building reserves, relocating people in the reserve area, educating the public on conservation, putting poachers on trial, and planting thousands of acres of bamboo.

Because the giant pandas' natural habitat is found only in China, the Chinese government is responsible for its upkeep. The departments within the Chinese government, which oversee the giant panda projects, need to work together to solve the many problems that they face.

The giant pandas' food supply is bamboo. Because they need a huge amount of bamboo to survive, large areas of bamboo forests must be made available for them. Over the years, some of China's population of more than a billion people have slowly moved into the giant pandas' feeding area and have cut the bamboo forests so that they can farm and build homes. It is difficult to explain to poor farmers that living in these areas causes great problems for these animals. If bamboo becomes scarce, giant pandas have nowhere to go for a new supply because their habitat has been greatly reduced in size. Reserves should have animals and plants only. People make it difficult for giant pandas to survive. It is important to discover new ways to help people and giant pandas live together.

The logging industry has also caused much harm to the bamboo forests. Although the loggers may not be interested in the bamboo when they remove the trees from the forest, they destroy the giant pandas' protection and shelter. Scientists know the loss of other trees in the bamboo forest affects the growth of a new bamboo crop.

People around the world love the giant panda. The People's Republic of China as well as the World Wildlife Fund have adopted the giant panda as their symbol. No one wants to see China's national treasure disappear. Educating the world about the giant panda's extinction has begun to pay off. People have begun to realize that their favorite zoo animal may not be here for their grandchildren to enjoy, and children have learned that if the giant panda disappears, many other animals and plants will also disappear.

For many years giant panda skins have been sold on the black market. As much as $20,000 has been paid for a skin. Killing giant pandas was big business for people known as poachers. For hundreds of years the giant panda made a lot of poachers very rich. In the past few years the Chinese government has written laws that make poaching giant pandas a crime punished by death.

Giant pandas must beware of hunters as well as poachers. Many times traps—better known as snares—that are set out for other animals instead catch the giant panda. Many giant pandas die each year from these traps. Once more the government has been educating hunters about setting traps in panda territory.

Many researchers feel the biggest problem of the giant panda is their trouble with breeding in captivity. In the People's Republic of China, the Peking and Ch'eng-tu zoos have had some success with the birth of giant pandas. But keeping them alive is also a problem. Researchers continue to work in these areas of study, hoping that more giant pandas in zoos will give birth and that the newborns will grow into healthy adults.

As one can see, the giant panda must overcome many problems if it is to remain as a species. History has proved many times that when everyone works together, great things can be done. Two hundred years from now there may be giant pandas in zoos everywhere for the whole world to enjoy.

From *Investigating Science Through Bears,* ©1994. Teacher Ideas Press, P.O. Box 6633, Englewood, CO 80155-6633.

Giant Panda Bear Activities

Activity No. 1
China's Pride and Joy—
The Giant Panda

The giant panda, a national treasure of China for more than 3,000 years, is now an endangered species. Students should learn that a global effort was undertaken to study how the giant panda's food supply, along with China's population growth, has played an important role in the giant panda's decline in numbers.

Background Information

The giant panda bear is one of the most loved bears in the world; however, it is also one of the rarest bears. The giant panda bear is found only in the People's Republic of China. Reserves containing the natural habitats of the giant panda bear have been set aside in the Szechwan, Kansu, and Shensi provinces of central China.

The giant panda bear eats large quantities of the bamboo plant, but humans need the land for farming. Without these acres of bamboo forests, the giant panda bear will have difficulty finding enough to eat to survive. The result is a conflict between humans and the giant panda bear. Although giant panda bears survive in zoos, their reproduction rate is very low in captivity. These factors contribute to the overall decline in the numbers of giant panda bears in the wild and in captivity.

Information about the giant panda bear can be obtained by writing to National Zoological Park, Washington, DC 20008-2598.

By studying the physical characteristics and structure (including the unique paws) of the giant panda bear, along with the bear's environment and food supply, integration of life science and earth science learnings can be accomplished. Investigating Chinese calligraphy and creating posters about the future of the giant panda bear provide the opportunity for the use of language-arts skills for student enrichment.

The Panda and China

In learning about the endangered giant panda bear, students will:

- locate the People's Republic of China on a world map;
- identify the regions of China where the giant panda bear lives;
- discuss how the giant panda bear's habitat and food supply have caused it to become an endangered species;
- discuss the relationship between humans' need for land and the survival of the giant panda bear;
- build a habitat for the giant panda bear living in captivity or one that is like where it lives in the wild;

- plan and create a poster campaign to save the endangered giant panda bear;

- study the importance of the so-called thumb of the giant panda bear;

- identify and use Chinese calligraphy to create and illustrate a giant panda bear short story.

Materials
- world map
- giant panda pictures
- magazines
- paints and crayons
- paste and glue
- poster board
- Giant Panda Bear Facts Pack
- map of the People's Republic of China
- marking pens and pencils
- brushes and scissors
- throwaway and recyclable materials from home and lawn for habitat
- learning sheets:
  No. 1. Poster Planning—The Endangered Giant Panda Bear
  No. 2. Chinese Characters—Giant Panda Bear Story
  No. 3. The People's Republic of China Map

Preparation
1. Display a large map of the People's Republic of China.

2. Collect and display pictures of the giant panda bears, Chinese people, China's terrain, bamboo forests, and so on. Create an Oriental atmosphere in the classroom.

3. Collect materials needed for building a giant panda bear's habitat as it would appear either in the wild or in captivity. These materials should include throwaway and recylable items found around the house, garage, and lawn.

4. Display maps, books, and magazines related to China for the students to study. Books and magazines may be obtained from the school library, and maps are available from travel agencies, and so on.

5. Display Chinese items such as clothing, dishes, and chopsticks.

6. Prepare:

   - Giant Panda Bear Facts Pack

   - Learning Sheet No. 1: Poster Planning—The Endangered Giant Panda Bear

   - Learning Sheet No. 2: Chinese Characters—Giant Panda Bear Story

   - Learning Sheet No. 3: The People's Republic of China Map

Procedure
1. Create an Oriental atmosphere in the classroom with pictures of the giant panda bear in its natural environment in China.

2. Display a world map and a map of the People's Republic of China. Ask the students to read and discuss the Giant Panda Bear Facts Pack; they will locate on the maps where the giant panda bears live.

3. Divide the students into groups of three or four, depending on the size of the classroom. Each group of students should be given a question from the list below to investigate. The Giant Panda Bear Facts Pack will be used to help them determine appropriate answers to the questions. Each group may then present their questions and answers in a classroom discussion. The following questions are to be investigated and may be written on note cards or on the chalkboard before the assignment.

   • Giant panda bears need enormous supplies of bamboo plants. Why is this important? What type of digestive system allows the bear to eat large amounts of bamboo plants? What other types of food is the giant panda bear able to eat? What foods are fed to the bear in captivity?

   • Giant panda bears do survive in captivity. Why is this possible? What are the problems that the zookeepers must watch for while the bears are in captivity? Will having the giant panda bears in captivity in zoos take them off the endangered-species list and keep them off? Why or why not?

   • Giant panda bears have an interesting body structure. What are some unique characteristics they have? What makes their paws special? Compare the physical characteristics of the giant panda bear with those of the bears of North America. How are the giant panda bears' structure and physical characteristics adapted for its living in the mountainous areas with significant climatic changes?

   • Giant panda bears are on the endangered-species list. How did they get on this list? How has man affected the survival or decline of the giant panda bear? What is the future for the giant panda bear in the modern world?

   After the groups have completed their investigations of the questions and compiled their answers, conduct a classroom discussion. Compile all the answers and information on chart paper to permit sharing during classroom discussion.

4. Using learning sheet 3, The People's Republic of China Map, the students may draw in the lines that represent the different provinces in the republic. After studying the People's Republic of China map and reading about the bears, the students should shade in the areas where the giant pandas are found. The students may then complete their maps by coloring lightly and labeling the provinces and by locating and identifying the capital city of the People's Republic of China.

5. After discussing the bear and its habitat, the students may select the type of bear habitat they wish to build. The choices are 1) a habitat found in the wild of China's mountainous areas, or 2) a habitat that would be created in a zoo setting. The habitats are to be built from the materials collected for this project.

6. As the discussion continues, create a poster as outlined on learning sheet 1, Poster Planning—The Endangered Giant Panda Bear. Display the completed posters for all the school's students to see.

7. The students may conclude the project by using learning sheet 2, Chinese Characters— Giant Panda Bear Story, to study Chinese characters related to the giant panda bear. Students should develop a short story using Chinese characters as part of their written story about the giant panda bear. The story may be illustrated with a picture of the giant panda bear eating bamboo.

Bear Extensions

1. Invite a local horticulturalist to visit the classroom. Discuss the different types of bamboo that are found in your area. Select bamboo plants from your local nursery, and let them grow in the classroom as part of the life-science learning.

2. Arrange to have a Giant Panda Bear Day during the study of this bear. Display stuffed pandas, games, clothing, dishes, books, and so on. Children owning panda-motif clothing should be encouraged to wear it, and the rest of the class should dress in black and white.

Vocabulary Words
- bamboo
- extinction
- calligraphy
- endangered
- Wolong Natural Reserve
- Shensi Province
- Kansu Province
- Szechwan Province
- the People's Republic of China

Learning Sheet No. 1
Poster Planning—
The Endangered Giant Panda Bear

Student Copy

Name:_____

Date:_____

Outline for Poster Planning

1. Theme (Title)

   • What do you want to say on your poster?

   • What animals do you want in the picture?

   • What plants need to be in the poster?

   • What or who is the giant panda's greatest enemy?

2. Drawing (Design)

   • Draw on practice paper the design that you want to use that will tell the story of the endangered giant panda.

   • Draw your design on poster board with a pencil.

3. Coloring (Colors)

   • Go back to your practice copy and color it with crayons, colored pencils, paints, or markers in the way you want your final poster to look.

4. Poster (Final Complete Design)

   • Reproduce the final poster from the practice copy on your poster board.

5. Display

   • Display the Endangered Giant Panda Bear poster for the other students to see. A contest for the most informative and original posters will be judged by the principal or another faculty member.

From *Investigating Science Through Bears,* ©1994. Teacher Ideas Press, P.O. Box 6633, Englewood, CO 80155-6633.

Learning Sheet No. 2
Chinese Characters—
Giant Panda Bear Story

Student Copy

Name:_____

Date:_____

The Chinese language is written quite differently from other languages. Instead of using letters to form words, strokes are drawn. Different strokes are drawn together to form characters, which stand for ideas. Although 50,000 characters are found in the Chinese language, most young schoolchildren know only several thousand.

China

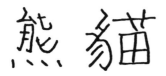

Giant Panda

Writing Chinese characters is an art known as calligraphy. Students spend many hours practicing these characters. Being able to write characters well is a sign of a well-educated person in China. Use the Chinese characters shown here to create a short story about the giant panda. Use one or more characters from the list in your story. Use English words in the story too. Continue the story with both Chinese characters and English words. Then draw and color a picture that tells about the story. Your teacher will provide the necessary paper for the project. Read the stories to the class. Display the completed projects.

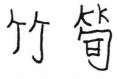

Bamboo Shoots

Zoo

Paws

Learning Sheet No. 3
The People's Republic of China Map

Student Copy

Name:_____

Date:_____

Directions

- Outline in green the *country* of the People's Republic of China.

- Name the three provinces of China where giant pandas live. _____, _____, and _____. Locate these provinces on the map above, and color them yellow.

- Locate Beijing, the capital of the People's Republic of China, on the map, and circle it in blue.

- Ch'eng-tu and Beijing zoos have giant panda bears in captivity. Underline these cities with red.

- Find the Wolong Natural Reserve on the map. Color it pink.

Activity No. 2
We Are Going to China
to Visit the World of the Giant Panda

Many people in North America have the natural habitats of bears literally in or near their own backyards. Others can travel to national parks to see North American bears living in their natural habitats. To see the giant panda bear in its natural habitat, North Americans must travel by airplane or boat to the People's Republic of China. In this activity, students learn about the preparations that must be made before leaving the United States or Canada to visit a foreign country such as China. After the final plans are made and all preparations are completed, the students may embark on a simulated airplane trip to the People's Republic of China.

Background Information

Airline travel is a way of life in the 1990s, which means that any part of the world is only hours away by airplane. This activity is designed to integrate many skills related to real-life travel experiences, including 1) using official documents needed for overseas travel, 2) purchasing an airline ticket, 3) experiencing simulated activities related to airports and airline travel, 4) observing the changes of the Earth while traveling in the air, 5) becoming familiar with different cultures in the world, and 6) anticipating a visit to a Chinese wildlife reserve to see the giant panda bear in its natural habitat.

Life and earth sciences are explored as the giant panda bear's environment is studied. Science and social studies are interrelated, and one cannot study life or earth science without discussing where it occurs. Social skills are required in order for people to successfully interact with other people in many situations, including those in this activity.

Foreign Travel Planning

In learning about making the preparations to visit a foreign country such as China, students will:

- locate the People's Republic of China on a world map;

- locate on a map of the People's Republic of China the Chinese provinces, major cities with zoos, and reserves where giant panda bears are found;

- plan a trip to the People's Republic of China with the help of a travel agency;

- learn about the official documents necessary for traveling outside the United States and Canada;

- determine the type of clothing and other items needed for a safe and pleasant trip;

- experience life aboard a simulated airplane trip during a long, overseas flight;

- record information about the trip to the People's Republic of China, including travel planning, airport experiences, in-flight experiences, cultural differences, and so on. A journal or diary may be used to record this information.

Materials

- The Giant Panda Bear Facts Pack
- world map
- used airline ticket and passport
- travel brochures and posters of China, major Chinese cities, airports, airplanes, and giant pandas bears
- travel films or videos
- Chinese newspapers
- camera with film
- paints, crayons, markers, and brushes
- glue, scissors, and large pieces of cardboard
- stove, dryer, or refrigerator boxes
- suitcase
- snack foods and clean, Styrofoam meat trays for airline food trays
- learning sheets:
  No. 1. Panda Airline Ticket
  No. 2. Passport Application
  No. 3. Student Passport
  No. 4. Making a Student Passport
  No. 5. I'm-Going-to-China Checklist
  No. 6. I'm-Going-to-Take-a-Trip Game
  No. 7. Flying High

Preparation

1. Collect from a local travel agency some travel brochures, travel posters, airline schedules, ticket information, and passport applications related to travel to the People's Republic of China. Invite a travel agent to visit the classroom to discuss traveling overseas to China.

2. Compile maps of the People's Republic of China, world maps, films, videos, slides, and music related to China.

3. Borrow library books related to China, the giant panda bear, airplanes, and so on, and have them on display for students to use as supplemental enrichment material.

4. Prepare the following for classroom activities:

   - Giant Panda Bear Facts Pack

   - Learning Sheet No. 1: Panda Airline Ticket

   - Learning Sheet No. 2: Passport Application

   - Learning Sheet No. 3: Student Passport

   - Learning Sheet No. 4: Making a Student Passport

   - Learning Sheet No. 5: I'm-Going-to-China Checklist

   - Learning Sheet No. 6: I'm-Going-to-Take-a-Trip Game

   - Learning Sheet No. 7: Flying High

Procedure

1. Prepare the classroom by decorating it with posters and pictures of China, giant panda bears, airplanes, and related materials that suggest a Chinese atmosphere. The classroom may be divided into parts to designate the different events that will take place. The classroom areas may represent 1) a North American airport, 2) a Chinese airport, 3) an airplane of Panda Airlines, and 4) a giant panda bear in a wildlife reserve in China.

2. Display library books, pictures of Chinese foods, chopsticks, Chinese clothing, and so on for supplemental enrichment. Playing Chinese music would add a touch of authenticity to the classroom atmosphere during continuing studies of the giant panda bear.

3. Provide students with journals in which they may record classroom events relating to each activity. Their journal entries should include their thoughts while traveling on the simulated airplane trip, information they thought was interesting, and new learning experiences that they encountered. At the completion of all the activities, the students should review their entries about the new things investigated during their simulated trip.

4. Read and discuss the materials posted in the different parts of the classroom in order to familiarize the students with the content that is displayed. Read orally or review the Giant Panda Bear Facts Pack to provide the students with information on both life and earth science as they relate to the giant panda bear. This information will assist the students in perceiving the total picture of the giant panda bear in its environment.

5. Carry out the following learning experiences:

Panda Airline Ticket

After studying the travel brochures and airline schedules, the following questions need to be discussed before filling in the airline ticket form shown in learning sheet 1:

- What city in China will be your destination?

- What is the cost of traveling to this city?

- Why are some flights less expensive than others?

- Does the time of day affect the ticket price?

- Is your flight a direct flight to your destination?

- If your flight is not a direct flight, how many stops are there?

Discuss the effect of these questions on ticket pricing, then decide which flight is the least expensive and most convenient for students. Using an old, used airline ticket as a guide, the students should fill in the flight information for the Panda Airlines ticket shown in learning sheet 1. The students may then cut out the tickets. The tickets are to be saved for the simulated airline flight. The students should also fill in the baggage tag shown in learning sheet 1 and save it for their traveling bag.

Passport Application and Student Passport

When traveling outside the United States or Canada, an American or Canadian citizen must have a passport. The passport has the person's picture on it. This official document states and shows that the passport holder is a legal citizen of the United States or Canada. All countries in the world require their citizens to carry a passport when traveling to most other countries.

To travel to these countries a passport application must be obtained and completed. This application is available from U.S. post offices. As a preliminary activity, the students should complete the passport-application form provided in learning sheet 2, and return it to the teacher. After the applications are reviewed, photos should be taken of each student for inclusion on their passport.

To make a student passport (see directions in learning sheet 4) students should:

- use a 9-x-12-inch (3.5-4.7-centimeter) piece of construction paper.

- fill in Student Passport Sheet from learning sheet 3.

- cut out the passport and picture from learning sheet 3.

- glue the passport information sheet onto the lower half of the construction paper. After it dries, fold the construction paper, top to bottom.

- glue the photograph onto the front of the passport.

- save the passport for the simulated trip to China.

Exploring an Airport and a Commercial Passenger Airplane

If your school is located near an airport, visiting the airport and walking through a passenger airline with a tour guide would be an enriching experience. Contact the public-relations branch of available airlines to investigate this possibility. If a tour can be arranged, invite the students while touring the airport to list the jobs that are necessary in order for the airplanes to fly, the airport to operate, and the people to eat both on the ground and in the airplane.

If the school is not located near an airport, there are excellent films for students to view that can substitute for a real visit. These include *Airplane Trips by Jet*, *Airplanes Work for Us*, and *Airplanes: How They Fly*. There are other fine travel films available through the local community library or travel agencies.

It takes many people to run an airplane efficiently. List on chart paper the different jobs people have on an airplane, and discuss their relative importance. Continue by listing other types of employment available at the airport. Discuss the importance of the support jobs as they relate to the safety of the passengers. Students should record in their journals the information that they obtain during these discussions.

Trip Planning

Before the simulated airplane trip, all students should fill in the I'm-Going-to-China Checklist found in learning sheet 5. Since additional considerations are necessary when traveling for two or more weeks in a foreign country, the following questions should be discussed:

- What is the season of the year?

- What will the weather be like?

- What will be the high and low temperatures?

- Will there be lots of walking after arriving in China?

- What clothes will be needed?

- How much luggage is permitted?

- Where are the places in China where the giant panda bear can be found?

- What are additional items that will be needed when traveling overseas?

- Where do tourists sleep at night in China?

- What will the hotels in China be like?

- What kinds of food will be available?

When traveling overseas, the amount of luggage permitted is often limited. So when choosing clothing, the weather and changing temperatures should be carefully considered because of limited space for packing. There are many places to visit in China: Beijing—the capital—the Ch'eng-tu Zoo, and the Wolong Natural Reserve will be on the list.

After itemizing the things that the students plan to take on their trip, play the listening game I'm-Going-to-Take-a-Trip, which is included in learning sheet 6.

A Simulated Trip to the People's Republic of China

To simulate an airplane trip to the People's Republic of China, use the following steps:

- Set up the classroom to look like the inside of an airliner. Students may want to use stove or dryer boxes to make the nose of the plane. Place several chairs facing into the open end of the box. This will be the cockpit. Students may want to design instrument panels out of cardboard to attach to the open end of the box. Set up several desks to act as the work area for the flight attendants, and don't forget to give them chairs to sit on during takeoff! Behind the work area, place chairs in rows. Leave an aisle in the middle. At the back of the plane there should be a refrigerator box marked Bathroom. Cut a door into the box for easy access. Baggage may be stored at the back of the plane.

- Because the class is playacting this airplane trip, students may want to bring luggage to make this dramatization more lifelike.

- It takes many people to run an airplane efficiently. Students may apply for the jobs to be pilot, copilot, navigator, baggage handler, ticket taker, and flight attendant. Each student should check in the encyclopedia for a job description for each job. Discuss with the students the importance of their jobs. Emphasize that a successful flight happens only when everyone works together.

- Discuss how the flight attendants should instruct the passengers on how to use the oxygen masks and flotation cushions in case of emergencies. Emphasize the importance of the seat belts in the cabin of the airplane.

- Please check with the students to see if they have their ticket, passport, and luggage. Each piece of luggage should have a baggage ticket. Have the students cut out the baggage ticket, fill in their name and address, and tie it on their luggage.

- All the airplane personnel should take their appropriate places, and the trip may begin.

- Passengers should check their luggage with the baggage handler. The luggage should then be taken to the back of the airplane.

- The ticket taker should take the tickets and check passports.

- The flight attendants should prepare the passengers for takeoff. The moment of departure has arrived!

- The pilot, copilot, and navigator may then welcome the passengers to the flight, and the flight attendants should inform the passengers about the safety rules for the flight.

- Snacks may be served to the passengers. The students should bring in healthy snacks from home for this activity, and the flight attendants should fix the snacks at their work

From *Investigating Science Through Bears,* ©1994. Teacher Ideas Press, P.O. Box 6633, Englewood, CO 80155-6633.

areas. Snacks may be served on trays borrowed from the cafeteria or on clean, throwaway meat trays.

- The flight is very long. To pass the time, movies are often shown on overseas flights.

- When the movie is over, passengers may enjoy reading travel brochures and books about China or the giant panda bear. Remind the students to continue writing their observations in their journals.

- The passengers should be sure to look out the windows during daylight hours. Notice the different features of the Earth over which the airplane is flying, such as oceans, mountains, valleys, rivers, and land shapes.

- Many hours have passed, and the airplane is ready to land. The pilot should wish the passengers a wonderful trip, and the flight attendants should prepare everyone for landing.

- As the passengers leave the airplane, talk about meeting in the airport to discuss their journal entries.

Flying High

In flying from one part of the world to another, people have the experience of eating different types of food in the different countries. Leaving the United States or Canada on an overseas flight to Frankfurt, Germany, the airline may serve American foods. However, while having a layover in Frankfurt, German foods are available to the passengers. After leaving Germany for the People's Republic of China, the airline might serve German food, or they might introduce the passengers to Chinese foods.

The students should fill in the form in learning sheet 7 to indicate the types of food they think will be served on their flight to China. List on the chart the foods the students say might be served and what foods they hope are served. Discuss and compare the differences between Chinese and American diets.

Upon arriving in China on the simulated overseas flight, students should write in their journals what events they think might occur next—riding a bicycle, visiting a zoo, eating Chinese foods, and so on. Summarize these ideas on a chart.

Bear Extensions

1. Invite into the classroom a Chinese student from a local college or the parents of Chinese students in your school. Natives of China are wonderful resources to speak about their homelands. And they might bring in and share foods of their culture!

2. Invite into the classroom local travelers who have visited China, and ask them to share their experiences and pictures with the students.

Vocabulary Words

- Beijing
- Ch'eng-tu
- Wolong Reserve
- travel agency
- passport
- application

- baggage
- brochures
- simulation
- tourist
- reserves

Learning Sheet No. 1

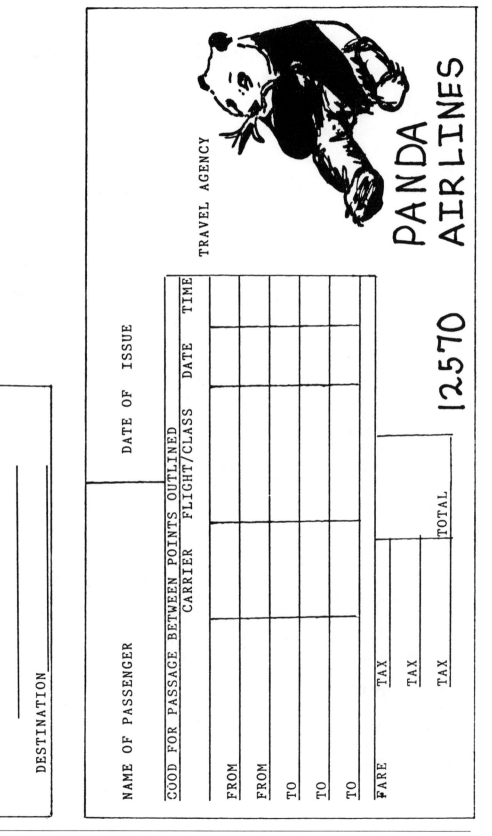

Learning Sheet No. 2

UNITED STATES DEPARTMENT OF STATE

APPLICATION FOR ☐ PASSPORT ☐ REGISTRATION

SEE INSTRUCTIONS—TYPE OR PRINT IN INK IN WHITE AREAS

1. NAME FIRST NAME   MIDDLE NAME

LAST NAME

2. MAILING ADDRESS

STREET

CITY, STATE, ZIP CODE

COUNTRY   IN CARE OF

☐ 5 Yr.   ☐ 10 Yr.   Issue
R D O DP   Date _____
End. #   Exp. _____

3. SEX   Male Female

4. PLACE OF BIRTH City, State or Province, Country

5. DATE OF BIRTH   Mo. Day Year

6. SEE FEDERAL TAX LAW NOTICE ON REVERSE SIDE   SOCIAL SECURITY NUMBER

7. HEIGHT Feet Inches

8. COLOR OF HAIR

9. COLOR OF EYES

10. (Area Code) HOME PHONE

11. (Area Code) BUSINESS PHONE

12. PERMANENT ADDRESS (Street, City, State, ZIP Code)

13. OCCUPATION

14. FATHER'S NAME   BIRTHPLACE   BIRTH DATE   U.S. CITIZEN ☐ YES ☐ NO

15. MOTHER'S MAIDEN NAME   BIRTHPLACE   BIRTH DATE   U.S. CITIZEN ☐ YES ☐ NO

16. TRAVEL PLANS (Not Mandatory)
COUNTRIES   DEPARTURE DATE
    LENGTH OF STAY

17. HAVE YOU EVER BEEN ISSUED A U.S. PASSPORT?   YES ☐   NO ☐   IF YES, SUBMIT PASSPORT IF AVAILABLE. ☐ Submitted

IF UNABLE TO SUBMIT MOST RECENT PASSPORT, STATE ITS DISPOSITION: COMPLETE NEXT LINE

NAME IN WHICH ISSUED   PASSPORT NUMBER   ISSUE DATE (Mo., Day, Yr.)   DISPOSITION

SUBMIT TWO RECENT IDENTICAL PHOTOS

FROM 1" TO 1-3/8"   2" × 2"

18. HAVE YOU EVER BEEN MARRIED? ☐ YES   ☐ NO   DATE OF MOST RECENT MARRIAGE   Mo. Day Year

WIDOWED/DIVORCED? ☐ YES ☐ NO   IF YES, GIVE DATE   Mo. Day Year

SPOUSE'S FULL BIRTH NAME   SPOUSE'S BIRTHPLACE

19. IN CASE OF EMERGENCY, NOTIFY (Person Not Traveling With You) (Not Mandatory)   RELATIONSHIP

FULL NAME

ADDRESS   (Area Code) PHONE NUMBER

20. TO BE COMPLETED BY AN APPLICANT WHO BECAME A CITIZEN THROUGH NATURALIZATION

I IMMIGRATED TO THE U.S. (Month, Year)   I RESIDED CONTINUOUSLY IN THE U.S. From (Mo., Yr.) To (Mo., Yr.)   DATE NATURALIZED (Mo., Day, Yr.)

PLACE

21. DO NOT SIGN APPLICATION UNTIL REQUESTED TO DO SO BY PERSON ADMINISTERING OATH

I have not, since acquiring United States citizenship, performed any of the acts listed under "Acts or Conditions" on the reverse of this application form (unless explanatory statement is attached). I solemnly swear (or affirm) that the statements made on this application are true and the photograph attached is a true likeness of me.

Subscribed and sworn to (affirmed) before me   (SEAL)   X

Month Day Year

☐ Clerk of Court or
☐ PASSPORT Agent
☐ Postal Employee
☐ (Vice) Consul USA At _____

(Signature of person authorized to accept application)

(Sign in presence of person authorized to accept application)

22. APPLICANT'S IDENTIFYING DOCUMENTS ☐ PASSPORT ☐ DRIVER'S LICENSE ☐ OTHER (Specify)

ISSUE DATE   EXPIRATION DATE
Month Day Year   Month Day Year

PLACE OF ISSUE

No.

ISSUED IN THE NAME OF

23. FOR ISSUING OFFICE USE ONLY (Applicant's evidence of citizenship)

☐ Birth Cert.   SR   CR   City   Filed/Issued:
☐ Passport   Bearer's Name:
☐ Report of Birth
☐ Naturalization/Citizenship Cert.   No.:
☐ Other:
☐ Seen & Returned
☐ Attached

APPLICATION APPROVAL

Examiner Name

Office, Date

24.

FEE _____ EXEC. _____ POST _____

FORM DSP-11 (12–87)   (SEE INSTRUCTIONS ON REVERSE)   Form Approved OMB No. 1405-0004 (Exp. 8/1/89)

FOLD

Learning Sheet No. 3

WARNING: Alteration, addition, or mutilation of entries is prohibited. Any unofficial change will render this passport invalid.

NAME- NOM

SEX-SEXE   BIRTHPLACE-LIEU DE NAISSANCE

BIRTH DATE-DATE DE NAISSANCE   ISSUE DATE-DATE DE DÉLIVRANCE

WIFE/HUSBAND-EPOUSE/EPOUX   EXPIRES ON-EXPIRE LE

MINORS-ENFANTS MINEURS

SIGNATURE OF BEARER- SIGNATURE DU TITULAIRE

Passport Photograph

IMPORTANT; This passport is not valid until signed by bearer. Persons included herein may not use this passport for travel unless accompanied by the bearer.

Learning Sheet No. 4
Making a Student Passport

Student Copy

Name:_____

Date:_____

12" (4.7cm)

9"
(3.5 cm)

← CONSTRUCTION PAPER

WRITE OR TYPE IN INFO.

← PASSPORT WORKSHEET

CUT OUT

CONSTRUCTION PAPER

← FOLD AFTER GLUE DRIES

GLUE COMPLETED PASSPORT WORKSHEET

PHOTO

GLUE

GLUE YOUR PHOTOGRAPH ONTO PASSPORT

Learning Sheet No. 5
I'm-Going-to-China Checklist

Student Copy

Name:_____

Date:_____

It will take two or more weeks to complete the round-trip to China. You are limited to one large suitcase and one shoulder bag for the trip. The questions below will help you decide on the items needed.

What Clothes Shall I Take?

List the clothing you plan to take with you on your trip.

_____

_____

_____

_____

_____

_____

_____

What Shall I Pack?

Taking the right clothes when traveling is important. List three factors that will determine the clothes you need.

Whom Shall I Ask?

Who could tell you the type of clothes to wear when visiting China? Name two sources you can ask.

Where Shall I Go?

The People's Republic of China has many places for tourists to visit. Choose three places to visit that will have the giant panda bear.

What Special Items Shall I Take?

What items will help to record all the exciting events? How will you show your friends where you went? List three items that will record your trip.

_____

_____

_____

Learning Sheet No. 6
I'm-Going-to-Take-a-Trip Game

Teacher Guide

This is a listening game that children of all ages enjoy. Because the game depends on the students remembering a lot of words, the size of the group should be limited to 25 participants.

1. Students should sit in a circle.

2. The first student says: "I'm going to take a trip. I'm going to China. In my suitcase, I am going to take a _____."

3. The second student repeats exactly what the first student said, plus the student adds: "and a _____." The second student adds what he or she is going to also take on the trip.

4. Each student repeats what the students have said before, and adds an item to take on the trip. This game continues until everyone in the circle has had a turn. By the time it is the 25th student's turn, children will be listening very quietly and mentally checking to see if they remember all 24 items that everyone is taking on the trip.

5. Regardless of age, everyone does well with this game. The more students who play, the more fun everyone has.

Learning Sheet No. 7
Flying High

Student Copy

Name:_____

Date:_____

FLYING HIGH
MEALS IN THE SKY

Food is an important part of an airline flight. All flights serve food. If your trip is short, a light snack will be served. On longer flights of several hours, a meal is served. Overseas flights that take many hours may have meals and snacks.

Your trip to China will take 16-18 hours flying time from Chicago, Illinois or Montreal, Canada. From the United States, you will fly to Frankfurt, Germany. You may have to wait hours before your flight leaves for China. Talk with a travel agent about the types of meals and snacks that an airline serves. Then list the foods that might be served on each part of your trip.

Flying to Frankfurt

Meal No. 1	Meal No. 2	Snacks

At the Frankfurt Airport

Meal No. 1	Meal No. 2	Snacks

Flying to China

Meal No. 1	Meal No. 2	Meal No. 3

Vocabulary for
Giant Panda Chapter

application—a request made in person or in writing.

baggage—trunks, bags, or suitcases packed for traveling.

Beijing—capital of China, with a population of 5,400,000.

black market—the illegal business of buying or selling goods in violation of price controls.

bleat—the cry made by a sheep, goat, or calf.

captivity—the condition of being held in an environment other than the animal's natural one; some animals cannot bear captivity and die after a few weeks in a cage.

Ch'eng-tu—city of central China, with a population of 1,800,000.

coniferous—any of various evergreen cone-bearing trees, such as pine, spruce, hemlock, or fir.

consume—to eat or drink available food or water.

DNA (deoxyribonucleic acid) genetic fingerprinting— a process whereby scientists study a living organism's cell structure to find its characteristics that make it different from any other living organism.

elevation—the height to which something is raised.

forepaw—a front paw.

hibernation—to spend the winter sleeping or resting.

hollow—a low place between hills.

independent—thinking or acting for oneself; not influenced by others.

Kansu—a province located in central China that includes a wilderness area containing giant panda bears.

laboratory—a place with special equipment where scientific experiments and tests are done.

migrate—to go from one region to another with the change in seasons.

nursery—a place where newborn animals are cared for in a zoo; a piece of ground or place where young plants are raised for transplanting or sale.

nutritious—healthy food for the body; nourishing; valuable as food.

offspring—the young animal; a descendant.

paddock—a small, enclosed field near a house that is used for exercising animals.

passport—a paper or book giving a person official permission to travel in a foreign country under the protection of that person's government.

pika—any of several small, tailless, harelike mammals of the mountains of North America and Eurasia.

pith—the central, spongy tissue in the stem of certain plants.

policy—a plan of action; a way of management.

radial sesamoid bone—pertaining to or near the radius or forearm; small bone that develops in a tendon or in a capsule of a joint; a wristbone on a panda's paw that acts like a human thumb.

reserve—a place set aside for a particular purpose, use, or reason.

rodent—any of a group of animals with large front teeth that are used for gnawing.

Shensi—a province of central China that includes a wilderness area with giant panda bears.

simulation—an imitation; the assuming of a false appearance.

Szechwan—a province of south-central China that includes a wilderness area with giant panda bears.

thicket—shrubs, bushes, or small trees growing close together.

tourist—a person traveling for pleasure.

transcontinental—crossing a continent.

urinating—the act of discharging liquid waste from the body.

Wolong Natural Reserve—China's largest giant panda bear natural reserve, which is located in Szechwan province, and is 800 square miles (2,222 square kilometers) in size.

Teacher Educational Resources

Books

Bailey, Bernadine. *Wonders of the World of Bears*. New York: Dodd, Mead, 1975.

Catton, Chris. *Pandas*. New York: Facts on File, 1990.

Charman, Andrew. Illustrated by C. Forsey. *The Book of Bears*. New York: Gallery Books, 1989.

Collins, Larry R., and James K. Page, Jr. *Ling-Ling and Hsing-Hsing. Year of the Panda*. Garden City, N.Y.: Anchor Press, 1973.

Domico, Terry. *Bears of the World*. New York: Facts on File, 1988.

MacClintock, Dorcas. Photographs by E. Young. *Red Pandas—A Natural History*. New York: Scribner, 1988.

Preiss, Byron, and Gao Xueyu. *The Secret World of the Pandas*. New York: Harry Abrams, 1990.

Schaller, George B. *The Giant Pandas of Woolong*. Chicago: University of Chicago Press, 1985.

Sheldon, William G. *The Wilderness Home of the Giant Panda*. Amherst, Mass.: University of Massachusetts Press, 1975.

Walker, Ernest P. *Mammals of the World*. Baltimore, Md.: Johns Hopkins University Press, 1975.

Magazine Articles

Caras, Roger. "Pandas on Their Home Ground." *GEO, The Earth Diary* (August 1981): 54.

Clark, G. "Panda Bears." *Time* (May 11, 1987): 79.

Dolnick, E. "Panda Paradox." *Discover* (September 1989): 70.

Drew, L. "Are We Loving the Panda Bear to Death?" *National Wildlife* (December 1988-January 1989): 14.

Drew, L. "Lonesome Panda." *Newsweek* (September 19, 1988): 87.

"Essay Panda Bears." *Discover* (February 1986): 40.

McPhee, A. T. "Scientists Help Save Wild Pandas." *Current Science* (November 3, 198): 4.

O'Brien, S. J. "The Ancestry of the Giant Panda." *Scientific American* (November 1987): 102.

"Pair of Pandas Are a Double First." *New Scientist* 129, no. 1758 (March 2, 1991): 15.

"Panda Bears." *Natural History* (January 1987): 14.

"Panda Bears." *Science News* (October 5, 1985): 216.

Preiss, Bryon, and Gao Xueyu. "The Secret World of Pandas." *Life* 13, no. 13 (October 1990): 72.

Robert, L. "China Bans Panda Loans." *Science* (September 23, 1988): 1594.

Robert, L. "Conservationists in Panda-Monium." *Science* (July 29, 1988): 529.

Annotated Bibliography
for Giant Panda Bears
and the Study of Life Science

Children's Books

Barrett, Norman. *Pandas*. New York: Franklin Watts, 1988.
The book presents the story of the panda in the Washington, D.C., zoo and focuses on the everyday life of the panda including the growing-up, eating, playing, and sleeping time of this charming creature. Also discussed are the facts and records of the pandas in China, as well as the lesser known red panda. Efforts on saving the panda from extinction are also discussed. Nonfiction.

Coerr, Eleanor. Illustrated by K. Mizumura. *Biography of a Giant Panda*. New York: G. P. Putnam's Sons, 1975.
This book details the giant panda's life cycle in its natural habitat in the animal kingdom in the mountains of China. A delightful account of the giant panda's antics and methods of survival that make this rarely seen animal one of the most unusual in the world. Nonfiction.

Cook, Susannah. Illustrated by Richard Orr. *Bears and Pandas*. New York: Franklin Watts, 1977.
Environments, life cycles, food, habits, and varieties of bears and pandas are discussed. Nonfiction.

Filstrup, Chris, and Janie Filstrup. Photographs by D. Deland and A. Newman. *China from Emperors to Communes*. Minneapolis, Minn.: Dillon Press, 1983.
The facts about Chinese history, art, traditions, social life, and recreation, including a chapter on Chinese-Americans, a glossary of Chinese terms, and a map of China. Nonfiction.

Green, Carl, and William R. Sanford. *The Giant Panda*. Mankato, Minn.: Crestwood House, 1987.
    This beautifully photographed book is part of a series, Wildlife, Habits, and Habitat. The life of the giant panda is examined in great detail. Several pages highlight the birth of a panda cub at the Wolong Natural Reserve. Nonfiction.

Grosvenor, Donna K. Illustrated by G. Founds. *Pandas*. Washington, D.C.: National Geographic Society, 1973.
    This book presents a short summary of the panda's home in China. It tells how Ling-Ling and Hsing-Hsing were given to the United States. It then discusses their life in the National Zoo in Washington, D.C. Nonfiction.

Hoffman, Mary. *Animals in the Wild—Panda*. Milwaukee, Wis.: Raintree Publishers, 1984.
    This book describes the giant panda in its natural surroundings and describes its life and struggle for survival. Nonfiction.

James, Ian. *Inside China*. New York: Franklin Watts, 1989.
    This book presents the life-style of the people of China in 1989. The contents include discussions on the land; the people and their history; towns and cities, family life, food, sports, and pastimes; the arts, farming, and industry; and on how China is looking to the future. Also included are facts about China and maps of China. Nonfiction.

Martin, Louise. *Panda: The Wild Life in Danger Series*. Vero Beach, Fla.: Rourke Enterprises, 1988.
    The book discusses the giant panda, why it is an endangered species, and the efforts by the World Wildlife Fund and other people to save the giant panda. Nonfiction.

Sadler, Catherine Edwards. Photographs by A. Sadler. *Two Chinese Families*. New York: McClelland and Steward, 1981.
    This book depicts life in modern China by focusing on the daily activities of two children from different families. Nonfiction.

Wang, Zhongui. *Giant Pandas*. East Sussex, England: Wayland Publishers, 1981.
    Beautiful photographs show the giant panda in its captive habitat as well as in its natural habitat. The book also gives detailed information about the giant panda's life and its habits. Nonfiction.

Wexo, John Bonnett. *Giant Pandas*. Mankato, Minn.: Creative Education, 1989.
    A complete story of the giant panda, what they do for fun, their bamboo food source, their habitat, how panda mothers care for their cubs, their body structure and special features, and the future of the giant pandas. Nonfiction.

Xugi, Jin, and Markus Kappeler. *The Giant Panda*. New York: G. P. Putnam's Sons, 1986.
    Photographs and text depict the characteristics, habitat, and behavior of giant pandas, including their feeding habits and reproduction and the current efforts to protect and breed them in captivity. Nonfiction.

Magazine Articles

Ferguson, Dorothy. "Ning-Ning and the White Bears." *Ranger Rick*, 24, no. 10 (October 1990): 12-15.

Miller, Claire. "China's Precious Pandas." *Ranger Rick*, 23, no. 7 (July 1989): 22-30.

"Panda Bears." *National Geographic World* (December 1986): 12.

"Panda Pumps Iron." *National Geographic World* (March 1989): 22.

Santos, Robin L. "Protecting the Pandas." *U.S. Kids* (December 1991-January 1992): 3.

Schaller, G. B. "First World." *Omni*, August 1988, 6.

Wexo, John Bonnett. "Giant Panda." *Zoo Books*, 11, no. 2 (November 1993): 1-14.

Films and Videos

Airplane Trip by Jet. Film, 16 mm, 11 min., Encyclopaedia Britannica Educational Corporation, Chicago, 1975.
　　Transcontinental jet flight shows airport personnel, ground and flight crews, a modern airport, jetliner equipment, and cabin facilities. Nonfiction.

Airplanes—How They Fly. Film, 16 mm, 10 min., Encyclopedia Britannica Educational Corporation, Chicago, 1978.
　　This film demonstrates the basic principles of aircraft flight through animation, a model airplane, and the flight taken by two children in a light plane. Nonfiction.

Airplanes Work for Us. Film, 16 mm, 11 min., Distributed by Churchill Films, New York, 1980.
　　This film depicts some of the common and uncommon uses of aircraft. It points out that in addition to carrying passengers, mail, and freight, airplanes and helicopters are used for fire-patrol rescue work, weather patrol, construction of power lines, and crop dusting. Nonfiction.

Airport in the Jet Age. Film, 16 mm, 10 min., Encyclopaedia Britannica Educational Corporation, Chicago, 1981.
　　This film explores a jet airport, showing ground crews, flight crews, traffic control, and many other services. A variety of equipment involved in preparing jet planes for flight are also discussed. Nonfiction.

The Last Emperor. NTSC VHS Videocassette, 104 min., Hemdale Film Corporation, Columbia Pictures Industries, Hollywood, 1987.
　　This commercially available video is a story of the last emperor of China. It provides a picture of the people and their country in the early 20th century. Fiction.

Pandas. Film, 16 mm, 23 min., Distributed by National Geographic Society, Educational Services, Washington, D.C., 1983.
　　Travel to China, where American and Chinese researchers work in the wild to save one of the world's most engaging and elusive animals. Learn about breeding efforts and about the panda's uncertain future. Nonfiction.

Pandas—A Gift from China. Film, 16 mm, 14 min., Distributed by Encyclopaedia Britannica Education Corporation, Chicago, 1972.

Ling-Ling and Hsing-Hsing are the two rare giant pandas presented as a gift to the United States in 1972 by the People's Republic of China. The camera records the bears in their home at the National Zoological Park in Washington, D.C. Nonfiction.

Save the Panda. Film, 16 mm, 59 min., Distributed by National Geographic Society, Educational Services, Washington, D.C., 1989.

This document is available in color video, CLV videodisc, and videos in Spanish and French. Over time, the number of pandas has dwindled due to human encroachment and climatic changes. Join the scientists as they track these rare creatures through nearly impenetrable bamboo in an effort to learn more about the panda, and ultimately increase its chances of survival. Nonfiction.

5

Other Bears

Overview of Other Bears
Around the World

There are little-known "other bears" living around the world. These bears include the sloth bear, the sun bear, the spectacled bear, the Asian black bear, and the brown bear of Japan. Students have the opportunity to see these bears only when they visit a zoo. This chapter provides facts packs that summarize biographical information about these bears that will enrich student learnings and present suggested research activities that provide life-science, social-studies, language-arts, and arts learning experiences for the student.

These relatively unknown bears live in the Southern Hemisphere, Europe, and Asia. Compared with the polar, black, and brown bears of the North American continent and the giant panda of China, limited research has been carried out on the other bears. These bears have many similar characteristics to those of the North American bears, yet they are quite different because of the effects of local climate, altitude, terrain, and so on.

The Other Bears Facts Pack are designed to provide the teacher with ideas that can stimulate the students' inquiring minds in the areas of the sciences, language arts, and art. These ideas can be developed into research activities that give the students an opportunity for investigating and comparing the various bears through divergent-thinking assignments for the student and the entire class.

While studying the life-science aspects of these bears, the students may investigate the tropical forests, major mountain ranges, habitats, food supplies, bear body characteristics, family structures, habitat environments, and the relationships between humans and the various bear species. Locating the homes of these other bears on the world map provides the students with social-studies information relating to terrains and the peoples who inhabit these other countries. Social-studies activities might also address the economic conditions, including the large populations in Japan and Europe, that are playing an important role in determining the survival of these lesser bears. Language-arts activities might include story writing, newspaper-article writing, and picture and poster construction through research related to each of the other bears.

Suggested Research Activities. The teachers may wish to develop specific activities that are 1) appropriate for the age level of their class, 2) designed to fit curriculum needs and requirements, or 3) structured to enrich a specific learning skill. The following are suggested research activities that meet these needs while fostering divergent thinking at both the student and class levels.

1. The *spectacled bear* of South America is an endangered species of the bear family because it is losing its home as civilization clears the tropical rain forests. Students may become news reporters, reporting to the class or the student body by means of a "news sheet" with the following information about the spectacled bear:

    - its location on maps

    - its type and availability of food supply

    - the source of its name

    - why it is called the "bear of the clouds"

    - its relationship with humans

    - what humans should do to the rain forests to protect this bear

2. The most unbearlike bear of all the bears is called the *sloth bear*. The sloth bear is found in India, where the climate is very warm. This bear may be of special interest to the students because it has traits that are contrary to those of all other bears. After identifying these differences during class discussions, the students could write letters from the warm-weather sloth bear to its friend the cold-weather polar bear regarding an upcoming visit to the polar bear's home. The sloth bear needs to know the following to ensure that its needs and safety are met:

    - how it gets to the polar bear's home

    - what kind of protection from the cold it will need

    - what food will be available for the sloth bear to eat

    - what kinds of enemies there are

    - what is necessary to take the bear's family on the trip

    - how humans affect the sloth bear's visit to the cold climates

3. The *sun bear* is the smallest of all the bears. This bear is found on the Malay Peninsula, which includes the areas of Sumatra, Burma, Borneo, and Thailand (countries near the equator). A classroom discussion about the unique body characteristics found only in the sun bear, the bear's habitats, and its food supplies provide information about this bear's survival capabilities. To provide learning experiences centered around the sun bear, the teacher may assign a story-writing activity based on a role-reversal approach. The students may then become sun bears for 24 hours and use their four senses to survive in the forest while recording what the sun bear might see, touch, smell, and hear.

4. A compare-the-bear activity employs a large wall chart to record information the students develop on all bears, including the bears identified in this chapter. All the bears of the world may be identified, and the students should then supply information on the following characteristics:

   - physical characteristics (weight, height, and so on)

   - type and nature of fur coat

   - food needs

   - climatic conditions of home territory

   - type of habitat

   - each bear's relationship with humans

   The result is a comprehensive look at the bears of the world, which in turn leads into a discussion of 1) the relationship of all bears with humans, and 2) why certain bears are becoming endangered species and what people can do to prevent this.

5. For older students, a research paper on one of these other bears might be created. This necessitates obtaining information from additional resources, including books from the school and community libraries. This activity introduces the students to the process of 1) gathering information, 2) organizing thoughts, and 3) writing clearly and concisely.

6. The brown bear family found in North America has relatives living in other parts of the world. An accelerated, investigative research project could be developed for the inquisitive student. The North American brown bear might be compared with the brown bears of the Kamchatka Pennisula of eastern Russia, the Asian brown bears of the northern mountains of India, and the brown bears of Japan. The information gathered could be tabulated and shared with the class as a learning experience for the student.

7. There are questions about the use and misuse of bears in captivity that many people are concerned about. These include the use of bears in circuses and the housing of bears in old, out-of-date zoos. Students might investigate the history of circuses, including the techniques the animal handlers have used to train their captive bears. Students might also review a number of zoos in North America, comparing the bad features of the old zoos with those of zoos built recently.

Other Bears Facts Pack

Spectacled Bear

What's in a Name? The scientific name for the spectacled bear is *Tremarctos ornatus*. This bear is the sole survivor of a short-faced bear family whose ancestors are traced back to the last Ice Age. The light-colored rings around the eyes make this bear look as if it is wearing eyeglasses, thus giving it its name.

Geographic Location. The spectacled bears are the only bears living on the South American continent. They live in the heart of the Andes in Venezuela, Colombia, and the coastal foothills of Ecuador, Peru, and Bolivia. Researchers who have spent years living in the spectacled bears' habitat have rarely seen them. Although spectacled bears roam on or near the rain forest floor, they prefer the ridge lines where they can avoid people. Therefore, spectacled bears travel in the high, cool, dense foliage covering the mountains in what are known as the Andean cloud forests. Spectacled bears are excellent tree climbers, which allows the bears to stay aloft in the treetops for several days eating and sleeping. The rain forests create warm, humid, and foggy clouds above the forest floor at higher elevations, thus creating the cloud forests where the spectacled bear can travel without being seen.

The Life of a Spectacled Bear. In the spectacled bear family, the adult male may accompany the mother and cubs as part of a group, but the mother and father do not travel as lifetime pairs. They only seek each other out at mating time in the spring.

A young female spectacled bear gives birth to her first set of cubs at age four. She usually gives birth to two cubs, but food supplies and inbreeding are contributing factors that determine if she has only one or as many as three cubs. The spectacled bear mothers are very protective of their cubs. If a mother bear becomes alarmed and senses danger, her young cubs may ride on her back, or she may hold an individual cub in her paw against her body and run on three legs. A frightened and alarmed spectacled bear may give an owl-like screech.

Cubs are usually born in the month of January, which is summer in South America. Each cub weighs between 8 and 11 ounces (227-311 grams) at birth. The cubs are born blind, hairless, and helpless, but in about a month the cubs are ready to travel outside the nest where they were born.

Hibernation. Spectacled bears do not hibernate as do the bears of North America. The year-round warm and humid climate in which they live is the factor that makes true hibernation unnecessary for spectacled bears. The female builds a den or nest before the cubs are born. She prepares the ground under large rocks or under the roots of trees for her nest. The South American rain forest vegetation provides a different environment from that found in the Northern Hemisphere, and the spectacled bears have successfully adapted for survival in this climate.

Size. By the time the cubs become adults, they weigh between 175 and 385 pounds (80-175 kilograms). As found with all bears, females are smaller. When standing on all four feet, the male measures 30 inches (76 centimeters) tall at his shoulders. From his nose to the tip of his tail, the male can measure as much as 7.5 feet (2.7 meters). The spectacled bears have large skulls equipped with strong teeth and powerful jaws, and they have 13 pairs of ribs—one fewer than other bears.

Feet. Their feet are designed with long claws, which allow the spectacled bears to be excellent climbers and to spend much of their time in trees moving from limb to limb for days at a time.

Skin and Fur. The spectacled bears are covered with shaggy black fur. Because the spectacled bears live in a warm climate, their fur coats are thin compared to the coats of bears that live in the Northern Hemisphere. The light-colored fur around their eyes extends from their cheeks to their chest.

The Spectacled Bear's Habitat. The spectacled bear's home range, territory, and movement are controlled by the available food supply and the presence of humans. Attempts have been made by Ecuador and Peru governments to establish national parks and sanctuaries that would allow the spectacled bears to move freely through the Andes mountain ranges. This rare and endangered bear is protected by laws, but hunting and poaching continues.

Food Supply. The spectacled bear's food supply is dictated by their being omnivores. Their heavy jaw muscles and large, flat molars help them chew very tough plants, such as palm leaves, cacti, nuts, and orchid bulbs. Fruit, honey, sugarcane, and some vegetables delight their taste buds. And cattle, llamas, ants, mice, birds, and rabbits are sometimes included in their diet.

The taste for fruit encourages the spectacled bear to climb fruit trees and spend several days eating and sleeping in the fruit trees. It is not uncommon to see the bear climbing carefully to the end of a limb to reach a bunch of fruit. The limbs that are broken off in these attempts lodge in the trees and are used to make resting spots between meals.

Spectacled Bears and Humans. People living in South America know about the spectacled bear mainly through legend. Most have never seen one. The spectacled bear held an important place in the religious beliefs of the ancient Incas. As Europeans came to South America, the spectacled bear became a sign of strength and manhood. Today, the beliefs about this bear are a combination of Indian and European thought. Indian guides, in fact, are eager to travel with researchers, because seeing a spectacled bear means the Indians are close to their gods.

As respected as the bear is, the presence of humans has reduced the spectacled bear population. Researchers estimate that only 2,000 spectacled bears exist in the wild. Three factors contribute to the reduced number of spectacled bears in the wild: 1) large companies have been cutting the rare and valuable trees found in the rain forest, 2) farmers are clearing more and more land for farming, and 3) hunting and poaching continue since bear parts bring in money for the poor mountain people. In addition, the bears' taste for crops and livestock have reduced their population because pesticides on crops can kill whole families of bears, and farmers shoot those spectacled bears that kill cattle. Experts feel that the spectacled bear will survive, and, fortunately, the bears do breed in captivity. So people will be able to continue viewing the bear with the glasses.

Sloth Bear

What's in a Name? The sloth bear has the scientific name of *Melursus ursinus*. Two hundred years ago, scientists from Europe first saw this strange-looking animal in the countries of Southeast Asia. They mistook it for another tropical American animal called the sloth. For many years, the sloth bear was known as the nameless animal. Finally, after years of study, scientists decided that the nameless animal was really a bear.

Geographic Location. The sloth bear lives in Southeast Asia in the forest areas on the island of Sri Lanka and in the countries of India and Nepal. This area is near the equator and provides a warm, humid climate and yearly monsoon rains. It is estimated that the sloth bear population worldwide is between 7,000 and 10,000.

The Life of a Sloth Bear. The family structure of the sloth bear is opposite from that of the North American bears. The adult male sloth bear is often part of the family group. He is gentle with the cubs and spends time with them while they are growing. North American bears live alone, but the sloth bears live in groups. They communicate with one another by making faces and lots of noise. Roars, howls, squeals, huffs, and gurgles can be heard when sloth bears meet.

Because the weather in Southeast Asia is very warm, the sloth bears are able to breed at varying times of the year. In India, the mating season is in the spring; however, on the island of Sri Lanka off the tip of India, the mating season can be year-round. Most sloth bear cubs are born in December or January in nests the mother bear has built in a cave or under large rocks. Two or three cubs are born completely helpless and blind. After three weeks, they are able to see. Within a month, the cubs travel with their mother through the forest. They no longer use their birthing nest.

The sloth bear carries her cubs on her back. They hold on to their mother's shaggy fur as they ride through the forest. If the cubs become frightened, they bury their faces in their mother's fur. Sloth bear cubs have a special place to sit while riding on their mother's back, and they always ride in the same spot. The cubs continue to ride on their mother's back until they are a third of her size. The cubs stay with their mother for two or three years.

Hibernation. The sloth bear lives in the topical forests of Southeast Asia where it is warm and humid throughout the year. The temperature ranges from 80° to 85° F (26.6°-29.4° C). Twice a year, this area of the world has heavy rains known as the monsoons. The rains and winds cause damage to the sloth bear's habitats. The sloth bear does not hibernate, but during the monsoon season it becomes lazy and inactive and goes into caves during this rainy period.

Size. The adult male sloth bear weighs about 300 pounds (136 kilograms). Females are smaller. The sloth bear stands 3 feet (1 meter) high at the shoulders and grows to be about 6 feet (1.8 meters) long.

Feet. The sloth bears have long claws for digging in the sun-baked soil. These claws are white, blunt, and curved measuring up to 3 inches (7.6 centimeters) long. The bottom, or pad, of the foot is bald, and the pad tips are connected by hairless webs.

Skin and Fur. The sloth bear has long, shaggy, messy, black fur that always looks like it needs brushing. On the chest of the bear, there is a large white or yellow Y-shaped patch of hair. Because of the extra hair on its neck and back, the sloth bear looks like it is wearing a mane. This bear has longer and shaggier hair than most other bears. Yet the bear has very little hair on its belly or on the insides of its legs. When not eating, the sloth bear is often found sleeping in the hot sun. Its fur permits cooling of the skin, so the heat does not bother the bear. While resting, the sloth bear often sucks its paws, making buzzing and humming sounds.

Speed. The sloth bears are usually slow when walking, but they can run faster than a human when they are frightened.

The Sloth Bear's Habitat. The sloth lives in the tropical forests of Southeast Asia. It is very warm in these forests, and the heavy rains of the monsoons keep the forests humid and moist. The tropical forests provide delicious food for the sloth bear to eat. With its very long and narrow muzzle and a large set of lips, the sloth bear can suck its favorite food—termites—from their homes. Inside the sloth bear's mouth, the front teeth are missing. With its long muzzle and its large lips, the missing teeth form a perfect "vacuum cleaner" for the sloth bear. When the sloth bear breaks open a termite nest, dust flies, loud blowing noises are heard, and the ends of the bear's nose close so that dust does not enter. When termites are not available, the sloth bear eats other insects.

The sloth bears share the tropical forests with many other animals, birds, and reptiles. Some of these include Bengal tigers, elephants, buffalo, wild boars, leopards, and giant lizards. More than 400 species of birds, including the macaws and the cockatoos, exist with the sloth bear, as do snakes such as the python, the cobra, and the viper.

Sloth bears are excellent tree climbers. They have been known to steal eggs from a bird's nest and to climb trees for fruit and honey. As do most bears, the sloth bear loves honey. They will use their tree-climbing ability to raid bees' nests to get at the honey inside—and the bees will not stop a sloth bear until it has eaten all the honey! Other foods that the sloth bear enjoys eating are sugarcane, corn, and yams. Sloth bears have even been known to damage fields of sugarcane and yams.

Male sloth bears travel throughout their habitat marking their territory by scraping their claws across the base of the trees. They also rub their bodies across the marks they have made to leave their scents. Because the sloth bears are usually nocturnal, they sleep during the day and travel and feed at night.

Sloth Bears and Humans. At one time, the sloth bear was considered a big-game animal and was hunted like the Bengal tiger, the elephant, and the wild boar. Laws have been enacted that protect the sloth bear from big-game hunters, but these laws do not protect them from the farmers and villagers of their environment. Usually the sloth bears are not bothered by the farmers unless the bears raid the farmers' fields.

The countries of India and Sri Lanka are very crowded with people who are looking for new land to build homes and raise crops for food. Consequently, these people are moving into the forests, clearing the lands of trees, and forcing the sloth bears to move to find new habitats. The cutting of timber in the sloth bears' habitat does great damage to the bears' home. When the trees that provide shelter and a food supply for the sloth bear are cut, the bears must find other sources of food and cover elsewhere.

The sloth bear is going to have a struggle to survive. Of the three tropical bears, however, the sloth bear has the best chance of survival. There are more sloth bears than there are sun bears or spectacled bears. Unlike the sun bear, the sloth bear does not attack humans and is usually left alone. Unfortunately, all three tropical bears live in countries where people are struggling to make a living, and saving wildlife is not considered important.

Sun Bear

What's in a Name? The scientific name for the sun bear is *Helarctos malayanus*. The sun bear is also known as the Malay or honey bear. The word *Malay* comes from the section of the world where this bear is found, and the use of the word *honey* comes from the yellowish patch of sun-shaped fur found on the sun bear's chest.

Geographic Location. The sun bear lives in the forests of the Malay Peninsula, Java, Sumatra, Borneo, Thailand, and Burma. These countries are on or above the equator in Southeast Asia. The sun bear makes its home in the hot and humid rain forests, where it rains more than 100 inches (254 centimeters) each year. The temperatures are warm all year-round, with the average ranging between 78° and 82° F (25.3°-27.8° C).

The Life of a Sun Bear. In the sun bear family, the sun bear father remains as part of the family group. The male sun bears are often seen with the female sun bears and the cubs while looking for food. The females have their first cubs at age three. Sun bears are able to breed anytime during the year. After about 100 days, two cubs are born. The cubs are very small at birth, weighing about 7 ounces (198 grams). They are born blind and hairless, and their skin is so thin that it is nearly transparent. They are unable to walk for the first two weeks.

The mother sun bear nurses the cubs on her milk for most of their first year of life. In order for the cubs to urinate and defecate, the mother sun bear must constantly lick them. The cubs' digestive systems are not fully mature until they begin to work on their own, which usually occurs by the time the cubs are three months old. Sun bear cubs raised in captivity without a mother must be sponged with water several times a day. If they do not receive this stimulation, the cubs will not survive.

As the young sun bears grow, they can be very noisy and playful. They make humming sounds with their paws in their mouths. Researchers compare this behavior with thumb sucking in human youngsters. When sun bear cubs are about four months old, they travel with their mother while searching for food. Although adult sun bears spend a lot of time in trees eating and resting, the cubs are born and raised on the ground under branches and heavy ground cover.

Hibernation. The sun bear does not hibernate. The climate in their environment is warm year-round, so there is no need to rest while cold or rainy weather passes. Mother sun bears make nests under branches and heavy ground cover, and then use them only until the cubs are old enough to travel while looking for food.

Size. The adult sun bear weighs between 65 and 140 pounds (27-64 kilograms). This bear is small and only grows to about 4½ feet (137 centimeters) in length. In the wild, it rarely weighs more than 100 pounds (45.4 kilograms). Those sun bears living in zoos weigh more because of the proper diets they are fed there.

Eyes and Ears. The sun bear has small, beadlike eyes and small, rounded ears.

Feet. The sun bear's feet have no hair on their soles, and the gray-colored claws are long and sicklelike in shape. When the sun bear is walking, its legs have a bowlegged look.

Skin and Fur. The body of the sun bear is covered with short, thick, black hair. Its coat is very heavy, even though it lives in a hot and humid climate. The sun bear's fur does not allow water, dirt, or mud to sink into the bear's skin, so its fur coat always looks clean and shiny.

Speed. The sun bear moves with lightning-fast speed across the floor of the jungle as it searches for food to eat. And the bear eats on the run after finding food.

The Sun Bear's Habitat. Most research carried out on the sun bear takes place in the zoos around the world. Sun bears are seldom seen in the wild. As a result, the only way that scientists can tell anything about the sun bear's territory is to rely on claw marks found on trees. These marks tell them that the sun bear lives in the area under study.

Much of the sun bear's life is spent in a tree. Not only do trees supply food, but they also offer a resting place. It is not uncommon to see a sun bear in a zoo sunning itself on a hot and humid afternoon. The sun bear is an excellent climber and moves up and down trees quite easily. The broken branches from the trees are used to make large nests near the trunk of the tree.

The sun bear's neighbors include elephants, tigers, wild pigs, rhinoceroses, tapir, crocodiles, and lizards. In the bear's neighborhood, there are more than 8,000 flowering plants and trees.

Food Supply. The sun bears eat many different types of food. These bears are called omnivores, because they eat both plants and animals. Honey, the bear's favorite food, is at the top of their food list. The sun bear's extra long, narrow tongue allows them to eat honey, comb, and bees—all at the same time! Small rodents and birds, lizards, insects, termites, and grubs—wormlike larva—are also part of the sun bear's menu. The sun bear is nocturnal, so few people have seen them eating. Although the sun bear spends hours looking for food, it is difficult to find in the sun bear's habitat because food and dead animals rot quickly in the humid environments of the tropical forest.

Sun bears can get into a lot of trouble eating coconut palm hearts. The heart of the palm is a large bud found at the top of the coconut palm tree. Once this part of the tree is removed, the tree usually dies. One sun bear, by slowly working night after night, can seriously damage an entire crop of coconut palms. The wise farmer soon catches on to what is happening to his trees and will shoot the bear.

Sun Bears and Humans. In developing countries there is little money for the research and conservation of animals. Money that is spent in these countries to help preserve the native animals usually comes from international conservation organizations. These groups of concerned people from around the world give time and money for the research of well-known, endangered animals such as the giant panda, the tiger, and the elephant. These efforts indirectly help the sun bear by preserving areas where it can live and obtain food.

Sun bears are found in many zoos around the world. They do not live well in enclosed places and will suck their feet and make loud whining noises while in their cages. Many times they become violent and damage their zoo habitats by tearing down walls and ruining their surroundings with their powerful forepaws.

The Future for Sun Bears. What will happen to the sun bears in the future? Scientists have placed them on the endangered-species list. Their habitats are growing smaller each year because of the logging industry—some of the world's finest furniture is made from the wood found in the tropical forests of the sun bear's habitat. When the trees are cut, the climate changes. It becomes drier, and forest fires become common.

There is still a spark of hope, though. Sun bears have been found in areas where it was thought they had become extinct. For example, researchers in India have reported seeing the sun bear for the first time in years. Because it is difficult to observe and count sun bears in the wild, letters have been sent to different governments asking about the sun bears in their part of Southeast Asia.

Laws have been written to protect the sun bear, but they are difficult to enforce and poaching is still a problem for the sun bears. Because sun bear cubs are in demand as pets, poachers take great chances to capture them, and, unfortunately, the mother bear is often killed during the capture of the cubs. The problem is that many people who live in the sun bears' home areas are poor and starving, and conserving endangered species means nothing to them. It will be difficult for the sun bears to survive.

From *Investigating Science Through Bears,* ©1994. Teacher Ideas Press, P.O. Box 6633, Englewood, CO 80155-6633.

Asian Black Bear

What's in a Name? The scientific name for the Asian black bear is *Selenarctos thibetanus*. This bear has several names, depending on where it is found. The scientific name means the moon bear of Tibet. The Asian black bear is also called the Tibetan black bear, the Himalayan black bear, and the Japanese black bear because it is found in these areas. The bear's large, white, crescent-shaped mark on its chest lends the moon bear its name.

Geographic Location. The Asian black bear is found in forested and mountainous areas in Iran, Afghanistan, Pakistan, Bangladesh, Laos, China, Taiwan, India, and the Japanese islands of Honshu, Kyushu, and Shikoku. The climates and seasons found in these countries and areas are similar to those found in North America. And the wintry, snowy conditions they encounter are the same as those encountered by the black bear of North America.

The Life of an Asian Black Bear. The Asian black bear, or moon bear, family structure is similar to that of the North American black bear. Researchers have gathered much information about the Asian black bear. Although most of it is from bears in zoos or in captivity, field research has taken place in Japan.

When they are three years old, the females begin to breed between the months of March and December. After seven or eight months, two or three tiny cubs are born weighing about 8 ounces (223 grams) each. The cubs' eyes open in about one week after birth, and in a month or two they are ready to follow their mother as she searches for food. The cubs live with their mother for two or three years. Researchers have seen the Asian black bear mother with two sets of cubs at one time. In captivity, these bears have been known to live as long as 33 years. The Asian black bear father is not a part of the family group, which is the same as in the North American black bear family.

Hibernation. If the Asian black bear is living in countries where the temperatures are warmer and a good food supply is available, it may sleep for only a short period of time in hibernation. In fact, some of the bears living in the warmer areas stay active all winter. The pregnant female, however, almost always makes a den in hollow logs or hollowed trees for her sleep period. The Japanese researchers have recorded that the Asian black bear in Japan hiberantes in the deep snow, making a den that has more than 3 feet (1 meter) of insulating snow to cover it. The altitude of the bear's habitat is a factor in den building. In the areas of lower altitude and warmer temperatures, the bear uses hollow logs and trees. In the higher, colder altitudes, the Asian black bear builds its dens in the snow.

Size. The moon bear is a medium-size bear, similar in size to the North American black bear. The average weight of the moon bear is between 200 and 255 pounds (90-115 kilograms). Its body length is between 55 and 65 inches (140-165 centimeters). A large male Asian black bear might weigh more than 400 pounds (180 kilograms) and measure 77 inches (195 centimeters) in length. The females are smaller.

Skin and Fur. The moon bear's body is covered with jet-black fur. Its muzzle is tan or brown, and its chin is whitish in color. The hair on the bear's neck and shoulders is thick and long with a manelike look. The moon bears living in the southeastern part of India have shorter and thinner coats. Those living at the higher altitudes in the northern regions have more underhair, or a thicker fur coat.

Feet. The claws of the moon bear are strong and allow it to peel bark from trees for eating. These powerful claws are useful for climbing trees in the bear's search for food. The Asian black bear makes a bear nest in cherry, beech, oak, and dogwood trees. The bear sits on branches at a fork of a tree and bends branches backward to reach the tree's fruit. In wet and cold weather, the moon bear uses its powerful claws to build so-called basking couches of twigs and branches so that it can sleep in the tree. Sleeping in the trees saves the bear's body heat by getting it off the cold ground. Some bear nests have been found as high as 65 feet (20 meters) off the ground. An Asian black bear's nest is constructed similarly to a bird's nest, but is much, much larger.

The Asian Black Bear's Habitat. The Asian black bear usually sleeps in caves or hollow trees during the day, then it comes out at dusk to look for food. Although some of the bears are nocturnal, others are active all day.

Food Supply. The Asian black bears in India and Tibet are carnivorous, and they kill sheep, goats, cattle, and large adult buffalo. They also eat termites, beetles, larvae, honey, fruits, nuts, and berries. In Japan, the bear eats plant foods all year. They eat beechnuts, oaknuts, wild cherries, dogwood, ants, and acorns. The Japanese black bear gnaws on tree bark to get to the sapwood of the cedar and the Japanese cypress trees. Unfortunately, this can kill the trees. It is reported that bears can debark up to 40 trees in one night.

Asian Black Bears and Humans. The Asian black bears are always in trouble with humans. They raid and kill farm animals and eat grain. These moon bears have bad tempers and will even attack people. Each year, many people in Asia are mauled and killed by this bear. In Japan each year, two or three people are killed, and another 10 to 20 are injured. When people are in the forests to collect wild bamboo shoots, they are in the moon bear's habitat. And the bears do not tolerate people.

Because the moon bear is feared, hunting seasons for the bear have been established in many countries. The governments encourage killing and trapping of the bears. At the present rate of hunting, the moon bear will only survive for another 10 to 20 years in Japan.

In Chinese regions of the Himalayan Mountains, the Chinese believe that the moon bear's meat, bile, and bones have medicinal powers. So many bears are killed to supply these items.

In India a different threat exists for the moon bear. The hunters kill the mother moon bear and capture the cubs. Then they muzzle the cubs and train them to ride bicycles and to dance for street performances and circuses.

The Future for the Asian Black Bear. There are no serious conservation efforts currently being enforced to save the Asian black bear. But if no future conservation plans are considered, the only moon bears that will exist will be those found in zoos.

Teacher Educational Resources

Books

Bailey, Bernadine. *Wonders of the World of Bears*. New York: Dodd, Mead, 1975.

"Bears." *Compton's Encyclopedia*. 1989 ed. Vol. 3, 116-118.

"Bears." *Grizmek's Encyclopedia of Mammals*, 1990 ed. Vol. 3, 477-507.

"Bears." *The New Encyclopaedia Britannica*. 1991 ed. Vol. 2, 11.

Domico, Terry. *Bears of the World*. New York: Facts on File, 1988.

MacDonald, David. *The Encyclopedia of Mammals*. New York: Facts on File, 1984.

Shepard, Paul, and Barry Sanders. *The Sacred Paw*. New York: Viking Penguin, 1985.

Walker, Ernest P. *Mammals of the World*. Baltimore, Md.: Johns Hopkins University Press, 1975.

Annotated Bibliography for Other Bears and the Study of Life Science

Children's Books

Bailey, Bernadine. *Wonders of the World of Bears*. New York: Dodd, Mead, 1975.
    This book summarizes and describes the characteristics and habits of various species of bears. Nonfiction.

Charman, Andrew. Illustrated by Chris Forsey. *The Book of Bears*. New York: Gallery Books, 1989.
    The contents of this book include all true bears, endangered bears, and the barely bears. Each bear is discussed, and the book is very readable for elementary students. Nonfiction.

Cook, Susannah. *A Closer Look at Bears and Pandas*. New York: Franklin Watts, 1977.
    Environments, life cycles, food, and habits of a variety of bears and pandas are discussed. Nonfiction.

Penny, Malcom. *Wildlife at Risk: Bears*. New York: Bookwright Press, 1991.
    A simple introduction to bears, how they live, why they are becoming endangered, and what is being done to reverse this trend. Nonfiction.

Whitehead, Robert. *The First Book of Bears*. New York: Franklin Watts, 1966.
    The history and habits of bears in general and of the grizzly, black, brown, Kodiak, polar, sloth, sun, and spectacled bears in particular. Nonfiction.

6

Bears in Literature

Many wonderful children's books have been written about bears. Authors have stretched the imaginations of the young reader by creating make-believe adventures that center around a warm, loving character—the bear. But as the reader matures, the bears they read about and come to know take on a different persona. Bears possess the characteristics of wild, fearsome real animals.

The books listed below give the reader a large variety of fictional situations in which the bear plays the central character. Many of these books are beautifully illustrated and have been written especially for the younger reader. However, it must be remembered that older students also enjoy picture books. Most people have never outgrown their love of being read to. It must be interesting for an older reader to hear again a picture book that the person first heard as a beginning student. Several years of schooling, as well as life experiences, may alter the person's understanding of the plot and characters in the reread book.

As you read through the annotated bibliographies, you will notice that many of the books mentioned have recent publication dates. During the past few years, there have been a number of outstanding bear books published. Mixed with old favorites, this list introduces some interesting new bear characters.

Bear Anthologies

If you are looking for a wide variety of bear material, these two books furnish a cross section of bear literature. Both supply material for the young and older students. In easy to read formats, these books could be easily adapted for classroom literature study.

Bond, Michael, *Book of Bears*. New York: Viking Penguin, 1971.
　　Michael Bond, author of *The Adventures of Paddington*, has collected bear literature from around the world. Folktales, fables, and mythology are included.

Osborne, Mary Pope. Illustrated by Karen Lee Schmidt. *Bears, Bears, Bears*. Englewood Cliffs, N.J.:
   Silver Press, 1990.
   Songs, poems, and stories are found in this bear treasury. Authors such as Maurice Sendak,
Arnold Lobel, and A. A. Milne have added their works to this beautifully illustrated collection.

Bear Poetry Collections

There are many splendid poems about bears. Many of these verses are found in anthologies of
children's poetry. Listed below are a few of the authors' favorite collections. For the true lover of
bears, these volumes are a must for your library.

Goldstein, Bobbye S. *Bear in Mind: A Book of Bear Poems*. Illustrated by William Pene Du Bois.
   New York: Viking Kestrel, Viking Penguin, 1989.
   The author has selected a variety of well-known bear poems for this collection. Real bears as
well as teddy bears are celebrated. Some of the poems featured are "The Adventures of Isabel" by
Ogden Nash, "Advice for Hikers" by Isabel Joshlin Glaser, "Grizzly Bear" by Mary Austin, and
"Polar Bear" by William Jay Smith. Each poem is uniquely illustrated.

Prelutsky, Jack. *The Random House Book of Poetry for Children: A Treasury of 572 Poems for
   Today's Child*. Illustrated by Arnold Lobel. New York: Random House, 1983.
   This is a wonderful book for any serious lover of children's poetry. Although the subject area
of the poems included in this volume is extensive, some of the more well-known poems can be found
here. Jane Yolen's "Grandpa Bear's Lullaby," Gail Kredenser's "Polar Bear," and Rose Burgunder's
"Joyful" are a part of this collection.

Prelutsky, Jack. *Read-Aloud Rhymes For the Very Young*. Illustrated by Marc Brown. New York:
   Alfred A. Knopf, 1986.
   Everyone is always looking for a poetry book with wonderful poems and come-alive illustrations. For the person who wants to introduce a young child to the wonderful world of poetry, this is
the book. Two hundred poems were especially chosen for the young reader. Jack Prelutsky has
included "My Teddy Bear" by Marchette Chute and "My Teddy Bear" by Margaret Hillert. Beautifully illustrated.

Bear Picture Books

Many of the books on this list are known as picture books. Children of all ages will enjoy looking at the beautiful illustrations as well as listening to them. Some of these books are appropriate for beginning readers. Students in the third, fourth, and fifth grades will be able to read them independently.

Alexander, Martha. *And My Mean Old Mother Will Be Sorry, Blackboard Bear*. New York: Dial, 1972.
Anthony, a young boy, has great difficulty with his mother. He runs away with his imaginary friend, Blackboard Bear. This is one of a series of four books.

Ambrus, Victor. *Never Laugh at Bears: A Transylvanian Folk Tale*. New York: Bedrick-Black, 1992.
A delightful tale of intrigue taking place in the Transylvanian countryside. Based on an ancient folktale.

Bond, Michael. *A Bear Called Paddington*. Illustrated by Peggy Fortnum. Boston: Houghton Mifflin, 1960.
A modern classic. Paddington, a bear from Peru, warms the hearts of young readers the world over as he bravely participates in wild adventures. This book is the first in a series of 10 stories.

Brett, Jan. *Berlioz the Bear*. New York: G. P. Putnam's Sons, 1991.
Berlioz and his fellow magicians are pleasantly surprised as they get ready to play for the town ball. Beautiful pictures accompany this interesting story.

Brett, Jan. *Goldilocks and the Three Bears*. New York: Sandcastle Books, 1987.
This is the traditional story of Goldilocks and the three bears. Lost in the woods, a tired and hungry girl finds the three bears' house, helps herself to food, and goes to sleep.

Carlstrom, Nancy White. *Better Not Get Wet, Jesse Bear*. Illustrated by Bruce Degan. New York: Macmillan, 1988.
One of several books about the antics of Jesse Bear. This book is written in rhyme.

Cazet, Denys. *A Fish in His Pocket*. New York: Orchard Books, 1987.
Russell, a young bear, worries about the fish in his pocket.

Clise, Michele Durkson. *My Circle of Bears*. San Diego, Calif.: Green Tiger Press, 1981.
Antique bears are beautifully photographed in vintage clothing. Each bear's life history is given. Older children would enjoy this book. The author's latest book is *No Bad Bears*.

de Beer, Hans. *Ahoy There Little Polar Bear*. New York: North-South Books, 1988.
Lars, the little polar bear, continues his adventures as he is scooped up into a fishnet and lands on a ship. This book comes in miniature size. *Little Polar Bear* is also by de Beer.

Degan, Bruce. *Jamberry*. New York: Harper & Row, 1988.
A story of a boy and a bear written in rhyme. Colorful illustrations. A good book for rhyming activities.

de Regniers, Beatrice Schenk. *How Joe the Bear and Sam the Mouse Got Together*. Illustrated by Bernice Myers. New York: Lothrop, Lee, & Shepard, 1965.

A bear and a mouse become good friends in spite of different ideas. This is a classic story of an enduring friendship.

Elish, Dan. *Jason and the Baseball Bear*. New York: Bantam-Skylark, 1990.

Whitney, the polar bear from the local zoo, gives Jason pointers on how to be a good baseball player.

Freeman, Don. *Corduroy*. New York: Viking Penguin, 1969.

Corduroy, a department-store teddy bear, looks for someone to buy him. *A Pocket for Corduroy* is the sequel.

Gammell, Stephen. *Wake Up, Bear—It's Christmas!* New York: Viking Penguin, 1981.

A hibernating bear wakes up on Christmas and has a surprise visitor.

Gauch, Patricia Lee. *Christina, Katerina, and the Great Bear Train*. Illustrated by Elise Primavera. New York: Putnam, 1990.

An ideal book for children with new babies in their family. Christina is unhappy about her new sister, so she takes her bears for a journey.

Gretz, Susanna, and Alison Sage. *Teddy Bears Cure a Cold*. New York: Macmillan, 1984.

William the teddy bear comes down with a cold. His friends take care of him, but he chases them away because he is ill.

Hall, Derek. *Polar Bear Leaps*. Illustrated by John Butler. New York: Sierra Club/Alfred A. Knopf, 1985.

Baby Polar Bear goes fishing with his mother and learns that a leap to safety can save his life.

Heine, Helme. *Prince Bear*. New York: McElderry Books, 1989.

This German tale, translated into English, recounts how in yesteryear any bear in the forest could change into a prince and any princess could change into a bear. The story holds interesting consequences.

Hoff, Syd. *Grizzwold*. New York: Harper & Row, 1963.

This easy-to-read story has become a classic. Grizzwold, a huge bear, decides his forest home is too small. He sets out to find a more suitable home but returns to the place he loves best.

Houston, James. *Long Claws, an Arctic Adventure*. New York: Puffin Books, 1981.

Followed by a huge polar bear, an Eskimo brother and sister make a dangerous trip across the frozen tundra to take a caribou back to their hungry family.

Kantrowitz, Mildred. *Willy Bear*. Illustrated by Nancy Winslow Parker. New York: Parents' Magazine Press, 1976.

The night before school begins a small boy talks to his teddy bear, Willy, about his uneasiness in going to school for the first time.

Kennedy, Jimmy. *The Teddy Bears' Picnic.*
Illustrated by Alexandra Day. La Jolla,
Calif.: Green Tiger Press, 1983.
The traditional song, "The Teddy Bears
Picnic," is beautifully illustrated and writ-
ten as a story. A record is included.

Kesey, Ken. *Little Tricker the Squirrel
Meets Big Double the Bear.* Illustrated
by Barry Moser. New York: Viking
Penguin, 1990.
Little Tricker watches as Big Double
terrorizes the forest animals one by one.
Little Tricker gets revenge.

Kimmel, Eric. *Bearhead.* Illustrated by
Charles Mikolaycak. New York: Holiday House, 1991.

An adaption of a Russian folktale. Bearhead is put through a series of tests by an evil witch,
Madame Hexaba. His honesty and cleverness get him through.

Kimmel, Eric. *The Chanukkah Guest.* Illustrated by Giora Carmi. New York: Holiday House, 1990.
On the first night of Chanukkah, Old Bear wanders into Bubba Brayna's house and receives a
delicious helping of potato latkes when she mistakes him for the rabbi.

McCloskey, Robert. *Blueberries for Sal.* New York. Viking Penguin, 1948.
This classic children's tale tells of the parallel adventures of a young girl and a bear cub as they
hunt for blueberries with their mothers.

McCully, Emily Arnold. *The Evil Spell.* New York: Harper & Row, 1990.
Edwin, the youngest member of an acting troupe, gets his chance to have a starring role. Opening
night gives him a bad case of stage fright. Family support pulls him through.

McCully, Emily Arnold. *Zaza's Opening Night.* New York: Harper & Row, 1989.
Zaza leaves her family and the theater to audition for a television series. She finds out that
television is not her cup of tea.

McPhail, David. *The Bear's Toothache.* Boston: Little, Brown, 1972.
A bear with a terrible toothache visits a little boy as he seeks relief from this pain.

Minarik, Else Holmelund. *Little Bear.* Illustrated by Maurice Sendak. New York: Harper & Row,
1957.
A classic for children who are beginning to read. Little Bear is the first in a series of bear
adventures. The characters are small forest animals that appeal to preschoolers as well as first- and
second-graders.

Morgan, Michaela. *Edward Loses His Teddy Bear.* Illustrated by Sue Porter. New York: E. P. Dutton,
1988.
The beautifully illustrated book tells the story of a little boy's search for a lost teddy bear.

Murdocca, Sal. *Christmas Bear*. New York: Simon & Schuster, 1987.
   Bear comes to rescue Santa when his sleigh upsets on Christmas Eve.

Murphy, Jill. *Peace at Last*. New York: Dial Books for Young Readers, 1980.
   This miniature book tells young readers of Mr. Bear's night in which he tries to find peace and quiet so that he can go to sleep.

Patz, Nancy. *Sarah Bear and Sweet Sidney*. New York: Macmillan, 1989.
   A story of bear love between elderly bears, Sweet Sidney and Sarah Bear.

Peet, Bill. *Big Bad Bruce*. Boston: Houghton Mifflin, 1977.
   This is one of students' favorite bear stories. Bruce, the bully bear, never picks on anyone his own size. One day he is reduced in more ways than one by a tiny but mighty witch.

Ratnett, Michael. *Jenny's Bear*. Illustrated by June Goulding. New York: G. P. Putnam's Sons, 1992.
   A beautifully illustrated book that tells of Jenny and her great love for teddy bears. Although she has collected hundreds of bears, she wants a real one.

Rosen, Michael. *We're Going on a Bear Hunt*. Illustrated by Helen Oxenbury. New York: McElderry Books, 1989.
   Brave bear hunters go through grass, a river, mud, and other troubles before they have an encounter with a bear.

Ross, Katherine. *Bear Island*. Illustrated by Lisa McCue. New York: Random House, 1987.
   Two animal friends set off in a boat for adventure on the high seas. After becoming shipwrecked they find an island of their own.

Ryder, Joann. *White Bear, Ice Bear*. Illustrated by Michael Rothman. New York: Morrow Junior Books, 1989.
   A polar bear tells of his daily routine—wandering and feeding on the Arctic ice floes.

Schoenherr, John. *Bear*. New York: Philomel Books, 1991.
   A young bear realizes that his mother is no longer there to take care of him. This is the story of his adventures on his own. Beautiful illustrations.

Simon, Carly. *Amy, the Dancing Bear*. Illustrated by Margot Datz. New York: Doubleday, 1989.
   Amy dances the night away, making excuses for why she can't go to bed.

Sivulich, Sandra Stoner. *I'm Going on a Bear Hunt*. Illustrated by Glen Rounds. New York: E. P. Dutton, 1973.
   The popular preschool chant and fingerplay is taken from this adventure.

Sungard, Arnold. *The Bear Who Loved Puccini*. Illustrated by Dominic Catalane. New York: Philomel Books, 1992.
   Barefoot, a young bruin, living in the deep forests of Minnesota, falls in love with opera and goes to the city to become a star.

Thayer, Ernest Lawrence. *Casey at the Bat*. Illustrated by Wallace Tripp. New York: Platt and Munk, 1989.

The book is based on Ernest Lawrence Thayer's poem "Casey at the Bat." Casey is portrayed as a bear, and the whimsical illustrations make this a delightful book to read.

Tolhurst, Marilyn. *Somebody and the Three Blairs*. Illustrated by Simone Abel. New York: Orchard Books, 1990.

The author wrote this book for her son, because he was upset at the way Goldilocks treated the baby bear. This is a reversal of the Goldilocks story.

Waber, Bernard. *Ira Sleeps Over*. Boston: Houghton Mifflin, 1972.

Ira is going on his first sleep over, and the important question is, Should he take his teddy bear?

Wadell, Martin. *Can't You Sleep, Little Bear?* Illustrated by Barbara Firth. Cambridge, Mass.: Candlewick Press, 1988.

Little Bear spends the night telling his father he can't sleep. Nothing helps until his father takes him outside, and he sees the moon and stars light up the sky.

Ward, Lynd. *The Biggest Bear*. Boston: Houghton Mifflin, 1952.

A classic children's story about a boy named Johnny and the bear cub he adopts. It emphasizes why it is difficult to try to tame something that is wild.

Wells, Rosemary. *Peabody*. New York: Dial Press, 1983.

Annie has a teddy bear named Peabody. Everything goes well until Annie gets a new exciting toy.

Wells, Rosemary. *The Story of Smokey the Bear*. New York: Little Golden Books, 1954.

The true story of Smokey the Bear.

Chapter Books

By the time students have reached the third grade, most are ready to read chapter books. The character of the bear in chapter books is often quite different from the bear in picture books. In picture books, the bear is usually portrayed as a lovable teddy bear. As a character in the chapter book, the bear is usually a real animal. The teddy bear as a dominant character in more sophisticated literature is seldom seen.

Listed on the following pages are stories in which bears play an important role. In most cases, the bear is characterized as an animal living in the woods. Of course, Winnie-the-Pooh and Baloo from *Jungle Book* are exceptions.

Curwood, James Oliver. *The Bear.* New York: Newmarket Press, 1916.
     This children's classic tells the story of an orphaned bear and a huge grizzly as they form a bond and flee the guns and dogs of two hunters.

Dalglesch, Alice. *The Bears of Hemlock Mountain.* Illustrated by Helen Sewell. New York: Aladdin Books, 1952.
     This small tall tale tells of Jonathan's adventures with the bears on the mountains near his home.

Kipling, Rudyard. *The Jungle Book.* New York: Viking Penguin, 1896.
     A wonderful read-aloud favorite, with Baloo the bear as one of the main characters. Older children enjoy reading this book to themselves.

McCafferty, Jim. *Holt and the Teddy Bear.* Illustrated by Florence S. Davis. Gretna, La.: Pelican, 1991.
     Based on the true story of the origin of the teddy bear, *Holt and the Teddy Bear* is a mixture of fact and fiction. The story tells of Holt Collier's pleas for Teddy Roosevelt to spare the life of a bear—which led to the creation of the teddy bear.

Milne, A. A. *Winnie-the-Pooh.* Illustrated by Ernest H. Shepard. New York: E. P. Dutton, 1926.
     Often considered a read-aloud book for younger children, *Winnie-the-Pooh* is a wonderful chapter book for the middle-grade reader. The adventures of this lovable bear and his forest friends have entertained readers for generations.

Morey, Walt. *Gentle Ben.* New York: E. P. Dutton, 1976.
     Science and environmental topics are found throughout this adventure story. The author introduces a young boy who adopts a huge brown bear. This exciting tale tells of the problems of adopting wild animals and of uncaring adults.

Stearns, Pamela. *Into the Painted Bear Lair.* Illustrated by Ann Strugnell. Boston: Houghton Mifflin, 1976.
     This beautifully written story tells of a plot that deals with life choices such as friendship and honesty. A young boy deals with a female knight and a ferocious bear.

Tripp, Jenny. *The Man Who Was Left for Dead.* Illustrated by Charles Shaw. Milwaukee, Wis.: Raintree, 1980.
     The true story of a man's survival after being attacked by a grizzly bear and left to die by his companion.

7

Bear Parties in the Classroom

Teddy bear events are highlights of every child's life. The age of the participant may vary from 1 to 100, but the excitement and love for the teddy bear is always present. This chapter presents a variety of activities that allow the classroom teacher to use this universal love for the teddy bear in the study of a variety of learning areas.

To provide learning opportunities, the classroom teacher may schedule a Gala Affair involving the students at different times of the year. The teacher may incorporate real bear information along with a related science activity. Preparation could include discussions of real bears and a science activity, depending on the theme that the teacher wants to emphasize.

This chapter provides a variety of suggested activities that allow the classroom teacher to explore real bear information in conjunction with the fantasy and psychological impact of the teddy bear. The four bear parties can be used at any time throughout the school year. The parties create unique atmospheres in the classroom that give the students memorable experiences.

Gala Affair No. 1: "The Teddy Bears' Winter Holiday"

The winter holiday season is a great time for the bears and teddy bears in the classroom. Children and teddy bears are inseparable when one speaks of holiday activities. As the classroom takes on the holiday atmosphere, teddy bear and real bear activities help complete the winter holiday spirit. Activities and crowd pleasers are listed that create an exciting learning environment for the classroom.

The Teddy Bear Winter Holiday Tree

The North American-style Teddy Bear Winter Holiday Tree can be the highlight for December. Any size pine tree—real or artificial—may be used. A large branch may also be used in place of trees. The colonial tradition was to use a large branch that was decorated. Holidays in the Southern Hemisphere's warm weather might find teddy bears hanging on palm trees or flowering bushes. Students in the classroom throughout the world may enjoy creating a teddy bear tree as a theme for a winter holiday and to display their teddy bears. Ask students to bring in their favorite teddy bear. Small bears are easier to hang on the tree. Of course, the teddy bears must have name tags with both the student's name and the teddy bear's name. Students should place their bears on the tree. All other decorations must be bear related. After the tree is completed, take a group picture of the students around their Teddy Bear Winter Holiday Tree to record this memorable experience.

The Teddy Bear Cookie House

This activity is centered around the making of a cookie house by the students. It requires planning to assemble the needed supplies. Necessary supplies include:

- ½-pint (227 gram) milk cartons

- firm, 9-inch (28-centimeter) paper plates

- 4-x-6-inch (10-x-15.2-centimeter) pieces of cotton batting, poly batting used in quilts, felt, or heavy fiber interfacing

- small bottles of white glue

- plastic picnic knives

- waxed paper

- 2 boxes of teddy-bear-shaped cookies

- 2 boxes of regular graham-cracker squares

- assorted candies

- large plastic bags with ties

- 2 16-ounce (454-gram) cans of prepared white frosting (Note: This frosting amount is enough for a class of 22.)

Ask the students to save their juice or milk cartons from their cafeteria lunches. When the students bring their ½-pint (227 gram) milk cartons to the classroom, rinse them out with water and let them dry. Later, restaple the cartons shut. When you have all the supplies assembled, you are ready to begin the project. Use the following directions for the Teddy Bear Cookie House:

- Have the students wash their hands and be seated quietly.

- Give each student a 9-x-24-inch (22.8-x-61-centimeter) piece of waxed paper. They may create their cookie house on this.

- Pass out a paper plate and a carton to each student. Set these on the waxed paper.

- Glue the carton to the middle of the paper plate with white glue, and give it a few minutes to dry. Meanwhile, continue passing out the other food items.

- Give each student four squares of graham crackers. These are glued to the sides of the carton. (White glue is firmer than frosting for holding the crackers to the carton.)

- Next, the felt or batting is glued to the top of the carton to form the roof of the house.

- Pass out the assorted candies and teddy-bear-shaped cookies, placing them on the waxed paper.

- Give each student a large tablespoon of frosting on the waxed paper. The plastic knives are used to put frosting on the cookies and candies so that they may be glued on the house for decorations.

- Students then complete the Teddy Bear Cookie House. If any candies and frosting are left, the students enjoy eating them. (Sometimes the houses are sparsely decorated because the leftovers are eaten first.)

- Let the houses dry for a couple of hours. Meanwhile, clean up the work areas or desks.

- After the houses are dry, the teachers or helpers should carefully slide the plate with the house into the large plastic bags, and tie the bag with the air puffed inside.

- Remember: The decorations on the house are edible, but the grahams *on the house* are not.

- A vegetable teddy bear house can be created with soda crackers or other shaped crackers. Decorate the teddy bear house with whole or cut vegetables. Cream cheese can be the frosting base for holding crackers and vegetables in place.

The Christmas Tree Teddy Bear Cake

Cake is a versatile food that can be created for all holidays. Any flavor of cake can be baked in this activity, because it is the shape that becomes the teddy bear cake. Using bear-shaped cooking pans is the easiest method. Canned frosting works well. Decorate the teddy bear cake with colored sugars. Be creative. Students may help decorate the cake; or the teacher may go solo—decorating while the students anxiously wait and watch the creation taking place! Eating the cake at the end of the day while reading teddy bear stories makes the winter holiday more meaningful. There are many traditional symbols that may represent the holidays in December and January. The teddy bear may reflect a country's national and ethnic traditions that add to the meaning for the younger students. Decorated cakes may be created to represent national or ethnic symbols as the winter holidays are celebrated.

Bear Bonus Recipe—Holiday Nog

The foods described in this activity are all items that can be purchased at the local supermarket. Teachers are creative, so finding supplies may be as easy as asking a parent.

- 10 cups (2.38 liters) milk

- 2 packages (4-serving size) instant vanilla pudding mix

- ½ teaspoon (2.4 cubic centimeters) peppermint extract

- In a blender combine half the milk, the pudding mix, and peppermint extract. Cover and blend until smooth. Pour into a large pitcher. Stir in the remaining milk. Cover and chill. Double the recipe; however, the blender will hold only one recipe portion at a time.

- Crush eight sticks of striped peppermint candy sticks or candy canes.

- When ready to serve, stir the chilled mix and pour into glasses. Sprinkle the crushed candy onto the drink. Serve with peppermint sticks or candy canes as stirrers. Makes 20 4-ounce (118-cubic-centimeter) servings.

Real Bear Stories

While involved with the winter holiday activities, Old Man Winter, Santa Claus, or his counterpart—depending on where one lives on this Earth—may be discussed. This is a great time to discuss the Arctic regions and their inhabitants. Polar bears make a good topic for science and social-studies discussions.

"Winter Holiday Bear Gala"
Science Activity

An applicable science activity related to the winter holiday bear party and the polar bear is the discussion of weather and the seasons throughout the world. Such a discussion of the weather around the world during the winter holiday season is a global experience. The seasons of the year can be discussed, highlighted by the fact that the people of the Southern Hemisphere have their summer weather during winter holiday time in the United States and Canada. Traditionally, people in North America think of snow, wind, and ice at the winter holiday time because they live in the Northern Hemisphere. With help from the students, the teddy bear will investigate the role of the meteorologist as different winter seasons throughout the world are studied.

Background Information

The Earth tilts on its axis as it orbits the sun. This movement controls the different seasons that occur in the Northern and Southern hemispheres. Because the different seasons occur on a regular schedule of spring, summer, fall, and winter as the Earth rotates, the holiday season of North America and Europe occurs in the winter season. Students living in these regions are aware of only the cooler

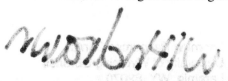

or cold months when the winter holidays take place. Discussing the different seasons naturally includes the discussion of weather. The students can become meteorologists and can analyze and predict the weather during the winter holidays.

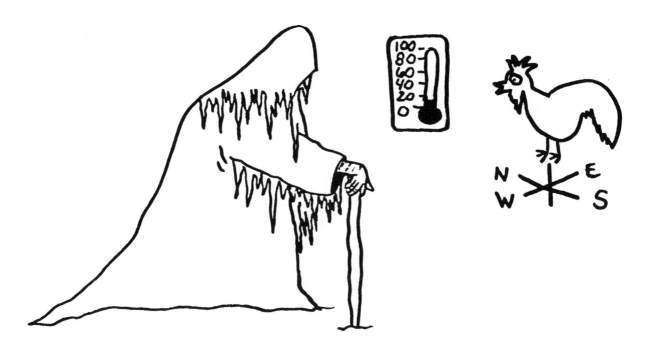

Materials
- world globes
- Celsius and Fahrenheit thermometers
- flashlights

Preparation
1. Use as many globes as possible for display so that the maximum number of students can simulate the sun with flashlights as the Earth moves around the globe.

2. Display large world maps to chart weather and climates at different cities on Earth for the holiday eve of Santa's travels.

3. Make available Fahrenheit and Celsius thermometers for practice in temperature reading in both scales.

4. Collect and save newspaper weather information pages for classroom discussion.

5. Collect weather-related charts and maps that can be found in the science texts and resource materials in the classroom.

6. Collect books from the school library that are related to seasonal changes and weather.

7. Assign each student a city on the world map. Ask each student to report on the city's weather and temperature for one week.

Procedure

1. About 10 days before the winter holiday vacation, begin studying the Earth as it moves around the sun and how it effects the weather.

2. The world map will be displayed. Students will select one of the cities plotted on the map to follow weather conditions for one week.

3. This science activity is designed to be a fun project as the students practice being meteorologists.

Bear Extensions

1. Discuss how different countries of the world celebrate the winter holiday season.

2. Discuss special transportation and equipment that might be used in a rainstorm in Perth, Australia, a sandstorm in the Sahara of northern Africa, or a snowstorm in Churchill, Manitoba, during the winter holiday.

3. Discuss how weather is different for the winter holiday season in many U.S. cities such as Key West, Florida; Seattle, Washington; Anchorage, Alaska; Los Angeles, California; Bangor, Maine; and Nashville, Tennessee. In Canada, this list of cities may include Edmonton, Alberta; Saskatoon, Saskatchewan; and Montreal, Quebec. Other cities around the world may include London, England; Rome, Italy; Stockholm, Sweden; New Delhi, India; and Lima, Peru.

4. Discuss how the winter holidays are celebrated in locations where there is no snow.

Vocabulary Words

- meteorologist
- weather
- seasons
- Celsius thermometer
- Fahrenheit thermometer
- Northern Hemisphere
- Southern Hemisphere
- temperature

Associated Bibliography

Following are books that help to put together a truly memorable winter holiday with a teddy bear set of activities:

- Catherall, Ed. *Exploring Weather*. Austin, Tex.: Wayland Publishers, 1991.

- Pattigrew, Mark. *Weather*. New York: Gloucester Press, 1989.

- *Ranger Rick's Nature Scope—Wild About Weather*. Washington, D.C., National Wildlife Federation, 1986.

Gala Affair No. 2: Baby Bear

Baby bear is devoted to the study of cubs in the wilderness and to the baby bears of children's literature. The discussion of baby bears should include information about the new cub and its first few months of life. The information about the new cubs of each kind of bear can be found in the preceding chapters. Bears in children's literature can be traced back many generations. Exploring the baby bears in the literature should enrich the students' learning. Bears in literature can be found in more detail in the Literature chapter.

Reading to the students will also enrich what they can learn about bears in literature. Students may explore the stories in the library, and then complete book reports. Becoming familiar with children's literature provides a lifetime experience for students. The activities as stated in the following paragraphs should give students a unique experience in the study of children's literature as it relates to the behaviors of real mother bears and their cubs.

Re-Creating Cub Story Favorites

This activity begins with the selection of the students' favorite bear cub stories in literature. Possible selections can be found in the Literature chapter. After reading about real or imaginary bear cubs, the students should illustrate their favorite part of the story and write a paragraph describing their picture. An alternative to drawing is the fabrication of a shoe-box model that re-creates the student's favorite scene in the story. A group activity may be developed from reading a fictional story about bears, dividing the story into parts. Each student group can then complete a series of models illustrating the story. After each group has finished its models, the students should display the pictorial story. An additional learning experience is possible by having the students present each of their model series in chronological order as a play to other classes.

The Teddy Bear Tea

Following is a suggested method for incorporating a "tea" into classroom activities. After a week of teddy bear activities the students will be excited that Friday has finally arrived. This can be the scheduled day for their Teddy Bear Tea. Ask students to bring all their bears to the classroom, which will make the celebration all the more exciting. Children who do not own a bear may bring a different stuffed animal, or see the teacher about Rent-a-Bear. The teacher may provide teddy bears for the children to rent for a day, for the price of a small classroom chore. Sometimes when the bears are well behaved, the teacher's bears may spend the weekend with their young renters. As the classroom begins to fill up with a variety of new and old bears, each child may pick one bear to tell about in front of the class. Children with many bears may find this is a difficult task. Once the bears are chosen, the students should take turns telling about their favorite furry creature. A blue ribbon is presented to each bear stating why it is unique and one

of a kind. After a morning of bear literature, poetry, and song, the students and their bears might choose to have a picnic lunch. Location depends on the weather.

After lunch, everyone should help to get ready for the Teddy Bear Tea. Children should bring their bears and teacups in for the occasion. Helpers should set up the tea table with a tablecloth, a flower arrangement, a tea service, milk pitcher, silverware, and all the necessities for a tea party. Children may bring cookies, tea sandwiches, and nuts from home. A helper can prepare the tea and assist with refills. Before the tea begins, a quick refresher course in manners should be given. Each child may go through the line asking the server for tea, sugar, or cream. The children and bears must use good manners, or they will not be served. After the children have gone through the line, they should return to the tea table for cookies, sandwiches, and gingerbread. Watching the children feed their bears certainly takes you back to your childhood!

"Beary" Good Food

The theme of the party is an English tea party. Consider serving foods at the tea that are of English origin. Gingerbread, for example, came to America from England with the early settlers. The English cooks say that gingerbread dates back to the very early history of England. There are many recipes for gingerbread. Choose your favorite.

Real Bear Stories

Studying bear cubs gives the students an opportunity to compare the size and the helplessness of newborn cubs with the cubs' size and development at the end of their first year. Information regarding each bear cub can be found in the preceding chapters. Charts, graphs, and pictures can be made into a bulletin board to provide a visual and pictorial story presentation for study.

Cub Behavior
Science Activity

Behavior concepts that are associated with mammals can be the basis for a science activity related to the study of bear cubs. Bear mothers, for example, have involuntary kinds of behavior controlled by instinct. Primary among these are the behaviors related to the feeding and protection of her cubs. The behavior of wild animals (such as mother bears with their cubs) is unchanged when in a zoo environment. However, there are some behaviors that can be altered in a zoo because of the environment's control by humans. Understanding the meaning of animal behavior—both instinctive and reflexive—helps the student to understand bear mothers and their relationships with their cubs.

Background Information

The bonding or imprinting of bear mothers and their cubs is very strong. Cubs are born weighing less than a pound, hairless, and with unopened eyes, so bear mothers are very protective. They stay in their dens until the cubs are large enough to be covered with fur and have developed vision.

Animals have many of the same reflexes as humans, including unconditioned reflexes that occur with no specific learning or experiences. Bears react to loud noises, surprises, or to animals entering their territories. Instinctive behaviors are actions that do not require learning experiences. Bear mothers instinctively care for and protect their cubs. They seek their own territory when looking for a den, even though they may wander several hundred miles before hibernating. Learned behaviors are actions that result from experience or practice. Cubs in captivity, for instance, can be trained, although they still have the instincts of the bear born in the wild.

Materials
- chalkboard
- pictures of bear mothers and their cubs
- construction paper

Preparation
- Collect pictures of bear mothers with their cubs.

- Have available the preceding chapters that discuss bear mothers and their cubs.

- If the science text of the class has a chapter discussing animal behaviors, utilize this good resource of information.

- Review and have available resource materials from the school library.

- Have construction paper available for the students to draw a picture of the bear mother and her cubs. Illustrations should demonstrate reflex, instinct, or learned behavior.

Procedure
- Begin by discussing the bear cubs and their mothers in the children's literature books. Select several of the students' favorite literature books, and discuss the relationships of cubs to their bear mothers. Brainstorm with the class about the behaviors that were instinctive and those that were learned. Make two lists on the chalkboard.

- Select one or several of the real bears discussed in previous chapters. Read and discuss the information related to the bear mother and her cubs in the wild. The relationships of mother bears to their cubs are generally the same for all breeds, but the panda bear and the sloth bear are unique in their handling of their cubs.

- List on the chalkboard the instinctive and learned behaviors of the real mother bears and their cubs in the wild. Discuss and compare the two lists, and then compare the real bears' behaviors with that of bears in the literature.

- After finishing a general discussion of reflexes, instincts, and learned behaviors, students should draw two pictures on construction paper that illustrate a reflexive or instinctive behavior and a learned behavior.

- Fold the construction sheet into two parts. Each half should have an illustration on behavior. Students should then write a sentence describing the pictures and labeling it an instinct or a learned behavior.

- Examples of each type of behavior are listed below. Brainstorm with the students and add to the list.

Instinct:
1. feeding milk to cub
2. helping newborn cub to stay warm
3. guarding new cubs when outdoors
4. catching fish for food
5. hunting food

Reflex:
1. cubs sent up trees at loud noises
2. cubs run if danger occurs
3. cubs smell food if it is present

Learned:
1. bears perform in circuses
2. bears respond to sounds of food being served in zoos at feeding time
3. bears eat from garbage dumps
4. bears steal food from campers

Bear Extensions

1. Visit a zoo where there are bear cubs and their mothers, and observe the behaviors of the animals.

2. Invite zoo personnel to visit the classroom to discuss bear mothers' relationships with their cubs.

3. Visit a circus that has performing bears, and then discuss techniques used for training bears. Explore the history of training performing bears, and discuss how early practices have been outlawed by world governments.

Vocabulary Words
- behavior
- instinct
- learned behavior
- social behavior
- reflex
- imprinting
- hibernation

Associated Bibliography

The following books lend a hand with the study of bear cubs:

- Ahlstrom, Mark E. *The Black Bear*. Riverside, N.J.: Crestwood House, 1985.

- Bendick, Jeanne. *How Animals Behave*. New York: Parents' Magazine Press, 1976.

- Brenner, Barbara, and Garelick Brenner. *Two Orphan Cubs*. New York: Walker, 1989.

- Brett, Jan. *Goldilocks and the Three Bears*. New York: G. P. Putnam's Sons, 1990.

- Buxton, Jane Heath. *Baby Bears and How They Grow*. Washington, D.C.: National Geographic Society, 1986.

- de Beer, Hans. *Ahoy There, Little Polar Bear*. New York: North-South Books, 1988.

- Irvine, Georgeanne. Photographs by Ron Garrison. *Zoo Babies: Nanuck the Polar Bear*. Chicago: Children's Press, 1982.

- Janice. *Little Bear's New Year's Party*. Illustrated by Mariana. New York: Lothrop, Lee, & Shepard, 1973.

- Johnston, Ginny, and Judy Cutchins. *Andy Bear*. Photographs by Constance Noble. New York: Scholastic, 1985.

- Matthews, Downs. *Polar Bear Cubs*. Photographs by Dan Guravich. New York: Simon & Schuster, 1989.

- Rockwell, Anne F. *The Three Bears*. New York: Thomas Y. Crowell, 1975.

- Tinbergen, Niko. *Animal Behavior*. New York: Time-Life Books, 1968.

- Ward, Andrew. *Baby Bear and the Long Sleep*. Illustrated by John Walsh. Boston: Little, Brown, 1980.

Gala Affair No. 3:
T.E.A. Month
(Trees, Earth, and Animals)

March and April have become months with important issues that need to be addressed in the classroom. These can include Arbor Day, Earth Day, the rain forest, and the endangered-animal issues.

These events are consistent with the preservation of the planet Earth. The giant panda bear is an example of an endangered animal that can be discussed in the classroom. Although each issue of T.E.A. can be discussed at great length, these issues need to be introduced with limited activities at the primary level or with extended activities for upper-class levels. Included at the end of this section are addresses of environmental and wildlife organizations that will provide additional information for students' research. Awareness of these issues is the first step in building toward more comprehensive studies at upper levels. The science activities that can be created to address the many issues involved in saving the Earth are endless. Only one of the many issues, groundwater, will be developed for a science activity in this section.

Earth Day Discussion

Begin this period with Earth Day as the main topic of discussion. This will help the students become aware that they are protectors of the environment of the planet Earth. General discussions can be held on natural resources, air, animals, forests, drinking water, and oceans. Understanding key words will generate the focus on the big picture—that of saving the planet Earth. As the discussions broaden, the Earth Day and Arbor Day events can coincide with the calendar dates for their observation. To support these two events, discussions are necessary on the history of both the Earth environmental movement and the history of Arbor Day.

Arbor Day Story

After the concept of the Earth's environment has been discussed, introduce the Arbor Day story. Arbor Day can be celebrated by the class planting a tree. This demonstrates to the students that they can personally do something that will help protect the Earth and provide clean air. To celebrate the Arbor Day event, four possible projects can be explored:

- Join the national Arbor Day organization by writing to The National Arbor Day Foundation, 100 Arbor Avenue, Nebraska City, NE 68410. They will provide tree seedlings for planting to membership cardholders.

- Include the student body by collecting an assigned amount of money—25 cents, for example—from each student for a whole-school project titled Planting a Tree. After the money is collected, contact a salesperson at a local nursery to supply a tree of significant size (to be planted by the professionals) that would be planted on the school property. Then the student body may participate in a tree-planting ceremony to celebrate Arbor Day.

- Another celebration activity for Arbor Day can involve the purchase of tree seedlings from a local wholesale tree farm (possibly they would consider giving reduced rates to the school) that can be given to the students on Arbor Day. Often, your school P.T.A. or P.T.O. groups will pay for the seedlings.

- The most attractive approach to the Arbor Day celebration is to have a local nursery donate the tree seedlings as a civic action for the benefit of the community. You can then make a celebration of Arbor Day by giving each student a tree seedling to be taken home and planted. The seedlings can be accompanied by handouts that discuss Arbor Day and cleaner air. Learning sheet 1 of this activity can be used by the student to make a record of the tree's progress during the various seasons.

What Are the Rain Forests?

An introduction to the rain-forest issue may be discussed at this point. This fits into the total picture of saving the natural resources, which in turn helps save the environment for people and the animals. The rain forests of the world are classified as Neotropical, Northwest Coast, African, and Southeast Asian. A list of environmental and wildlife organizations that offer detailed information on the rain forests of the world is provided at the end of this activity.

The Endangered Animals

The endangered-animal list is increasing each year. A discussion of animals that are classified as endangered needs to take place and should emphasize the concepts of how and why an animal can become endangered. At this point, the subject of the giant panda bear and its problems of survival may be addressed. See the Giant Panda Bear chapter for information and facts about the panda bear.

Creating a T.E.A. Bulletin Board

After addressing the issues of T.E.A. (Trees, Earth, and Animals), combine all the topics and make a large bulletin board that involves all the topics discussed in this section. The bulletin board can be a class project. *Save the Earth* is one title that can be used, although students may create their own. Make a list of trees and animals that are on the endangered-species list. Then

- let each student choose a tree or animal that is endangered;
- select a book from the library that tells and shows a story and a picture of the tree or animal;
- draw a large picture of the tree or animal on butcher paper or on a paper grocery bag that has been cut open;
- color or paint the items drawn;
- place the colored items on the bulletin board, and add a background of trees, land, water, flowers, plants, and sky to create a completed project;
- write a paragraph about their selection, and report to the class about it.

Bear Bonus Recipe—Garbage-Can Cookies

If leftovers keep accumulating in your refrigerators and cupboards, you may be tempted to throw them away—and so you add good food to the refuse in the town landfill. But with a little imagination, you can create delicious and nutritious cookies. The teacher can make the cookies with the help of the students. The easier solution is to have a parent of a student make the cookies. Here's how:

In a large mixing bowl combine:
    2 to 3 cups (470-695 cubic centimeters) flour
    1 cup (235 cubic centimeters) sugar or honey (to taste)
    1 cup (235 cubic centimeters) rolled oats
    ½ cup (117 cubic centimeters) granola (any kind)

Mix in:
    1 stick (117 cubic centimeters) butter or margarine
    2 eggs
    1 teaspoon (4.8 cubic centimeters) lemon peel
    ½ cup (117 cubic centimeters) orange juice
    1 to 2 tablespoons (14.6-29.2 cubic centimeters) peanut butter

Blend with:

    1 package of M&Ms or other small candies
    ½ cup (117 cubic centimeters) raisins, currants, or other dried fruit
    ½ cup (117 cubic centimeters) chopped walnuts

Drop tablespoons of cookie mixture on a greased cookie sheet, 2 inches (5 centimeters) apart, and bake at 350° F for 8 to 10 minutes. This recipe yields 24 cookies for everyone to enjoy.

Giant Panda Bear Day

As a concluding activity, the class can have a Giant Panda Bear Day. Students can bring their giant panda bear items to school for this event. There are many clothing items—sweaters, T-shirts, and sweatshirts—that can be worn. The students can also bring their giant panda teddy bears to share the school day with the students. The Garbage-Can Cookies above can be served along with a drink such as hot chocolate made with bottled water on this day to remind everyone of the T.E.A. events and activities.

Real Bear Stories

The giant panda bear should be the topic of discussion for the T.E.A. month of activity. The giant panda is on the endangered-species list, so studying this bear is important at this time. The facts and information about the bear can be found in the Giant Panda Bear chapter. The classroom discussion should include the People's Republic of China, so that the students understand that concern should be directed at endangered animals and plants from countries all over the planet Earth.

Water Testing Science Activity

Saving the Earth has become a major topic for science classes at all levels. The need to study pollution, for example, becomes greater each year. The pollution issues are endless, but one topic that affects every student is that of having clean drinking water. Exploring the water people use is a major undertaking. However, the teacher can assist the students in this small but dramatic activity in which direct, visual, and easily demonstrated profound results can be obtained. Demonstrate clean water being converted into polluted water so that students can observe the problems that are involved and what some of the solutions might be.

Background Information

Polluted water is found all around us in our lakes, streams, rivers, seas, and oceans. At the local level, students can see the streams and rivers as they become more and more polluted. The groundwater concept, however, is a bit more difficult to understand. The rain that falls from the sky does not run off until the ground is saturated with water. When that point is reached, the rain runs off as groundwater. It is important to discuss how groundwater becomes polluted by people dumping contaminants into the streams and lakes and the adjacent land areas. In addition, rainwater takes pollutants into the soil as it soaks into the ground. Humans, plants, and animals need clean water in the lakes and streams and nonpolluted soils to survive. Fish from polluted waters and plants grown in polluted soils are not healthy and are not safe to eat. It is important for students to learn the source of their community's water. And it is equally important for the students to learn how the water company treats the water so that students understand how safe drinking water is provided.

Materials
- large jar or pan
- throwaway junk from students
- seeds
- school drinking water
- construction paper

Preparation
- Ask local water company officials for handouts, films, or videos discussing clean water.

- Ask local or state environmental agencies for publications, handouts, and information on clean water and pollution control.

- Make available a large jar, pan, or bucket for creating a source of polluted water.

- Provide grain seeds that can be put in the polluted water to demonstrate food growth in polluted water.

- Contact local water company officials, and invite one of their representatives to present a program in the classroom.

- Use the students' science text as a resource.

- Review the school library for additional resources.

Procedure
- Display a jar of clean water from the school water fountain. Discuss the following:
  1. Where did the water come from?
  2. How was the water made safe for drinking?
  3. Are there still microorganisms in the water?
  4. Why could the water have been unsafe to use before the water company treated it?

- Continue the discussion by listing ways to clean up the water that will be used by the local water company.

- Display a chart of the water cycle that takes place on Earth. Discuss rainfall and how the rainwater soaks into the ground and then runs into the streams and rivers. Discuss how junk, garbage, chemicals, and so on pollute both the surface water and the underground water.

- Invite a local water company representative to speak, discussing how water is made safe for us to drink.

- Making polluted water in the classroom demonstrates how quickly dirty or contaminated water can be created.

- Without telling the students what is taking place, pass the large jar around to each student and ask each to throw something small into the jar—something that they would normally put into the wastebasket at the end of the day. Though teachers will get many questions about what they are doing, the teachers should not give any clues.

- Take the jar of garbage and junk, and fill it with water. Display the jar so that the students can observe it. Ask the students to identify what they are looking at. The answer is *polluted water*. Ask the students if they would wish to drink the water.

- Leave the jar of polluted water in a prominent location in the classroom. Check the contents of the jar at one day, one week, one month, and longer—if the smell doesn't get in the way.

- After this unsightly polluted water has set for a while, sprinkle some seeds (corn, beans, and so on) on top of the thickened mass. The seeds will germinate, sprout, and begin to grow. This is a dramatic completion to the activity but is also an easy demonstration that relates to everyday living. The display shows how important it is to have clean, safe drinking water and clean groundwater for growing food.

- The students should create a poster expressing how they define a water-pollution problem and how they would go about correcting the problem. One-half of the construction paper should be devoted to drawing a water-pollution problem. The other half of the construction paper should demonstrate how the water-pollution problem might be solved. Students should write a sentence explaining the problem and a sentence telling how the problem might be solved. Display the students' posters.

Vocabulary Words
- groundwater
- pollution
- purified water
- contamination
- water company
- pollutants

Associated Bibliography

The following books and articles provide additional information about T.E.A. activities:

- Cole, Joanna. *The Magic School Bus at the Waterworks*. Illustrated by Bruce Degen. New York: Scholastic, 1990.

- "Earth Day Special. All About Earth Day." *Ranger Rick*, April 1990.

- The Earth Works Group. *Fifty Simple Things Kids Can Do to Save the Earth*. Illustrated by Michele Montez. New York: Scholastic, 1990.

- Kostalos, Mary S., and Annette Alberth. *Weaving the Web—Networking for Environmental Education*. Pittsburgh, Pa.: Rachel Carson Institution, 1990.

- Livingston, Myra Cohn. *Earth Songs*. Illustrated by Leonard Everett Fisher. New York: Scholastic, 1986.

- *Ranger Rick's Nature Scope—Pollution: Problems and Solutions*. Washington, D.C.: National Wildlife Federation, 1990.

- Roettger, Doris. *Pollution, Recycling, Trash, and Litter*. Carthage, Ill.: Fearon Teacher Aids, 1991.

Environmental and Wildlife Organizations

- International Union for the Conservation
  of Nature and Natural Resources
  Avenue Mont Blanc
  1196 Gland, Switzerland

- National Audubon Society
  645 Pennsylvania Avenue SE
  Washington, DC 20003

- National Geographic Society
  P.O. Box 2895
  Washington, DC 20013

- National Wildlife Federation
  1400 16th Street NW
  Washington, DC 20036-2266

- Sierra Club
  730 Polk Street
  San Francisco, CA 94109

- World Resources Institute
  1709 New York Avenue
  Washington, DC 20006

- World Wildlife Fund &
  The Conservation Foundation
  1250 24th Street NW
  Washington, DC 20037

Learning Sheet No. 1
The Arbor Tree Story

Student's Name:_____

Kind of Tree:_____

Name of Tree:_____

Date Planted:_____

1. Picture of Tree When Planted:

2. Picture of Tree One Year Later:

Gala Affair No. 4:
Teddy Bear Picnic

May is devoted to finishing the activities of both the teddy bears and the real bears. The last week of school is an ideal time to spend the entire week with the bears. During the week the following items may comprise the concluding parts of the real bear and teddy bear activities. Literature, poems, and music are explored from chapters 6 and 7. The music department might be asked to help teach and sing bear songs with your class. Language-arts skills are included as the students write an illustrated bear story—either fact or fiction. Students and the teacher should read bear stories orally for the pleasure of hearing the stories. Students may also view films and videos of real bears and teddy bears.

An excellent resource book for addressing language-arts skills is:

- Costigan, Shirleyann. *The Giant Bears Skills Book for Language Arts*. Belmont, Calif.: Pitman Learning, 1985.

Math and science skills are brought together in the following two books:

- Costigan, Shirleyann. "Gummy Bears." *Primarily Bears Book 1*. Fresno, Calif.: Aims Education Foundation, 1987.

- Costigan, Shirleyann. *Teddy Bear Math*. Fresno, Calif.: Aims Education Foundation, 1989.

The social-studies review concludes the study of the real bears by stating where all the bears live throughout the world.

After bear week has been introduced as an official activity in your classroom, it may become an annual event. New students each year will look forward to the annual bear week.

Bear week is introduced by sending a letter home to parents giving them the details of the coming events at least two weeks in advance. (See A Sample Letter to the Parents, p. 119, as a reference.) The activities should include all subject areas with a touch of bears. One real bear activity can involve the construction of a habitat for the bear of the students' choice. The teddy bear activities can continue with events that emphasize health and safety, such as a visit from the local ambulance service. The paramedics might present a safety program with their teddy bear.

During bear week, a collage poster may be made in addition to the other art projects completed in art class. The art department might cooperate in making bear art projects with your students. At the end of the week, the students may decorate a bear cookie to be eaten at the Teddy Bear Picnic. The Teddy Bear Picnic should be a time to celebrate all the summer birthdays of the students. Bear Awards are presented at the picnic for the many activities that occur during the week.

Making a Habitat

The major real bear activity will be the making of a habitat for the bear of the students' choice from the earlier studies. The habitat is to be made from items found in the yard or from recyclables around the house or garage. Teachers will find that the creativity exhibited by the students in developing the habitats is excellent. All habitats should be displayed during bear week, and awards may be given. A list of ideas for various award categories is included in this section.

Creating a Poster

Making a teddy bear and real bear collage poster is a fun way to decorate the classroom. Each student is given a 9-x-12-inch (23-x-30-cubic-centimeter) or 12-x-24-inch (30-x-60-cubic-centimeter) piece of construction paper. The directions for the poster are:

- Fit and glue as many teddy bears and real bears as possible on the construction paper.

- Work must be neat.

- Count the number of bears used by the students.

The students with the most bears on their poster should win a Bear Award. First-, second-, and third-place awards should be given.

Special Teddy Bears Welcome

Students may bring as many teddy bears to school as their parents will permit. A bear may sit with the student all week. Each bear is labeled with a bear tag providing the student's name and the bear's name. Judging the teddy bears' size, color, dress, unusual clothes, and so on turns out to be the most exciting part of bear week! All students receive a Bear Award for at least two of their teddy bears. Check the handout Bear Awards, p.192, for a listing of ideas for awards.

Bear Cookie Decoration

Principles of design and color are developed in this activity. While creating this remarkable piece of artwork, the students may lick their fingers as much as they want! The 8-inch (20.32 centimeters) cookie suggested for this activity is prebaked by the teacher or a parent prior to the classroom activity. Canned vanilla frosting for the cookies works well and can be tinted to give a variety of colors to make decorating more interesting to the students. Decorating the bear cookie involves all the students. By having an impartial person such as the art teacher, school secretary, or principal do the judging, the excitement can be heightened! The students are very creative, and they can add available candies for accents. Such candies include cinnamon candies, string red licorice, raisins, and so on. The cookies are decorated the day before the Teddy Bear Picnic. Awards for the first-, second-, and third-place winners are given for the most creative and interestingly decorated bear cookie. However, judges may find it difficult to narrow the awards down to only three winners, so they may have to create special awards to fit the special cookie bears. See the handout Bear Awards for examples of special categories that have been found to be effective when there are more than three winners.

Celebrating Birthdays

Summer birthdays are celebrated at the Teddy Bear Picnic. During the school year, as students celebrate their birthdays, the authors give each student a stuffed birthday teddy bear. Each student with a summer birthday should be given their stuffed, birthday teddy bear at the picnic while being serenaded with the happy birthday song. This provides all the students in the class with their birthday teddy bear and a memorable experience.

Professionally Made Bears

As a special treat, invite a local designer (if available) who makes teddy bears for sale. This person can explain the art of teddy bear making, can relate about teddy bear collecting, and can tell about special teddy bears of the past and present.

The Picnic

Picnic times are usually planned for about 2:00 P.M. on the last day of the week. The following foods have been found over the past 10 years to be the students' favorites. Use your imagination!:

- peanut-butter-and-jelly sandwiches cut in bear shapes with a small cookie cutter
- Jell-O cut in bear shapes with a small cookie cutter
- a birthday cake made in the shape of a bear
- gummy-bear candy
- "beary punch" Kool-Aid

All awards and birthday bears are given to the students in a ceremony before eating the food. All food is served on bear-decorated paper products if available. Eating time is great fun! Playing the "Teddy Bear Picnic" song by Jimmy Kennedy adds to the mood of the event. Following the Teddy Bear Picnic, all teddy bears go home after a week of fun activities. The success of the picnic—come rain or shine—can be guaranteed through the help of parents. If it rains, push the tables or desks aside in the classroom, put the blankets down on the floor, and have a great picnic! But having the picnic outdoors—with lots of games added—is the ideal situation. But scheduling the picnic for the month of May enhances your chances of having good weather and a great picnic.

"Beary" Good Food—Sugar Cookies

The ingredients needed for the sugar cookies are found in the kitchen. These cookies should be made by an adult before the cookie-decorating activity is scheduled. Any roll-out sugar-cookie recipe can be used for any event that suggests the use for cutout cookies.

Real Bear Stories

Because the school year has been spent studying many bears, during the month of May there is the opportunity to review the habitats of each bear studied. If habitat construction is to be selected, give the students an opportunity to choose the bear whose habitat they will create. They should use items that are found around the house, garage, or yard. A display of the finished habitats may be made for other classes to see. The following books are helpful in discussing approaches to a bear picnic and party:

- Asch, Frank. *Happy Birthday, Moon*. Englewood Cliffs, N.J.: Prentice-Hall, 1982.
- Berenstain, Stan. *The Bears' Picnic*. New York: Random House, 1966.
- Bowden, Joan. *Bear's Surprise Party*. Illustrated by Jerry Scott. New York: Golden Press, 1975.
- Fischer-Nagel, Heiderose. *Life of the Honeybee*. New York: Carolrhoda, 1986.
- Hunt, Bernice Kohn. *The Busy Honeybee*. Illustrated by Mel Furukawa. New York: Four Winds Press, 1972.
- Lecht, Jane. *Honeybees*. Washington, D.C.: National Geographic Society, 1973.

Honeybee Science Activity

The bear's favorite food is honey. Bears will go after honey in hollow trees or in beekeepers' hives at every opportunity. Some bears eat the hive, bees, and honey, never caring that they are being stung on the nose while they are eating. Becoming familiar with the honeybees and their process of making honey gives the students a life-science experience. The discussion of honey production by honeybees—all leading to the honey-tasting event—exposes the students to a product produced in nature.

Background Information

Bears are enemies of the honeybees. They destroy the hives in their search for honey. The bees, however, have a social order that permits them to exist and produce honey in spite of the bears. This social order needs to be explored. Bees are insects that live in every part of the world except the North and South poles. There are 10,000 kinds of bees, but only honeybees make honey and wax that people can use. Bees are the only insects that make a food that human beings can eat. The wax is used for candles and lipstick. The honey is used for cooking and as a sweet spread on bread.

Materials
- bread or graham crackers
- honey in a wax cone
- pure honey
- napkins

Preparation
- Display pictures of real bears and honeybees.

- Select books from the school library for reading and discussion of honeybees.

- Prior to the honeybee study, order bear-shaped bread from a local bakery or from a teacher or room helper. This bread, needed for the tasting party after the honeybee study, can be created from frozen dough in the kitchen.

- Invite a local beekeeper to class to discuss the care of hives and honeybees.

- For tasting, have pure honey and the wax cone honey available.

- Display products that come from beeswax, and foods that are made with honey.

Procedure
- Discuss the life of the honeybee, how honey is made, and the relationship between the bees and the bears in nature.

- Discuss the job of being a beekeeper, and how beekeepers attend their hives. The presence of a real beekeeper with protective clothing enhances the classroom discussion.

- Have a display of products made from beeswax and foods made with honey.

- Assign the students the task of making a list of foods in their cupboards and refrigerators at home that are made with honey or have honey in them. Have them obtain this information by reading the labels on the containers.

- Review the bears' love for honey.

- After the discussion of bears and their love for honey, the students should be given the opportunity to taste honey on bread.

- Students may be given a piece of bread with a small serving of honey on it.

- This tasting of honey becomes a finger-licking experience, so don't forget the required napkins. Usually, a drink and a bathroom break are necessary as the class becomes sticky.

- To enhance the honey-tasting experience, the teacher may choose to read a story about Winnie-the-Pooh and his adventures with honey and bees.

Vocabulary Words
- beekeeping
- queen bee
- drones
- hives
- honeybee colony
- workers
- larva
- pupa

A Sample Letter to the Parents

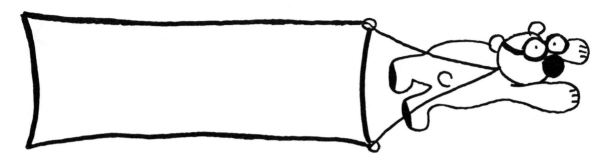

To: Parents of Second Grade Students
From: Second Grade Staff
Date: May 11

The week of May 21 is proclaimed Teddy Bear Week in grade two at Mount View Elementary. We will be celebrating this week with Bear Facts. We have been studying about real bears and bear habitats. The habitats are to be made at home from materials found around the house and lawn. The habitats will be due May 22nd. We will also include the following items in our study: literature, poems, social studies, math, movies, language arts, and videos all related to real bears or teddy bears.

Celebrating is most fun if students have teddy bears. The students may bring as many teddy bears as parents permit. Of course, students' names and bears' names must be on the bear name tags. *All* bears must go home Friday afternoon, May 25th.

Friday afternoon, May 25th, about 2:30 P.M. (rain or shine), we will have our *Teddy Bear Picnic*. We will also celebrate all summer birthdays that afternoon.

We are all going to have a "Beary" Good Time!!!

Bear Awards

All teddy bears are wonderful in the eyes of the students. Receiving a Bear Award is one of the highlights in the finale at the Teddy Bear Picnic. The following list provides ideas for awards, but remember that the award should fit the bear.

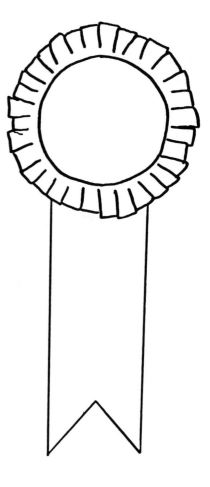

1. The fluffiest bear
2. The biggest bear
3. The cutest bear
4. The most loved bear
5. The funniest-looking bear
6. The smallest bear
7. The fattest bear
8. The skinniest bear
9. The most huggable bear
10. The oldest bear
11. The best-dressed bear
12. The biggest belly-button bear
13. The youngest bear
14. The best-talking bear
15. The most musical bear
16. The most colorful bear
17. The bear with the biggest heart
18. The largest bear family
19. The best polar bear
20. The best koala bear
21. The biggest brown bear
22. The biggest black bear
23. The easiest-to-love bear
24. The bear with the longest legs
25. The best hand-crafted bear
26. The best hand-puppet bear
27. The best grizzly bear named Harry
28. The best sugar-plum bear
29. The best blue bear with blue paws and blue eyes
30. The best bear with Christmas red mittens

From *Investigating Science Through Bears,* ©1994. Teacher Ideas Press, P.O. Box 6633, Englewood, CO 80155-6633.

Categories of Awards

The cookie-decorating contest is a highlight of the teddy bear events. The judging begins with a first prize, a second prize, and a third prize for the best-looking decorated teddy bear cookie. All students receive an award for their decorated cookie. The list below provides ideas for awards, but the judges should make an award fit the decorated cookie.

1. The most colorful cookie bear
2. The chocolately-chippiest cookie bear
3. The biggest smile on a cookie bear
4. The biggest, browniest cookie bear
5. The most icing on the cookie bear
6. The happiest cookie bear
7. The most creative cookie bear
8. The brownest-looking cookie bear
9. The cutest jacket on a cookie bear
10. The fanciest cookie bear
11. The nicest bow tie on a cookie bear
12. The best clown-dressed cookie bear
13. The pinkiest bear
14. The neatest-looking bear
15. The most athletic bear
16. The bear with the biggest pop eyes
17. Neapolitan-ice-cream bear (all 3 colors!)
18. The sweetest bear

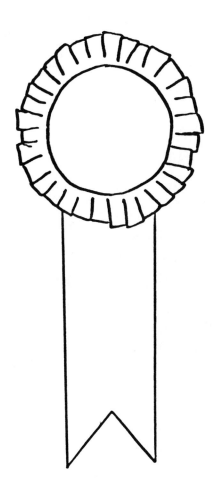

Criteria for Awards for
Bear Habitats

Awards for the bear habitats are difficult to define inasmuch as the habitats will reflect considerable creativity by the students. The list below gives the judges ideas for terminology to use for defining the various awards. The judges may need to make the award fit the bear habitat!

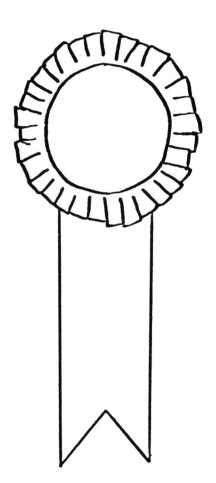

1. Best creative black bear setting
2. Best natural display of a grizzly habitat
3. Best hand-molded display
4. Best protected and presented natural habitat
5. Best use of materials to create a cave
6. Best natural setting for the polar bear
7. Most realistic use of a variety of materials
8. Most authentic use of natural materials
9. An interesting natural setting
10. An interesting use of a variety of materials
11. A realistic cave
12. Best creative display of a realistic bear activity
13. Best natural setting and authentic setting
14. Good use of a variety of materials

8

The Origin of the Teddy Bear

Over the years, many stories have been told about the origin of the teddy bear. Although Theodore Roosevelt, the 26th president of the United States, is usually credited with the creation of this toy, a German woman stricken with polio as a child actually made the "teddy" a bear before the famous Teddy Bear Incident involving the president.

In the 1880s, Margarete Steiff began to make toy animals for her little friends. Her new creations met with such success that by 1900 she had developed a whole line of soft animals and was employing most of the town's people. Margarete was then ready to expand her business. She hired her nephew, a recent college graduate with a degree in art, to help her develop this new line. As a student, Richard Steiff had spent many hours watching the brown bears at the local zoo. He thought a bear covered with furlike mohair and having movable limbs would be the ideal new toy for his aunt's business. His aunt—much to Richard's surprise—did not like the idea, claiming that the bear was much larger than the currently produced stuffed toys. Besides, mohair was expensive. A few brown bears were produced, but they were not actively marketed until a buyer arrived from the United States. The salesman was in desperate need for something "soft and cuddly" for the children back home. The

Steiff salesman showed the buyer Margarete's unpopular toy bear. The buyer immediately ordered 3,000 bears, and Margarete admitted to her nephew that he had had an excellent idea after all!

Even though Margarete Steiff made the first brown bear, it was President Roosevelt who catapulted it to fame. As the president of the United States, Roosevelt portrayed a bigger-than-life image to the American people. In his spare time, he liked to hunt grizzly bears with his friends. Besides being a great hunter, Roosevelt enjoyed observing the bear undetected and was knowledgeable about the bear's traits and its living and feeding habits. Being very particular about choosing his target, the president was careful not to shoot a bear that was too young or too old. This fact was brought to the nation's attention on November 14, 1902.

Roosevelt had traveled to the South to settle a boundary dispute between Mississippi and Louisiana. Since the local politicians knew of Roosevelt's great love of hunting, a trip was organized with the hope that the president would successfully shoot at least one bear. As the day wore on, no bears materialized, thus causing great anxiety among the hosts. After a long search, a small cub was brought to the president. Viewing the sad-looking animal, Roosevelt said "I draw the line at killing anything so small."

President Roosevelt felt that the encounter with the cub was quite unfortunate and seldom discussed it with his colleagues. The public would have soon forgotten the incident if it had not been for the political cartoonist Clifford K. Berryman. The now-famous cartoon Berryman drew shows Roosevelt standing with the young cub, with the caption on the cartoon reading "Drawing the Line in Mississippi." Because racial tension was developing in the South, the caption on the cartoon had a double meaning for many readers. Regardless of what the American people thought of the cartoon, the little cub was then known as Teddy's Bear. The popularity of an American president, coupled with the heartwarming incident involving the baby bear, laid the foundation for the manufacture of the most popular toy the world has ever known.

Morris Michtom, a Russian immigrant, owned a candy store in Brooklyn. He, with the help of his wife, was always making new items to sell in his shop. As a Russian, Michtom's childhood had been steeped in the many traditions of the bear. Reading about Roosevelt's encounter with the cub, Michtom thought he might create "the wonderful furry fellow" that the kindhearted president had refused to shoot. The newly designed bear was placed in the candy-store window, along with a copy of Berryman's cartoon. It was an instant success.

Michtom was ecstatic about the success of his bear, but he had a problem with its name. Along with a letter, a special bear was sent to the White House, asking the president for permission to use his name on the new toy. With the president's approval, the teddy bear went into production. Along with Steiff, 12 companies began to manufacture teddy bears.

We know the history of the teddy bear and the people who were involved with its development. To the children of the world, it doesn't matter which company produced the first teddy bear. They are happy that the teddy bear is as popular today as it was in the early 1900s. Although many children through the centuries have had bears in their lives, bears as toys were not universally popular until the 20th century and the advent of the teddy bear.

Appendix
Teacher-Made Modeling Clay

Teacher Reference

Warn students not to eat any of these clays!

Uncooked Colored Clay

1. Add food coloring to ½ cup (117 cubic centimeters) of water until you like the color.

2. Mix 1½ cups (352 cubic centimeters) of flour with ½ cup (117 cubic centimeters) of salt. Add colored water and ¼ cup (59 cubic centimeters) of vegetable oil. Knead thoroughly. Make several batches in different colors.

3. Make the shapes you want. Set them aside for a few days until they harden. Note: Gluten in flour holds bread together, and it holds your clay shapes together too.

Baking Clay

    4 cups (940 cubic centimeters) flour
    1 cup (235 cubic centimeters) salt
    1½ cups (352 cubic centimeters) water

Mix all ingredients together with hands. If the dough is too sticky, add more flour. Knead 4 to 6 minutes. Make desired shapes. Bake at 350° F (176° C) for one hour or more. The figures should be firm when done. Figures may be painted with a craft paint or tempera, or the dough can be tinted with food coloring. Spray with varnish, shellac, or lacquer to seal.

Top-of-the-Stove
Salt Clay

1 cup (235 cubic centimeters) salt
½ cup (117 cubic centimeters) cornstarch
¾ cup (175 cubic centimeters) water
food coloring

Combine salt and cornstarch in the top of a double boiler and place over boiling water. Slowly add water while stirring constantly. When the mixture has thickened to the point where it is hard to stir, place it on a cookie sheet to cool. When cool, knead until smooth. The clay will keep for an extended period of time if stored in an airtight container until ready for use. Any figures made from this recipe can also be painted using craft paint or tempera.

Top-of-the-Stove
Salt and Flour Clay

1 cup (235 cubic centimeters) salt
½ cup (117 cubic centimeters) flour
1 cup (235 cubic centimeters) water
food coloring

Combine the salt and flour in a pan; then add the water. Heat the mixture over a low heat. Stir the mixture constantly until it thickens. Then place on a cookie sheet, and allow to cool. If cooled mixture is too sticky, add flour. To keep until it is used, store the clay in an airtight container. Again, any figures made from this clay can be painted with craft paint or tempera to provide the desired effect.

Edible "Play Dough"

1 cup (235 cubic centimeters) peanut butter
1 cup (235 cubic centimeters) honey
1½ cups (352 cubic centimeters) powdered milk

Mix the ingredients well, and store in refrigerator. When ready for use, cover table with plastic cloth. Place mixture on cloth and divide into suitable sizes for the number of students participating. The pieces of "play dough" may be rolled in chopped nuts, chocolate sprinkles, or other cookie-decorating materials. Then form the dough into the desired shapes and figures. After the activity is over, the students may eat their "play dough" or take it home.

Index

About the Authors

Karlene Ray Smith is an elementary teacher in the Greater Latrobe School District, Latrobe, Pennsylvania. She has completed 19 years of instruction in the areas of home economics and elementary education. She received her B.S. in education from Seton Hill College, Greensburg, Pennsylvania, and has completed graduate work at Carlow College, Pittsburgh, and Indiana University of Pennsylvania. Her presentations, addressing science education at the elementary level, include papers given at both state and national science teachers conventions. She is currently involved in science instruction for elementary students. She is the mother of two children, and she and her husband reside in Greensburg, Pennsylvania, and are active in bareboat chartering on the Chesapeake Bay.

Karlene Ray Smith

Anne Hudson Bush

Anne Hudson Bush teaches in the Greater Latrobe School District, Latrobe, Pennsylvania. During the past 21 years she has taught in the primary grades, as well as reading remediation. She received her B.S. in home economics from West Virginia Wesleyan College, Buckhannon, West Virginia, her teacher's certification from Seton Hill College, Greensburg, Pennsylvania, and a Master's of Education, Reading Specialist Certification, from California University of Pennsylvania, California, Pennsylvania. She enjoys teaching science to young children and has presented papers on elementary science activities at both state and national science teachers conventions. Bush resides in rural Latrobe, Pennsylvania, and enjoys reading and gardening.